Patent Analytics

Jieun Kim · Buyong Jeong · Daejung Kim

Patent Analytics

Transforming IP Strategy into Intelligence

Springer

Jieun Kim
Graduate School of Technology
and Innovation Management
Hanyang University
Seoul, Korea (Republic of)

Daejung Kim
Bright College
Hankyong National University
Gyeonggi-do, Korea (Republic of)

Buyong Jeong
Trademark and Design Examination Bureau
Korean Intellectual Property Office
Daejeon, Korea (Republic of)

ISBN 978-981-16-2929-7 ISBN 978-981-16-2930-3 (eBook)
https://doi.org/10.1007/978-981-16-2930-3

This Springer imprint is published by the registered company Springer Nature Singapore Pte Ltd.
The registered company address is: 152 Beach Road, #21-01/04 Gateway East, Singapore 189721, Singapore

Foreword

In praise of *Patent Analytics: Transforming IP Strategy into Intelligence*

For years, designers and non-designers have been convinced that design cannot be measured. This presumption of immeasurability is so strong that no attempt has even been made so far. In this book, readers will understand that intangibles assets—design, branding—that appear to be completely intractable can be made tangible through data-driven analytics and visualisation techniques as well as through artificial intelligence approaches.

Why should decision-makers—business managers, IP professionals, and designers—read this book?

First, innovation, design, and user experience have become critical issues in major organisational decisions and present certain challenges—yet these issues do not seem to lend themselves to easy, practical tools for management. *Patent Analytics* visualises the strategic innovation path. Patent mapping becomes a measurement tool that informs uncertain decisions on innovation strategy. These analytical tools enrich *scientometrics* research and add scientific productivity to innovation portfolio decision-making.

Second, the book reveals *why* decision-makers should focus more on patent management. The big questions are, 'What is the decision you hope to resolve with improved patent management using these new tools?' and 'What will engineers and designers do if they learn, through the tools developed in this book, that their innovation impacts are higher or lower than expected?' *Patent Analytics* helps them trust their investment in innovation and design. This is not a 'feel-good' toolbox. Each chapter of the book teaches how citation analysis, patent networks, and visualisation techniques participate in building long-term portfolio growth. It provides empirical evidence on how to improve decisions in intellectual property (IP) leadership. It widens the possibilities for companies, compares their innovation and IP policies with competitors in their industry, and offers insights for proactive decisions. It helps one understand the past and document the present. This is a creative book that is relevant to business. The ideas developed in this research have a financial impact and provide invaluable insights to all innovators.

Third, this book is especially suitable for IP professionals, such as IP lawyers, data protection attorneys, technology transfer officers, IP commercialisation experts, and those tasked with data analytics and visualisation: clients' requests are becoming more and more data-driven, so it is imperative that companies respond appropriately. While the most essential component of the book discusses the practical apparatus and covers real-world business cases, the authors endeavour to attract academic readership—in particular, senior undergraduate and graduate students in the field of technology innovation management, and MBA programs specialising in business analytics or data science.

Finally, for the design community, *Patent Analytics* shows the power of mixing artificial intelligence and visualisation capacity. It makes the work of designers worldwide more tangible, perhaps even putting an end to the way designers have been protecting themselves by keeping their designs fuzzy or as 'trade secrets'. It shows the value of the design process in a dynamic way. Through Patent Analytics, the designer's work is made visible and accessible to all. Designers can therefore stop arguing that the value of design cannot be measured. This book explains that design is an activity always practised as part of a team, so the value of design input cannot be isolated from other actors, such as marketers or engineers.

I have always believed that working with designers made me a better manager. My research and model, 'Designence', has offered evidence of how the capabilities of designers complement business knowledge capital. Likewise, this book complements our 'Designence' model with its innovation indicators. When it comes to filing design patents and brand images, the business value of design outputs can be seen.

Patent Analytics shows how design is an active/proactive partner in IP strategies. It will help strategy consultants, while evaluating businesses through brands and IP intangibles, to change their way of seeing the integration of designers into innovation and R&D strategies; this is vital now in a world of digital transformation using user experience (UX) and service designers.

This book is a must-read for designers everywhere, as it bridges design leadership with the legal department. It will help them optimise innovation performance, following the examples of great companies. It shows the value of visualisation skills and artificial intelligence in strategic portfolio decisions, encourages all innovation managers to see the connections, illuminates the cross-pollination of design and technology, and shows how one category of products is influenced by other patents in another product category. It manages strategic pivot points and demonstrates the business value of long-term career and inventor talent paths.

Brigitte Borja de Mozota
Member, Chaire Diament UQAM Montréal,
Honorary Professor, University Paris X Director
Founder, Designence™
Metz, France

Contents

About the Authors

Jieun Kim is an associate professor at the Graduate School of Technology and Innovation Management, Hanyang University and co-directs an interdisciplinary research lab - Imagine X lab since 2013. She has a BA in Industrial Design from KAIST (2007) and an MS and PHD in Industrial Engineering from Arts et Métiers ParisTech, Paris (2008/2011), followed by the Leverhulme Research Fellowship (2012) at Royal College of Art in London. She was a visiting associate professor at Human Communication Technologies Lab, University of British Columbia (2020). She served as a general co-chair of ACM TVX 2018 and continued to contribute to many international design and innovation management communities as reviewers and speakers.

Buyong Jeong is a deputy director in the Korean Intellectual Property Office (KIPO). Before joining KIPO in 2015, he worked as a patent attorney at PLUS International IP Law firm (2009–2014). He has been involved in various projects and policies for the Trademark and Design Examination bureau of KIPO. His legal and practical expertise is supported by his academic background, having obtaining bachelor's and master's degrees in Industrial design from Korea Advanced Institute of Science and Technology (KAIST). He is the co-author of the Korean chapter for AIPPI Law Series: Design Rights, Functionality and Scope of Protection (by Christopher V. Carani / Wolters Kluwer 2017).

Daejung Kim is a data scientist specialising in intellectual property and a senior lecturer at Hankyong National University. He holds his Ph.D. in technology and innovation management from Hanyang University. He is a frequent speaker and consultant in strategic technology and management solutions for many law firms and corporate legal departments.

Abbreviations

AI	Artificial Intelligence
CNIPA	China National Intellectual Property Administration
CPC	Cooperative Patent Classification
EPO	European Patent Office
EUIPO	European Union Intellectual Property Office
IDS	Information Disclosure Statement
INID	Internationally agreed Numbers for the Identification of Data
IP	Intellectual Property
IPC	International Patent Classification
IPR	Inter Partes Review
JPO	Japan Patent Office
KIPO	Korean Intellectual Property Office
NPE	Non-Practicing Entity
PCT	Patent Cooperation Treaty
PTAB	Patent Trial and Appeal Board
PTO	Patent and Trademark Office
USPC	United States Patent Classification
USPTO	US Patent and Trademark Office
WIPO	World Intellectual Property Organisation

List of Figures

List of Tables

Chapter 1
Introduction

Abstract This chapter starts with a straightforward question: "*Can patents be regarded as big data?*" The number of patents has grown significantly in the last 230 years. Yet, views on patent data are complex and multifaceted. Through the prism of big data and data analytics, we demystify the complexity of patent data and address how to leverage patent analytics to discover relationships, trends, and patterns for decision -making in the context of business and innovation management. Finally, the chapter concludes with a detailed overview of the book to help readers navigate their way.

1.1 The Prism of Patent Big Data

1.1.1 The Vs to the Patent Big Data Paradigm

On June 19, 2018, the United States Patent and Trademark Office celebrated the issuance of patent number 10,000,000.[1] Patent 10 million is more than just a number. It represents the rich history and great achievement of the patent system over the past 230 years—since the first patent was registered on July 31, 1790. *How long will it take to record another 10 million patent*s? The number of patent applications for the last 30 years from 1988 to 2019 was equivalent to the number of patent applications from 1836 to 1987, which implies that it will not take long to break this record. Currently, the global patent dataset totals over 100 terabytes, with millions of new patents issued annually and made public every week. This ever-increasing volume shows no signs of slowing down. *Can patents be regarded as big data?* Let us first explore what do we mean by *big data*.

The term big data has become a buzzword over the years with its wide usage and moving definitions. The three Vs, which were originally coined by Laney (2001), have been used as a common framework to describe big data. *Volume* refers to the massive amount of data being generated, gathered, and processed. Data size is a major

[1]On June 19, 2018, the 10-millionth patent in the US was issued to Dr. Joseph Marron, an optical engineer from the Raytheon Company, for a real-time reading technology of a large laser radar.

J. Kim et al., *Patent Analytics*,
https://doi.org/10.1007/978-981-16-2930-3_1

part of big data. Yet, the volume that qualifies as big data has rapidly increased as everywhere data are growing. When applying the three Vs to patent data, the volume is snowballing. Throughout the patent lifecycle, they continue to be produced and piled up, ranging from the initial idea to prior art search, examination, maintenance, trial and litigation, license, and expiration.

Velocity refers to the speed at which data are generated and processed. Compared to the recent rise of big data in industry practices with relatively short collection periods, patent data have been accumulated for a long period of time at an increasing rate.

Variety refers to the number of data types. Patent data include a variety of data, including both structured and unstructured data, such as numbers (application date), categories (technology fields), text (claims), and images (drawings).

Along with high-volume, -velocity and -variety data, additional V's family of big data highlight the importance of data quality and its alignment with business goals: such as *veracity* (Schroeck et al. 2012), *value* (Dijcks 2013), and *visualization* (McCosker and Wilken 2014). Not to mention, patent data are the world's largest open repository of technical information, which establishes its importance between technology and business values.

1.1.2 Coping with Patent Big Data Complexity

The dimensions of big data have been mainly proposed in the data science and computing industry, but big data studies should take an interdisciplinary approach to address data complexity as well. According to the McKinsey Global Institute, big data refers to "*a very large and often complex dataset whose size is beyond the ability of typical database software tools to capture, store, manage, and analyze*" (Manyika et al. 2011, p104). The Big Data Commission (2015) defined big data as "a phenomenon that is a result of the rapid acceleration and exponential growth in the expanding volume of high velocity, *complex* and diverse types of data."

Notwithstanding the fact that the patent system is recognized as one of the most well-structured legal systems, patent data live with the system that is less structured and more complex.

Patent data are continually evolving by absorbing the technologies and business value of time in competitive relations. Every day patents are being filed and are expiring. Patents can be acquired and sold with explosive popularity in certain markets or sadly forgotten after being cited in various locations. Around half of the patents expire prematurely because they are not worth maintaining, or they may be invalidated or rejected due to nonpatentable subject matters, insufficient disclosures, third party oppositions. More importantly, changes in patent data may alternate their values or evolutions to technology relationships and business landscapes.

Complexity is a perceived quality that comes from difficulty understanding or describing many layers of interrelated parts (Fry 2000). What good is patent big data if we do not know how to use it to obtain needed information?

Benjamin J. Fry incites a novel concept of organic information visualization that helps identify hidden patterns in vast amounts of changing data in real-time. Organic information visualization refers to "a system that employs simulated organic properties in an interactive and visually refined environment to glean qualitative facts from large bodies of quantitative data generated by dynamic information" (Fry 2000, p19). He defined individual entities in an organic information system as nodes and determined a set of behavior rules governing interactions between nodes with visual elements. For instance, his *anemone* project envisions information as a complex, organic system that is both interactive and emergent. Based on website traffic data, a typical website's structure considers web pages as nodes and hyperlinks as edges connecting related pages. The edges become complex in response to the website's structure's growth, and the nodes—a web page—become thicker relative to the number of visitor log records. Through the changes of nodes and edges, we can delve deeper into complex data.

Fry's approach resembles a classic network representation derived from a social network analysis that measures network structure, connections, nodes, and other modeling network dynamics and growths (e.g., network density, network centrality, network flows). Unlike other big data analytics (e.g., web usage mining), network analytics complement likely unstructured complex patent data, natural language, and context-dependent.

Patent big data can be a subject worthy of network analytics for many reasons. First, it contains various individual entities, such as structured and unstructured data. Structured patent data are often derived from patent documents. At a high level, the presentation of bibliographic data on the front page is uniform regardless of its database. Examples of structured data include dates (priority, application and publication dates), text (patent title, applicants, and inventors), numbers (application and publication number), classification codes (the International patent classification and the Locarno classification), and citation information. Unstructured patent data comprises narrative text, including the patent title, claims, description, and drawings.

Second, patent data are made up of several rules to aggregate individual entities and form more complex structures. Classification is a special rule applied to patent data to subdivide technology into distinct units. A classification symbol (or code) is defined for each unit and group invention hierarchically. Multiple classification codes can be assigned as an index to observe the fusion and convergence of heterogeneous fields. Many patent search and analysis tools permit advanced filters capable of sorting or refining patent data based on a pair of rules, such as classifications, patent family, and citations.

Third, patent data engender growth and movement of information with continuing interactions of patent entities. It consists of cross-references between patents and collaborating inventor networks that enable us to assess the reliance on or impact patent data and identify innovation sources. The main difficulty in analyzing citation data is that they emerge over time, sometimes after the cited patent was filed, granted, or even reached full term. In addition, patent transactions (including licensing, litigation, and acquisition) can lead to changes in patent ownership over time. The number of patent transactions keeps growing, exchanging hundreds of billions of dollars per year. However, current decentralized data of the sale and transfer of ownership is difficult to monitor.

1.1.3 Harnessing Patent Big Data Analytics to Make a Difference

The rise of patent big data and analytic tools calls for current practice changes in the Intellectual Property (IP) industry, namely geared towards aiding patent examiners, inventors, attorneys, corporate legal professionals, technology transfer officers, IP commercialization experts, and legal tech enterprises.

In May 2018, the World Intellectual Property Organization (WIPO) held the first meeting involving directors of national patent offices to spark a conversation in pursuit of coherent Artificial Intelligence (AI) and IP strategy, management of IP big data, and the cooperative development of AI-based applications (WIPO 2020). Since then, WIPO has hosted a series of conversations with a wider range of stakeholders, including representatives of member states, academic, scientific, and private organizations. Marked advancements at hand include automatic patent classification, machine translation for patent documents (titles, claims, and descriptions), and image similarity searches (drawings and trademarks).

Coupled with international cooperation initiatives, private legal tech companies have continued interfacing law and technology. The biggest and most widely known database for the legal tech landscape is the Stanford CodeX Index (2020) in which a list of legal tech companies, including IP specialized service providers, are curated according to their main service categories and target stakeholders. The list comprises more than 1300 companies.

Different stakeholders approach patent data and analytics with different purposes. We define patent analytics as the data science of analyzing a large amount of patent information to discover relationships, trends and patterns for decision making rooted in the business context. The importance of accommodating interdisciplinary viewpoints in patent analytics includes:

- *Business managers and professionals* looking to improve their innovation portfolio and tooling with patent analytic techniques aiming to exploit highly detailed, accurate, and actionable insights on patent data to bolster informed decision-making.
- *Data analysts* who seek to gain a deeper understanding of the special structures, knowledge, and economic values that underlie patent data and close the gap between big data analytics capacities and the particular needs of legal professionals.
- *Legal professionals* need to harness the power of patent analytics to practically improve IP research and legal-services delivery and envisage the emerging legal technology landscape.

This book pivots us to the central question: Can patents be regarded as big data? We claim that patents are exciting subjects of big data and advanced analytics. In particular, patent analytics and artificial intelligence approach capable of demonstrating a contextual understanding of complex patent data could benefit a large range of stakeholders constituting the innovation ecosystem.

1.2 Overview of the Book

This book is organized into four major parts, followed by this introduction. Part I, *Patents as Data,* which spans Chaps. 2–4, guides readers in the evolution of the patent system from the historical beginnings to modern developments and provides a walk-through of patent documents highlighting key data fields for those with little knowledge of the intellectual property. Part II, *Network Analytics,* covers Chaps. 5–8 and presents an introduction of network analysis and a practical guide to research design involving patent data gathering and network analysis using free, open-source software tools. Part III, *Uncover Corporate Innovation with Patent Analytics,* covering Chaps. 9–13, expands the methodologies presented in Part II and provides five case studies of global companies: Dyson, Bose, Apple, Adobe, Samsung, and LG Electronics. The book concludes with Chaps. 14 and 15 in Part IV, *Future Developments with AI,* which deploys the latent intersection between artificial intelligence, intellectual property, and legal technologies and poses challenges for future patent analytics with AI. A brief summary of each chapter is provided in the following paragraphs.

1.2.1 Part I: Patent as Data

Chapter 2, *Brief History of Patents,* introduces critical episodes in the history of the patent system and laws from the nineteenth century. The history of the patent system has evolved with technology changes, industry demands, and lessons learned from accidents, notably the two great fires in the United States Patent and Trademark Office. These incidents catalyzed the emergence of the *claims, numberings,* and *citations system,* which is now a major contribution to the development of patent analytics. Tracing back the journey of 230 years of patent system elaborates the value of patent data through a historical lens.

Chapter 3, *Understanding Patent Data,* is designed for those with little knowledge of the intellectual property. Understanding the structure of patent documents and data fields is the first step for anyone who wants to open the door to patent analytics. Included is the explanation of what patent documents consist of and how utility patents differ from design patents and trademarks, using the examples of Apple's AirPods' patent documents. Some remarks on the different meanings and structure of patents, design, and trademarks are of particular interest to readers planning to use the data in interdisciplinary research.

Chapter 4, *Claims, "Legally, Less is More!* focuses on the structure and meaning of patent claims which defines the scope of protection of a patent. The anatomy of patent claims in a step-by-step manner guides readers to determine key claim elements and their structural and functional relationships. In addition, given that the protection scope of design patents is primally determined by ornamental shape, this chapter further explains how to define claims in design patents without a wordsmith and practical uses of a partial design claiming system.

1.2.2 Part II: Network Analytics

Chapter 5, *Basic Network Concepts.* provides basic building blocks for understanding network concepts, terminologies, and statistics. This chapter is designed to incite contemplations about patent citation or co-inventor network by selecting its structural properties and relations. More in-depth case studies are provided in Chaps. 9–13 in Part III.

Chapter 6, *Patent Citations Analysis,* discusses the value of patent citation networks, which relates to firms' hidden innovation activities and knowledge flows between technologies, individuals, firms, industries, or countries. In addition, this chapter recounts the story of the Apple-Samsung lawsuit using the citation network of iPhone's design patent. Finally, common pitfalls and best practices for using patent citation data are discussed.

Chapter 7, *Patent Data through a Visual Lens,* starts with an anecdote of a patent attorney coping with an increasing amount of patent data and reimagining legal service provisions with the emergence of data analytics and visualization tools. This chapter serves to inspire the disentanglement of the complex nature of patent data armed with a greater flexibility in data visualization techniques from basic charts to elaborate network visualization.

Chapter 8, *How to Study Patent Network Analysis,* starts with a guide to aid research design in conducting patent network analysis from the formulation of research questions to patent data collection and subsequent network analysis. It is designed for those with no programming language skills and provides a high-level overview of free, open-source tools that offer different functionalities for network analysis and visualization. Finally, Gephi and Dyson's patent data samples are used to exemplify a four-step patent network analysis—data collection (step 1), data cleaning and mapping (step 2), network analysis (step 3), and network visualization (step 4). This chapter is a must-read for anyone contemplating network analytics using the patent data.

1.2.3 Part III: Uncover Corporate Innovation with Patent Analytics

Chapter 9, *Is Innovation design- or technology-driven? Dyson,* explores the diversification in product innovation at Dyson, from the bagless vacuum cleaner to bladeless hairdryer. Multi-depth patent citation networks allow readers to both quantitatively and visually assess how Dyson's product innovations grow and are connected and what these connections mean for the company's next innovations.

Chapter 10, *Predict Strategic Pivot Points: Bose,* investigates Bose's four innovation pivots, which seem to have no connection with sound at all, such as suspension seats, high-tech cooktops, audio AR sunglasses, and sleepbuds. This chapter demonstrates Bose's core technology and emerging pivoting areas using a series of patent citation networks in 1972–2016.

Chapter 11, *Who Drives Innovation? Apple,* demonstrates a series of Apple's inventor networks derived from Periscopic and Kenedict to demystify the structure of Apple's internal innovation network. Particularly, this chapter deals with unanswered questions about Apple, such as how Apple's internal innovation networks formed, how they have evolved over the years, who the core inventors have been, or the extent to which Steve Jobs influenced innovation.

Chapter 12, *Knowledge Acquisition and Assimilation after M&As: Adobe,* investigates the evolution of Adobe's inventor network between 1988 and 2010 and 1988–2018, aiming to understand Adobe's innovation affiliation after the multiple acquisitions in pursuit of the Cloud Creative initiatives since 2011. Specifically, this chapter deals with two questions: how did technology and knowledge clusters evolve between pre–and post–M&A periods, and how much has the collaboration between inventors increased over time? A deep dive into Adobe's inventor network analysis sheds light on these questions.

Chapter 13, *Learn to Build Design Innovation Team: Samsung vs LG,* explores Samsung and LG Electronics' competitive landscape using in-depth network analysis of co inventors and the Locarno classifications in their design patents filed between 2014 and 2017 in Korea. This case study juxtaposes the clusters of design teams, product line-ups, and core-inventors of both companies and examines their different product diversification strategies and collaboration patterns.

1.2.4 Part IV: Future Developments with AI

Chapter 14, *Is Trademark the First Sparring Partner of AI?,* reviews the state-of-the-art AI advancements and their implementation in the trademark domain, and how these developments cope with the ever-rising number of trademark filing and the crowded trademark landscape is discussed. Finally, a use case guides how AI-powered trademark search tools incorporate brand protection and mitigate risks of infringements for global businesses.

Chapter 15, *Legal Technologies in Action,* deploys the latent intersection between intellectual property, legal services, and artificial intelligence. First, this chapter focuses on five areas of AI implications where the concerted efforts of the World Intellectual Property Organization and several national patent offices have been made: Automatic classification, machine translation, examination and formality checks, image search and recognition, and helpdesk bots. Next, how legal technologies are making new waves to change the delivery of legal services are discussed with the cases of Case text and Lex Machina.

References

Dijcks J (2013) Oracle: Big data for the enterprise. Oracle White Paper. Oracle Corporation, Redwood Shores.

Fry BJ (2000) Organic Information Design. Master Dissertation, Massachusetts Institute of Technology.

Laney D (2001) 3D Data Management: Controlling Data Volume, Velocity and Variety. META Group Research

Manyika J, Chui M, Brown B Bughin J, Dobbs R, Roxburgh C, Hung BA (2011) Big data: The next frontier for innovation, competition, and productivity. McKinsey Global Institute.

McCosker A, Wilken R (2014) Rethinking 'big data' as visual knowledge: The sublime and the diagrammatic in data visualisation. Vis Stud 29(2):155–164.

Schroeck M, Shockley R, Smart J, Romero-Morales D, Tufano P (2012) Analytics: The real-world use of big data. IBM Institute for Business Value, Said Business School, New York.

Part I
Patent as Data

Chapter 2
A Brief History of Patents

Abstract A patent system has encountered significant events over the past two centuries, which include considerable efforts to constitutionalize patent laws and unexpected great fires. These events engendered modern patent documents, containing *claims*, *numberings*, and *citations*. This chapter traces back the journey of 230 years of patent systems aiming to understand the value of patent data through a historical lens.

2.1 The Prelude of the Patent System

There are many stories about the origin of the patent system. The first account of rights comparable to patents is from the ancient Greeks. In 500 BCE, in the Greek city of Sybaris, the following decree was alleged to have been in force: "*If a cook invents a delicious new dish, no other cook is to be permitted to prepare that dish for one year.*" That said, the inventor (the cook) is given the privilege to use the invention exclusively within a year and shall reap the economic profits from this dish (EPO 2011). It resembles the aim of the current patent system to encourage innovation by providing a means to receive public recognition and promote competition.

The Venetian patent statute of 1474 is widely deemed to be the first statutory system in Europe (Nard and Morriss 2006). The statute is written in old Venetian dialect. The following excerpt is the reproduction of the Statute of Venice in 1474 in English.

> […] By authority of this Council, each person *in this city* who makes *any new and ingenious contrivance, not made heretofore in our dominion*, shall, as soon as it is perfected so that it can be used and exercised, give notice of the same to our office of State Judicial Office, it being *forbidden up to 10 years* for any other person in any territory and place of ours to make a contrivance in the form and resemblance thereof, without the consent and license of the author […].

The Venice patent law expressively states that patents are granted for inventions new to the country concerns and recognizes a minimum duration for patent rights.

In England, monopolies were historically granted by the Crown (i.e., the King or Queen) for all sorts of common goods (e.g., salt). In particular, during the reign of

J. Kim et al., *Patent Analytics*,
https://doi.org/10.1007/978-981-16-2930-3_2

Queen Elizabeth I (1558–1603), there were many abuses of the royal privilege. On his succession in 1603, King James I revoked all previous monopolies and introduced a new system that produced the first *modern* patent in 1617. An early patent on an invention granted in England is shown in Fig. 2.1, which was issued in 1617. This patent gave the inventors a monopoly on making and distributing precise maps of the major cities of England (EPO 2011).

Seven years later, the Parliament of England passed the Statute of Monopolies, which is notably the first statutory expression of English patent law. This Statute has a pivotal role in the modern patent system in that it represents the first measure to lay out the exceptions to the rules preventing any kind of monopoly of patent. In Sect. 6 of the Statute of Monopolies, "patents would apply to *any new manner of manufacture*," a manner of manufacture refers both to the creation of an object and the method for that object (Pila 2001). This Statute of Monopolies of 1624 became the foundation for later developments in patent law in England and elsewhere.

2.2 The First Patent with Claims

While earlier patent acts were crude by modern-day standards, the US Patents Act of 1836 was probably the first in the world to institute a formal system of examination and to include a statutory requirement for claims.

As technology further develops, it has been difficult to judge whether inventions infringe on others' patents by relying on a simple description or drawings only. Section 6 of the 1836 Act introduced a requirement that the potential patentee "particularly specify and point out the part, improvement, or combination, which he claims as his own invention or discovery." Nowadays, the claims are in many respects the most important part of the patent application.

Figure 2.2 shows the United States Patent and Trademark Office (USPTO)'s No.1. patent, a locomotive steam engine for use on rails and other roads (July 13, 1836), invented by John Ruggles (1789–1874). A four-page patent document consisted of the bibliographic data, such as the inventor, title of the invention, patent number, patent date, and a detailed description on the front page and the rest of the pages covering three claims and witness details. The patent document published in 1836 closely resembles today's patent document; however, some information such as names of applicants and assignees, terms, classifications, and references are not included.

2.3 The Great Fire and Patent Numbering

Patent numbering might deceive many readers. The British Patent No.1 issued in 1617 was the first numbered British patent (Fig. 2.1). However, it was not the earliest patent ever granted. Rather, it is the first patent that published the details of the invention.

A.D. 1617 . . . . N° 1.

Engraving and Printing Maps. Plans. &c.

RATHBURNE & BURGES' PATENT.

JAMES, by the grace of God Kinge of Englandie, Scotland, Fraunce, and Irelande, Defendor of the Faith, &c., to all justices of peace, mayors, sherriffs, bailiffes, constables, and all officers, ministers, and subiectes of vs, our heires and successors, to whome it shall or maie appertaine, and to everie of them, greetinge.

WHEREAS wee are informed that amongste forraine nations there are faire, curious, and artificiall descripcons, plott(, and mappes made and sett forth of their principall citties and townes of greatest note, which beinge exactlie drawne out in mettall and printed of, are dispersed and sent abroad into all partes, to the greate honor and renowne of those princes in whose domynions they are, and that of our cittie of London, being the chiefe and principoll in this our kingdome of England, there hath never been made or taken any true or pfecte descripcon, but false and meane draught(cutt out in wood, and soe dispersed abroade, to the greate disparagement and disgrace of soe famous and worthie a state: And whereas our lovinge subiecte, Aron Rathborne, Gentleman, practiconer in the mathematiques, hath a greate desire to take a pfecte survaie as well of the said cittie of London as of divers others places within this our kingdome of England hereafter menconed, and to make suche exacte plott(, mappes, and descripcons thereof as hath not been hitherto pformed by anie, and hath humblie besought vs that wee woulde bee graciouslie pleased to graunte vnto him our Royall lycence and priviledge, (the wante whereof, as

1s 6d

Price 25p

Fig. 2.1 British Patent No.1 issued in 1617

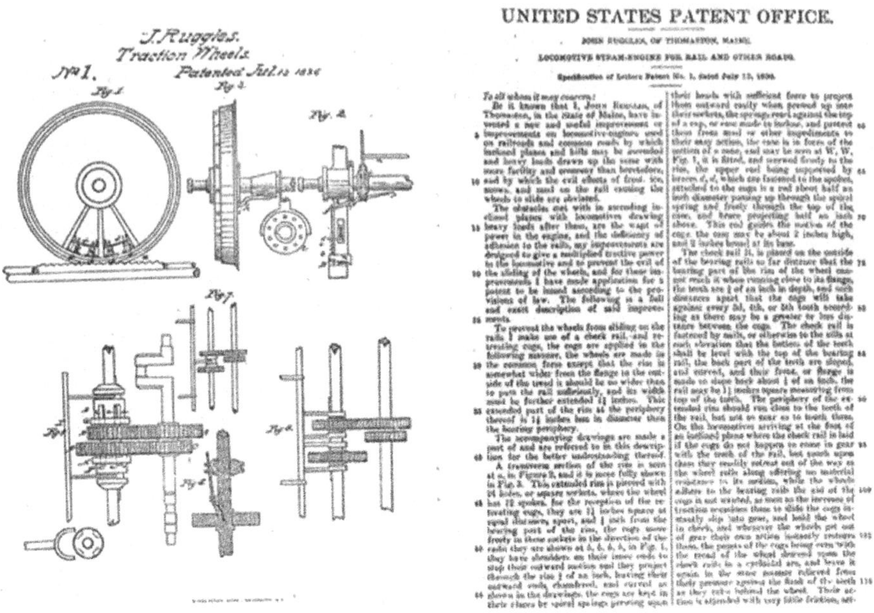

Fig. 2.2 US Patent No. 1 by John Ruggles (1789–1874) (July 13, 1836)

Also, the US Patent No.1 issued in 1836 is not the first genuine patent in United States. After the US Declaration of Independence in 1776, James Madison and Charles Cotesworth Pinckney formed the foundation to protect inventors and creators in Clause 8 of Sect. 8 in Article 1 of the US Constitution in 1787. The first US Patent Act became law in 1790. Thomas Jefferson, a *father of American invention,* played the prime role, as one of the founding members of Patent Trial and Appeal Board (PTAB) which leads to the decision about the granting of patents. On July 31, 1790, a three-man review board consisting of George Washington, the first US President, Thomas Jefferson, and Edmund Jennings Randolph, approved the de facto first patent US X1 (Dobyns 1994). This patent, entitled "In the making of Potash and Pearl ash by a new Apparatus and Process," was invented by Samuel Hopkins (1743–1818). Hopkins's patent document did not include the patent number or a detailed description of the invention, and instead, only included the matters pertaining to the grant of the patent (Fig. 2.3).

From 1790 to 1793, the U.S. adopted a substantive examination system. Since the enactment of the US Patent Act, three patents, 33 patents, and 11 patents were granted in 1790, 1791, and 1792, respectively. There was a growing trend at the time to criticize the examination process' unnecessary length and complexity though. From 1793, a non-substantive examination system was adopted until the revival of the examination system in 1836. Prior to 1836, patents were unnumbered and could only be accessed by patentee name or publication date.

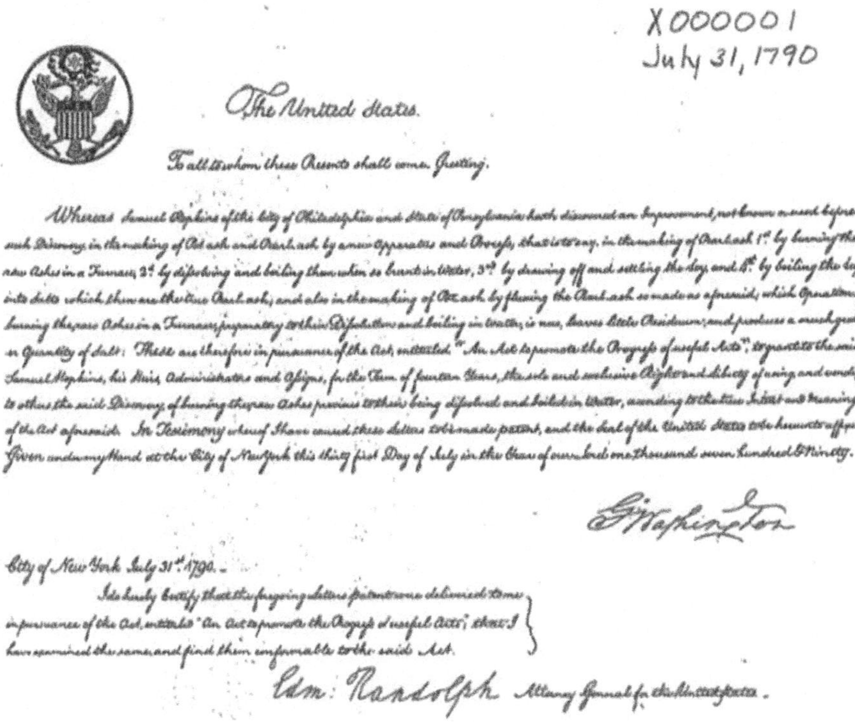

Fig. 2.3 US Patent X1 by Samuel Hopkins (1743–1818) (July 31, 1790)

The Patent Act of 1836 completely rewrote the US patent law. Patent numbering and archive systems are introduced for the sake of efficient examination processes. The US Patent No.1, under the Patent Act of 1836, was granted to John Ruggles, who also authored the Act of 1836. Unfortunately, the first great fire of the USPTO occurred during the winter of the same year.

On December 15, 1836, the fire started in the basement of Blodget's Hotel building in Washington, where the Patent Office was located at the time. Efforts to contain the fire proved unsuccessful, resulting in approximately 10,000 patent documents and 7,000 model collections, compiled over half a century, to be destroyed almost instantaneously. No copies or rosters were maintained by the government at the time. Despite massive efforts to reconstruct the collection with the inventors' copies, only 2,845 documents were taken back. All patents from 1790 to 1836 were listed later as X-Patents, with the prefix X in front of the number (Alan et al. 2015).

The second great fire of the USPTO occurred on September 24, 1877. Unlike the first fire, the patent office building was constructed to be fireproof, and duplicates of patent documents were stored in separate buildings. No patents were completely lost; however, around 136,000 models were damaged.

While the modern USPTO emerged from two great fires, the Patent Act of 1836 significantly transformed the patenting process, laying the foundations for the system we still use today. The Act ushered the very first professional patent examiners, the first PTAB, the first numbering system, and the first library of prior art.

The concept of the patent numbering system makes it possible to efficiently search and retrieve patent information that is publicly accessible worldwide. Today, all patent offices adopt the numbering system and assign a unique patent publication number to each patent. The patent number plays a pivotal role of establishing patent big data, proving an identifier (patent number) for each data object (patent). This resembles the Digital Object Identifier (DOI) system, which provides data linking and metadata for scholarly research.

2.4 Genesis of Citations

As in scientific publications, references are also given in patent documents. The first US patent with the reference listing appears to have been design patent US D146,275 (Design for condiment dispenser set, January 28, 1947), containing the basic information of the cited patent (patent number, inventor name, and date of filling) (Fig. 2.4). US 2,415,068 (Tube spacer and supporter, February 4, 1947) is presumed to be the first utility patent with citations (Fig. 2.5).

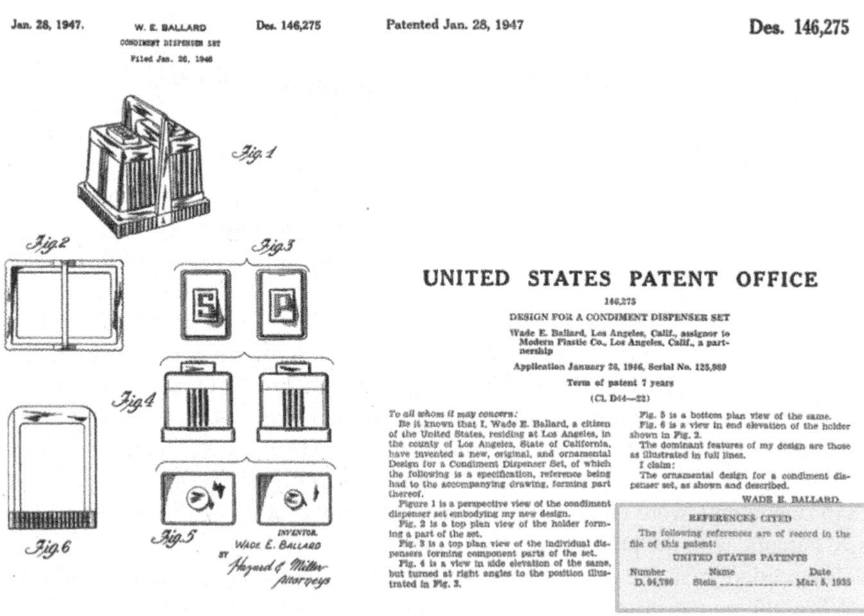
Jan. 28, 1947. W. E. BALLARD Des. 146,275
CONDIMENT DISPENSER SET
Filed Jan. 26, 1946

Patented Jan. 28, 1947 Des. 146,275

UNITED STATES PATENT OFFICE

146,275

DESIGN FOR A CONDIMENT DISPENSER SET

Wade E. Ballard, Los Angeles, Calif., assignor to Modern Plastic Co., Los Angeles, Calif., a partnership

Application January 26, 1946, Serial No. 125,989

Term of patent 7 years

(Cl. D44—22)

To all whom it may concern:

Be it known that I, Wade E. Ballard, a citizen of the United States, residing at Los Angeles, in the county of Los Angeles, State of California, have invented a new, original, and ornamental Design for a Condiment Dispenser Set, of which the following is a specification, reference being had to the accompanying drawing, forming part thereof.

Figure 1 is a perspective view of the condiment dispenser set embodying my new design.

Fig. 2 is a top plan view of the holder forming a part of the set.

Fig. 3 is a top plan view of the individual dispensers forming component parts of the set.

Fig. 4 is a view in side elevation of the same, but turned at right angles to the position illustrated in Fig. 3.

Fig. 5 is a bottom plan view of the same.

Fig. 6 is a view in end elevation of the holder shown in Fig. 2.

The dominant features of my design are those as illustrated in full lines.

I claim:

The ornamental design for a condiment dispenser set, as shown and described.

WADE E. BALLARD.

REFERENCES CITED

The following references are of record in the file of this patent:

UNITED STATES PATENTS

Number	Name	Date
D. 94,786	Stein	Mar. 5, 1935

Fig. 2.4 US D146,275 (Design for condiment dispenser set, January 28, 1947), where citation reference was firstly recorded

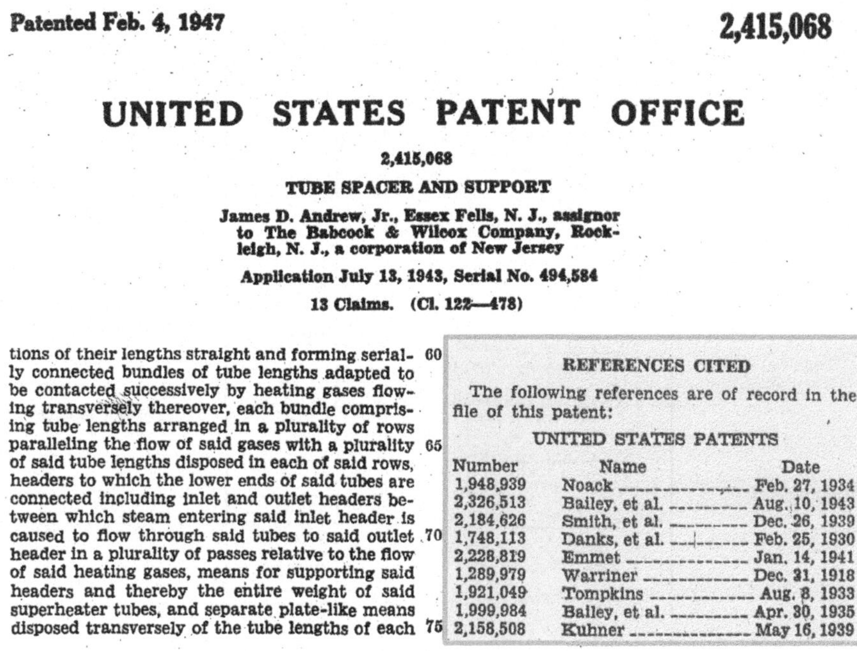
Patented Feb. 4, 1947 **2,415,068**

UNITED STATES PATENT OFFICE

2,415,068

TUBE SPACER AND SUPPORT

James D. Andrew, Jr., Essex Fells, N. J., assignor to The Babcock & Wilcox Company, Rockleigh, N. J., a corporation of New Jersey

Application July 13, 1943, Serial No. 494,584

13 Claims. (Cl. 122—478)

tions of their lengths straight and forming serially connected bundles of tube lengths adapted to be contacted successively by heating gases flowing transversely thereover, each bundle comprising tube lengths arranged in a plurality of rows paralleling the flow of said gases with a plurality of said tube lengths disposed in each of said rows, headers to which the lower ends of said tubes are connected including inlet and outlet headers between which steam entering said inlet header is caused to flow through said tubes to said outlet header in a plurality of passes relative to the flow of said heating gases, means for supporting said headers and thereby the entire weight of said superheater tubes, and separate plate-like means disposed transversely of the tube lengths of each

REFERENCES CITED

The following references are of record in the file of this patent:

UNITED STATES PATENTS

Number	Name	Date
1,948,939	Noack	Feb. 27, 1934
2,326,513	Bailey, et al.	Aug. 10, 1943
2,184,626	Smith, et al.	Dec. 26, 1939
1,748,113	Danks, et al.	Feb. 25, 1930
2,228,819	Emmet	Jan. 14, 1941
1,289,979	Warriner	Dec. 31, 1918
1,921,049	Tompkins	Aug. 8, 1933
1,999,984	Bailey, et al.	Apr. 30, 1935
2,158,508	Kuhner	May 16, 1939

Fig. 2.5 US 2,415,068 (Tube spacer and supporter, February 4, 1947)

In patents, inventors can itemize their references; however, this can be enforced by examiners as well as other stakeholders, which is different from the practice in scientific publications, in which the author is at leisure with their citations (EPO 2011).

The first patent application recorded in the European Patent Office (EPO) was EP 0,000,001A1[1] (December 20, 1978). A search report, including prior art search listings, is available on the last page of the patent document (Fig. 2.6). Compared to bare listings of citation found in the US patent document, the EPO's search report is enriched with a list of relevant prior art documents (citations) plus elements such as the corresponding claims for which a citation is relevant, technology areas searched, and examiner name. Notably, categories of cited documents are highly valuable data in the search report, which indicates whether the citation is particularly relevant if taken alone (category X—novelty) or if combined with another document of the same (category Y—inventive step). Category A, which is marked in EP 0,000,001, refers to technical background information.

It is important to note that the section entitled *reference cited* in a US patent (Figs. 2.4 and 2.5) appears to be similar to the search report of the EPO (Fig. 2.6), but not equivalent. In fact, when filing patents to the US, applicants have a duty to disclose

[1]A1 is one of the kind-of-document codes to represent. For instance, A1 refers to a publication of unexamined specification with search report), and B1 refers to a publication of grant of European patent.

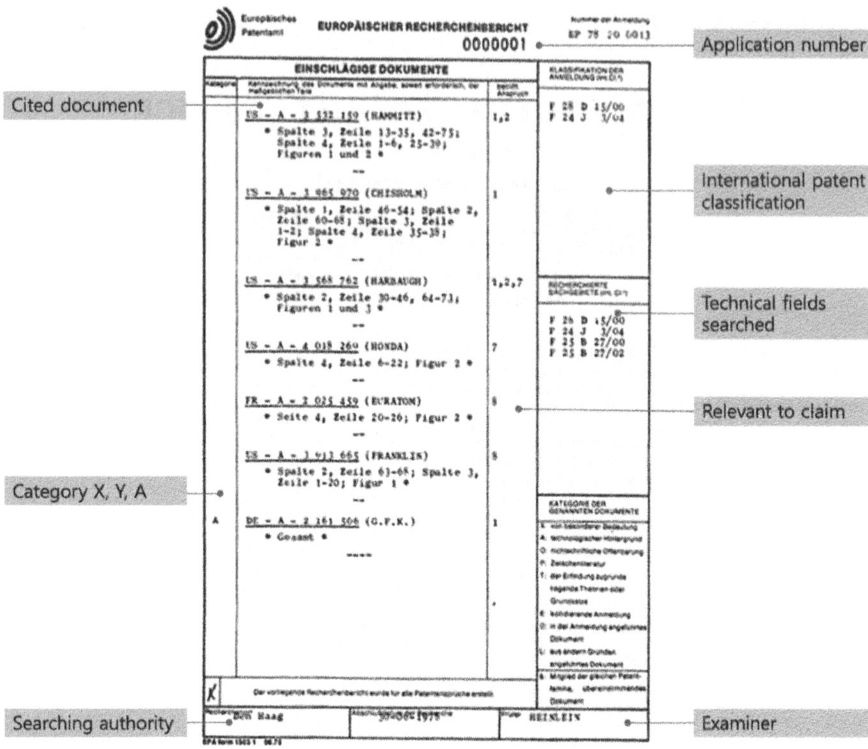

Fig. 2.6 A search report of the EPO's first patent EP0,000,001 A1 (December 20, 1978)

all known prior art or other information that may be applied to the invention. This unique requirement in the USPTO is referred to as information disclosure statement. If the relevancy of the references is deliberately mischaracterized or applicants do not meticulously write every related feature in the statement, applicants can charge for unenforceable conduct for failing to disclose prior art, which results in complete rejections as well as huge financial risks.

Despite the necessity to appropriately attribute credit, one ramification is that US inventors overwhelm their citations, some of which are arguably irrelevant. Beginning with the US patent documents printed after January 1, 2001, an asterisk (*) in the reference section indicates the prior arts that a patent examiner added during the office actions (OA). It is practical to focus on the key references that underlie a patent by noticing the differences between applicant and examiner citations. The USPTO instituted this change in hope of indicating "whether or not a reference was listed by the examiner will be helpful in compiling statistical data related to prior art submissions so that the USPTO can better consider whether changes are required to the rules governing prior art statements."

However, no patent systems are without problems. Interestingly, the European examination system does not enforce disclosure, yet the system is highly regarded for its completeness and quality search reports. Since adopting the citation system in 1947 and 1978, the USPTO and the EPO, respectively, have successfully built a wide corpus of patent citation data. Besides capturing patent documents individually, the advent of electronic databases and their built-in links facilitate greater ease in patent search and examination processes. More recently, mapping and network analysis with multiple generations of forward and backward citations have proven to be of crucial importance as a measure of innovation activities, which is discussed in Chap. 6 in more detail.

2.5 Summary

The history of the patent system has evolved with technology changes, industry demands, and lessons learned from accidents, notably the two great fires in the USPTO. These incidents catalysed the emergence of the claims, numberings, and citations systems, which is a major contribution to modern patent analytics.

From the perspectives of patent data analysts, a patent claim was the first data field of a patent document to set forth the scope of patent protection. Next, the idea of a numbering system allows for the efficient search and retrieval of patent data today. Finally, the patent citation system enables us to build a corpus of accumulative knowledge to industrial innovation, which constitutes intellectual and economic values. The subsequent chapters go into greater depth on each data field and their use in patent analytics: patent numbering (Chap. 3), claims (Chap. 4), and citations (Chap. 6).

References

Alan C, Carley MM, Jackson S, Myer A (2015) The USPTO historical patent data files: two centuries of invention. In: USPTO Economic working paper. https://www.uspto.gov/sites/default/files/documents/USPTO_economic_WP_2015-01_v2.pdf. Accessed 14 Sept 2020.

Dobyns KW (1994) The Patent Office Pony: A History of the Early Patent Office US Government Printing Office. Docent Press.

EPO (2011) Patent teaching kit. https://www.epo.org/learning/materials/kit/download.html. Accessed 14 Jan 2021.

Nard CA, Morriss AP (2006) Constitutionalizing patents: from Venice to Philadelphia. Int'l Rev L Econ 2(2):223–321.

Pila J (2001) The common law invention in its original form. Intell Prop Qtly (3) http://dx.doi.org/ https://doi.org/10.2139/ssrn.270909. Accessed 14 Jan 2021.

Chapter 3
Understanding Patent Data

Abstract Patent documents contain a wealth of information, including bibliographic data, technical disclosure, and legal information. Understanding the structure of patent documents and data fields is the first step for anyone who wants to open the door to patent analytics. With examples of Apple's AirPods patent documents, this chapter walks through each data field using patent documents encompassing patents, designs, and trademarks and identifies different types of patent data that characterize one another.

3.1 Patents, Designs, and Trademarks

Intellectual property (IP) refers to assets, such as given to patents, designs, trademarks, and other intangible properties that serve different protection purposes and coverages. Patents are granted for technical invention, ideas or concepts, and designs protect the visual appearance of a product. Trademarks relate to a corporate or brand identity, such as a brand name, logo, and symbol, in the marketplace.

The patenting system varies across countries. Under United States (US) Patent Law, there are three primary types of patents: utility, design, and plant. Utility patents are applicable to the type of patent that most people think of when referring to the word *patent*. Utility patents may be easily confused with utility models. However, utility models[1] are not as widely known as patents, though they are issued in some regional and national IP offices, such as the European Patent Office (EPO), Korean Intellectual Property Office (KIPO), and Japan Patent Office (JPO). The US patenting system does not elect to protect utility models as a type of patent.[2]

[1] Similar to utility patents, utility models protect new technical inventions. However, they are sometimes referred to as "minor inventions" or "short-term patents," which do not fulfill the patentability requirements, but may have an important role in a local innovation system.

[2] The terms and conditions for granting utility models are different from *traditional* patents. In most countries, utility models are granted under no substantive examination systems with shorter protection terms up to seven to ten years, compared to 20 and 15 years for utility and design patents, respectively.

J. Kim et al., *Patent Analytics*,
https://doi.org/10.1007/978-981-16-2930-3_3

In contrast, design patents are granted for a new, original, and ornamental characteristics of the product. They only protect the aesthetic aspects, but not the functional features of the product. Unlike the United States Patent and Trademark Office (USPTO), KIPO, and JPO where design patents are obtained after substantive patent examination, the European Union Intellectual Property Office (EUIPO)[3] adopts a Registered Community Design (RCD), where design rights are obtained by deposits that comply with the formalities. Regardless of whether designs meet the subject, matters concerned with legal requirements are decided later in the courts, if there is a legal dispute, that is, patentability and infringements. The requirement and duration of registered designs are not a perfect parallel to design patents in the United States. For the sake of simplicity, this book is grounded in the US patent system and *patents* are referred to as both utility patents and design patents throughout the book. If there is a need to explain them separately, each of them will be separated.

Patents are to protect creations by giving the patentee exclusive rights to exclude others from making, using, offering for sales, or selling in a country where the patents are in force. On the one hand, advantages are that patents serve to promote continuous innovation activities with the potential to gain economic profits, as well as provide legal measures for preventing infringements and compensation for damages or losses caused by unfair competition (EPO 2011). However, exercising these exclusive rights may discourage market competition or even obstruct follow-up inventions.

In exchange for these exclusive rights, patent law requires inventors to disclose their inventions to public. This disclosure becomes freely available online as soon as the patent is issued. In addition, the duration of patent protection is finite. In the U.S., the term of protection is 20 years for utility patents and 15 years for design patents.[4] After patents expire, they become part of the public domain.

Juxtaposed with patents, trademark rights can potentially last forever—available for renewal every 10 years—so long as the trademark is used in actual commerce. A trademark is an exclusive right for brand names and logos used in goods or services. Any sign capable of distinguishing goods or services can be used as a trademark, such as words, numerals, letters, symbols, colors, or combination thereof. Trademarks do not protect the goods or services themselves but play a role in preventing a competitor from marketing similar goods or services, which could lead to customer confusion. Hence, trademarks closely relate to customer loyalty, marketing, and brand assets.

As many companies pursue innovation through advancing technologies and product functionality, patents have been crowned as premier intellectual properties. However, the value of patents has been greatly exaggerated.

Figure 3.1 depicts the rate at which utility patents, design patents, and trademarks gain value over time. There is a clear upward trend in all IPs, but they vary in terms of function. Initially utility and design patents appear to be more valuable than trademarks, and design patents amass higher initial value than patents. This is partly

[3]Following the Brexit Agreement, EUIPO now comprises 27 EU member states from January 1, 2021.

[4]In the United States, design patents filed on or after May 13, 2015 are valid for 15 years, or 14 years if filed prior to May 13, 2015.

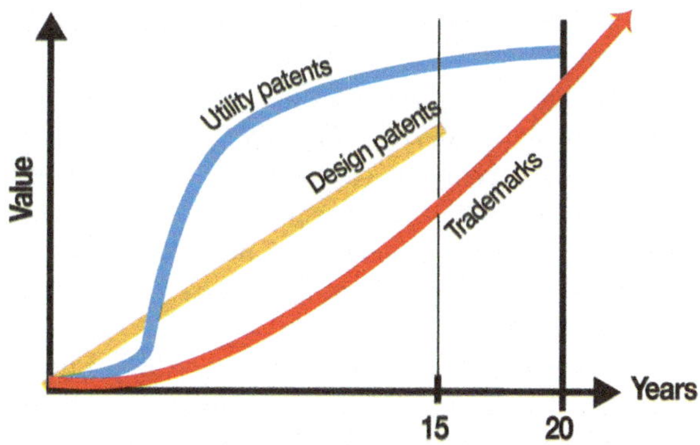

Fig. 3.1 Terms and value of utility patents, design patents, and trademarks

due to the prompt issuance of design patents, which are usually granted within a few months after filling, thereby making it possible to coordinate with product launch. In contrast, the utility patent pendency appears to fluctuate with technology. It is not uncommon for utility patents to be pending beyond two or three years. However, once issued, the value of utility patents dramatically increases and slowly equilibrates until the end of the protection term. Remarkably, the value of trademarks climbs slowly as brand equity develops and does not taper even after utility and design patents expire.

The values of intellectual properties change throughout the product life cycle (Fig. 3.2). During the initial stage of market entry, patents have a profound impact on competitive advantages by providing companies new ways to manifest their technological advances. However, with the market growth, the limits of technology can be reached, or at any point there may be a step change in technology. At the maturity

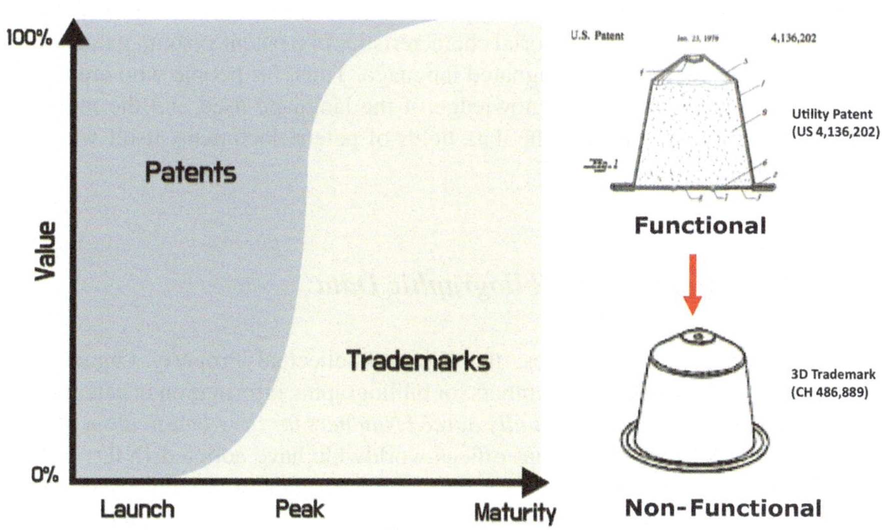

Fig. 3.2 Value transition in relation to product life cycles: examples of Nespresso capsules

stage, patents eventually attenuate their value and intangible values then reside in trademarks.

Mckenna (2012) explains this phenomenon using the IP value transference model where *transferring intangible values* follow from functional (patents) to non-functional elements (designs and trademarks). One such example is Nestlé's Nespresso coffee capsule. Nespresso's coffee machine and its compatible capsules have been strongly protected by multiple patents. However, these prime patents expired a decade ago. Now *what else...* than the end of patent protection for Nespresso?

Meanwhile, in an attempt to protect its original design (CH 486,889), Nestlé resisted and kept renewing its three-dimensional trademark on the Nespresso capsule such that Nespresso's intangible value resides in its designs and brands other than the functional aspects.

3.2 A Walk Through of Patent Data Fields

Understanding patents as a data source is the first step in patent analytics. Patents documents contain several data fields, including bibliographic data (e.g., title, applicants, filing dates), technical disclosure (e.g., abstract, descriptions, drawings), and legal information (e.g., claims, legal status) (Trippe 2015).

There are several barriers to extracting meaningful information from patents documents. First, patents are a double-edged sword: that is, protecting the exclusive rights of patent holders while disclosing the details of the discovery to the public. Thus, patent documents are intentionally obfuscated, using a complex sentence structure and technical and legal jargon, in a way that makes retrieving relevant information difficult. Second, due to the territorial characteristics of a patent system, patent documents are published in their designated language. Thus, for people who are new to the patent system and without knowledge of the language used and the industrial property laws applied, reading the data fields of patent documents itself would be the first challenge.

3.2.1 INID Codes and Bibliographic Data

To deal with these complexities, the World Intellectual Property Organization (WIPO) has standardized code numbers for bibliographic information in patent documents, which is called *Internationally agreed Numbers for the Identification of Data* (INID) (WIPO ST.9 2013). Patent offices worldwide have adopted INIDs in their patent systems, as shown in Fig. 3.3. The sample patent front pages issued from the EPO, USPTO, China National Intellectual Property Administration (CNIPA) and KIPO have the INID codes with parentheses in common. These concerted efforts allow the public to read important patent information regardless of the

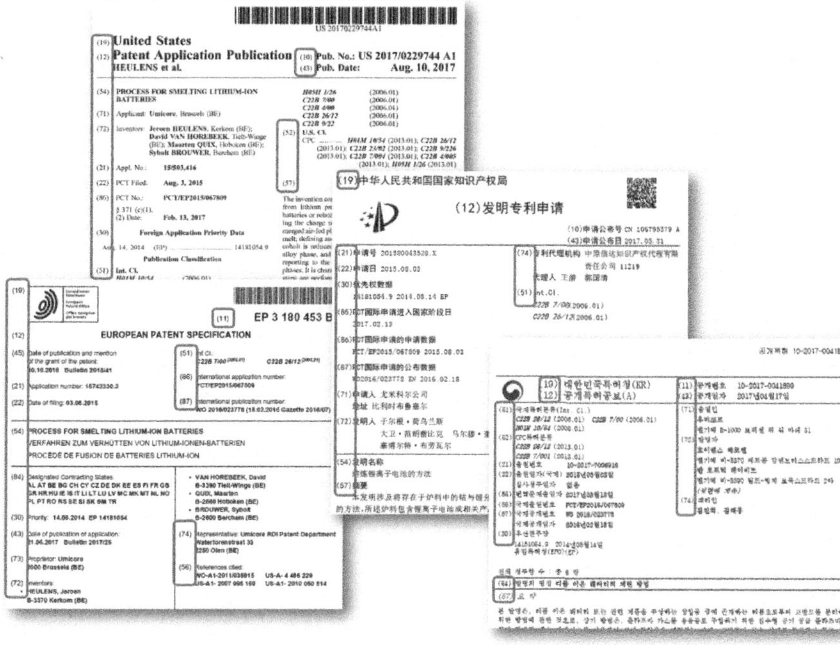

Fig. 3.3 Sample front page of patent document issued from the EPO, USPTO, CNIPA, and KIPO (in order from left to right)

language barriers and harmonize regional and national patents office databases with international standards.

The INID codes and corresponding patent data fields include type of document (12), title of the invention (code 54), date of publication (code 45), international technology fields (code 51), reference cited (code 56), names of applicants (code 71), and names of assignees (code 73).

Figure 3.4 shows the front page of US 9,967,644 utility patent (Apple's AirPods). We can walk through the bibliographic data through key INID codes as follows: US 9,967,644 was issued in the United States on May 6, 2018 (codes 12 and 45) under the title of the magnetic retention of earbud with cavity (code 54). The patent is technically classified in H04R 1/10 and H04R 1/34 based on the International Patent Classifications (IPCs) (code 51). A list of the prior art from the United States and foreign patents as well as non-patent literature are available in code 56. The applicant (code 71) and assignee (code 73) were both Apple Inc.

Patent documents also contain the legal and procedural status of patents. First, the priority date is deemed to determine the priority legally of all subsequent fillings of the same application anywhere else in the world (Oldham 2016). The INID code 65 indicates the prior publication date in the example patent, which is August 24, 2017. Second, under the US procedure, the processes of examining patents and of

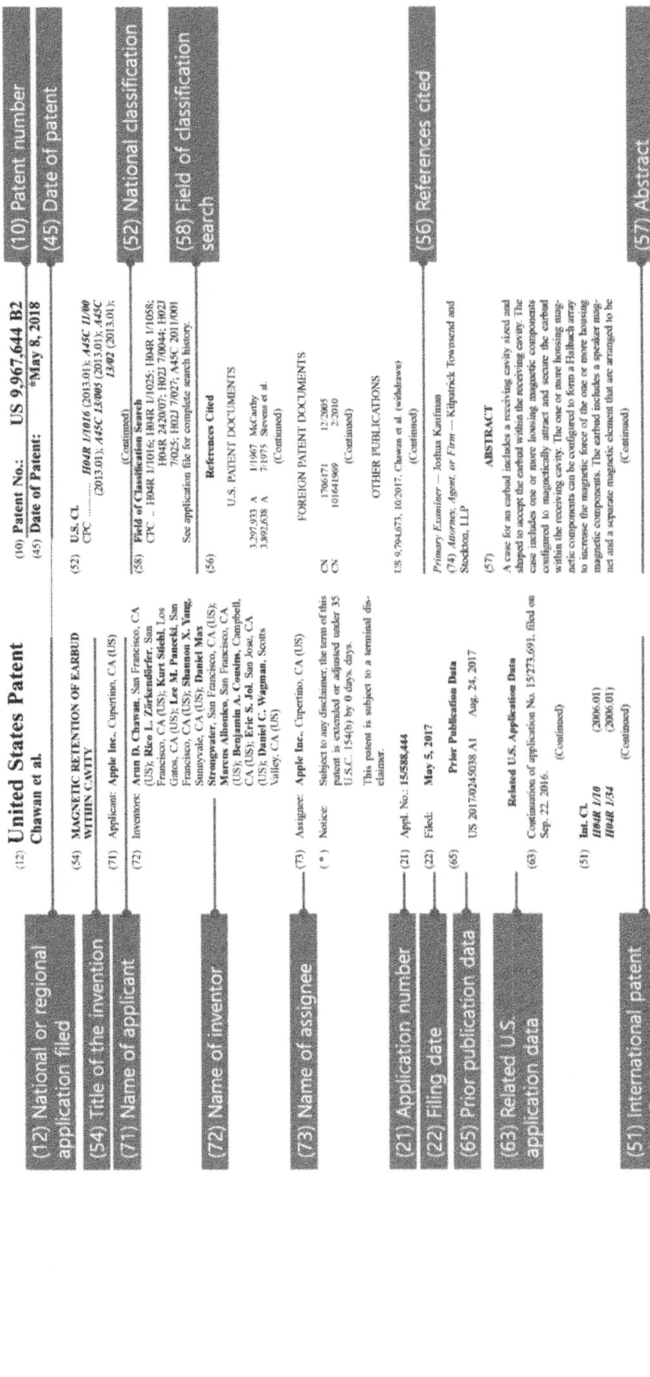

Fig. 3.4 Front page of utility patent of Apple's AirPods (US 9,967,644)

publishing the specification as filed at 18 months operate. However, the gap between the prior publication date (August 24, 2017, code 65) and the filing dates (May 5, 2017, code 22) was only four months. Presumably, Apple wished to expedite the prosecution process for some reasons, such as legal actions on patent infringement at the earliest. Refer to Chap. 10 for more details regarding the patent litigations between Apple's Beats and Bose.

Notably, the continuation of the application (code 63) informs that the patent was not a sole application but one of continuing applications to reinforce a corresponding prior-filed US provisional application. In addition, if there is a mismatch between applicants and assignees, it indicates the patent has undergone patent transactions, such as any form of patent licensing, sales, and acquisitions.

Table 3.1 lists the frequently used INID codes in patent analytics. Many of the codes have corresponding machine-readable tags, which are used to accelerate the updates on electronic databases and offer separate downloadable files. A full list and definitions of the INID codes are available in WIPO Standard ST.9 (WIPO ST.9 2013).

3.2.2 Patent Numbering System and Kind-Of-Documents

Patent documents are assigned unique identification numbers at each stage in the patenting process, such as an application, publication and patent numbers.

Referring to Apple's AirPods patent in Fig. 3.4, the application number (code 21) was assigned when the application was filed to the USPTO, which is 15/588,444. When an application is published (usually 18 months after it is filed), the publication number (code 65) US 2017/0245038 A1 is given. Finally, if the patent is granted, the patent number (code 10) is assigned, of which the format is US 9,967,644 B2. The elucidation of each numbering format is as follows:

- An *application number* is assigned in format of YY/NNN,NNN where the first two digits (i.e., YY) are the series code associated with the filing year and the six digits (i.e., NNN,NNN) are the registration numbers.
- A *publication number* is in the format of CC YYYY/NNNNNNN KD, where CC is the country code of the place of filing (e.g., US for the United States, see Table 3.2), YYYY indicates the publication year (2017/0245038 is published in 2017), NNNNNNN is a serial number, followed by a two-character kind-of-document codes (see Table 3.3).
- The typical format for a *patent number* is CC N,NNN,NNN KD where CC is the country, N,NNN,NNN is a sequential numerical string for the patent number, and KD means the kind-of-document code.

Table 3.2 provides a list of country codes given in WIPO Standard ST.3 (WIPO ST.3 2019). The two-letter country code denotes either country of filling, application, or publication. The country codes are also found in the fields of applicant (71), inventor (72), and assignee (73). These data are frequently employed in patent

Table 3.1 Key INID codes for patent analytics

Code	Description
(10) Identification of the patent document	
11	Patent number
13	Kind of publication (using kind-of-document code see Table 3.3)
(20) Data considering the application for a patent	
21	Application number(s)
22	Date(s) of filing the application
(30) Data relating to priority	
31	Priority application number(s)
32	Priority application date(s)
33	Country in which priority application was filed
(40) Publication dates	
45	Date of publication by printing of a granted patent
(50) Technical information	
51	International Patent Classifications (in the case of a utility patent) or Locarno classification (in the case of a design patent)
52	Domestic or national classification (e.g., Cooperative Patent Classification (CPC) and US Patent Classification System (USPC) for US utility patents; US design classification for US Design patents)
54	Title of the invention
56	Reference cited
57	Abstract or claim
58	Field of Search
(60) Additional information related to legally or procedurally related documents	
63	Number and filing date the earlier application of which the present patent document is a continuation number
65	Number of a previously published patent document concerning the same application (prior publication data)
(70) Identification of parties	
71	Name(s) of applicant(s)
72	Name(s) of inventor(s)
73	Name(s) of assignee(s)

Table 3.2 Two-letter of country and regional codes (WIPO ST.3 2019)

Code	Country/regional publishing authority
CA	Canada
CN	China
EA	Eurasian Patent Office
EP	European Patent Office
FR	France
GB	United Kingdom
JP	Japan
KR	Republic of Korea
US	United States
WO	World Intellectual Property Organization, Patent Cooperation Treaty

Table 3.3 Common US Kind-of-document codes (WIPO ST.16 2016)

Code	Definition
US Kind-of-document codes	
A1	Patent application publication
A2	Patent application publication (Republication, with new number)
B1	Publication of granted patent without prior A1 publication
B2	Publication of grant of patent following prior A1 publication
S	Design patent
P1	Publication of unexamined Plant Patent application
P2	Granted Plant Patent without prior P1 publication
P3	Granted Plant Patent following prior P1 publication
PCT Kind-of-document codes	
A1	International application (Published application with search report)
A2	International application (Published application without search report)
A3	International search report
A4	Later publication of amended claims
A8	International application (Republication of front page of specification)
A9	International application or international search report (Republication of entire specification)

analytic studies, such as identifying cross-country collaborations and geographic distribution of patenting activities.

The kind-of-document codes (e.g., A2, B1, S etc.) indicate the publication level and type of patent document (Adams 2020). Some frequent examples in use are: A1 (pre-2001 patents.), B1 (utility patent, not previously published), B2 (utility patent, previously published as an application), and S (design patent). For instance, US 2017/0245038 A1 is the US patent application publication No. 2017/0245038, where A1 refers to patent application publication. For the patent number, US 9,967,644 B2, US Patent No. 9,967,644 is published in the US, where there is previously published patent application publication (here, US 2017/0245038 A1).

Note that the interpretation of the kind-of-document codes requires considerable care because its practices vary in patent offices. Table 3.3 summarizes key kind-of-document codes for the US and PCT patent documents. The Patent Cooperation Treaty (PCT) is administrated by WIPO, where applicants file international applications to seek patent protections across multiple countries. Patent documents published by WIPO leads a patent number in the format of PCT/CCYYYY/NNNNNN KD or WO YYYY/NNNNNN KD.[5] Note that WO represents WIPO (technically the international bureau of the WIPO), YYYY is the year of application to the PCT system, and NNNNNN is a serial number, followed by the PCT kind-of-document codes. For a complete list available by county, please refer to WIPO Standard ST.16. Kind-of-Document codes (WIPO ST.16 2016).

One important lesson from the patent numbering system is that patenting activity in the past is reflected in patent numbers. Moreover, one patent can be assigned at least two or more numbers. For patent analytics, in order to use a patent number as a unique identifier, it should carefully deal with possible duplicate records and different numbering formats used in patent offices and electronic databases. In Chap. 8, we further walk through a few more steps needed to clean patent data fields in relation to research questions and intents for patent analytics.

3.2.3 Patent Classification System

A patent classification system is an arrangement of hierarchical categories for technology codes. The primary purpose is to assign an patent examiner administratively and support efficient patent searches by arranging patent documents systematically.

There are several patent classification systems. The International Patent Classification (IPC) and the Cooperative Patent Classification (CPC) are common and used by patent offices worldwide including the USPTO, WIPO, and EPO. In the case of design patents, the Locarno Classification (LOC) is destined to classify goods according to the industrial design they belong to. The design patent specific classifications and data fields are detailed in Sect. 3.3.

[5]Like many other patent offices, the WIPO has undergone several changes in PCT numeration. The current PCT numeration has been in force since December 31, 2003.

3.2.4 International Patent Classification (INID Code: 51)

The International Patent Classification (IPC or Int.Cl) is a hierarchical taxonomy developed and administrated by the WIPO for classifying patent documents. The IPC covers a wide range of technical and scientific vocabulary.

The IPC comprises eight sections from A to H, which are in turn subdivided into classes, sub-classes, groups, and sub-groups, and regularly revised to include new technologies, or the existing classification are divided into several subunits with a more narrowly defined scope. The latest edition of the IPC (in force as from January 1, 2021) comprises 8 sections, 131 classes, 646 subclasses, 7523 main groups, and 68,899 subgroups, of which the total number of groups is 76,422.

It is common for a patent to cover more than one IPC codes. For instance, Apple's patent is assigned two IPC classes: H04R 1/10 and H04R 1/34 that are related to earpieces and directional sound technologies. The structure and description of Apple's AirPods IPC classifications are shown in Table 3.4.

Table 3.4 Apple's AirPods IPC classes: H04R1/10 and H04R 1/34

Level	Number of subdivisions	Symbol	Description
Section	8	H	Electricity
Class	131	H04	Electric communication technique
Subclass	646	H04R	Loudspeakers, microphones, or like acoustic electromechanical transducers
Group	7523	H04R1	Transducers {loudspeakers or microphones}
Subgroup	68,899	H04R1/10	Earpieces; Attachments therefor
		H04R 1/34	for obtaining desired directional characteristic only by using a single transducer with sound reflecting, diffracting, directing or guiding means

3.2.5 Cooperative Patent Classification (INID Code: 52)

The Cooperative Patent Classification (CPC) system is an extension of the IPC and is jointly managed by the EPO and the USPTO. The assigned CPCs appear under the INID code 52 along with other domestic or national classifications (e.g., USPC of the USPTO, F-term of the JPO).

The CPC shares the general hierarchical structure of the IPC but has more subgroups than the IPC. The CPC has A–H sections and an additional Y section. The Y section generally tags new technological developments and cross-sectional technologies spanning across serval sections. For instance, class Y02 represents climate change mitigation technology (e.g., reduction of greenhouse gas emissions,

Table 3.5 Apple's AirPods CPC classes: H04R1/ 1016 and A45C 13/02

Level	Number of subdivisions	Symbol	Description
H04R 1/1016			
Section	9	H	Electricity
Class	120	H04	Electric communication technique
Subclass	628	H04R	Loudspeakers, microphones, or like acoustic electromechanical transducers
Group	10,633	H04R1	Transducers {loudspeakers or microphones}
Subgroup	254,795	H04R1/1016	Earpieces of the intra-aural type
A45C 13/02			
Section	9	A	Agriculture
Class	120	A45	Hand and traveling articles
Subclass	628	A45C	Purses, luggage, hand carried bags
Group	10,633	A45C 13	Details: Accessories
Subgroup	254,795	A45C 13/02	Interior fittings, means for holding and packing articles

waste management) and Y04 relates to information and communication technologies having an impact on other technology areas (e.g., smart grids technology).

Like IPCs, one or more CPC symbols that best represent the subject matter of the patent can be applied. Apple's AirPods patent is assigned four CPC classes (H04R1/1016, A45C 11/00, A45C 13/005, A45C 13/02). Table 3.5 shows the structure and descriptions of H04 H04R1/ 1016 and A45C 13/02, for example.

3.3 Same Same, but Different Design Patents

Figure 3.5 shows the front page of the design patent related to Apple's AirPods (US D801,314). Briefly, no differences are observed between the design and utility patent documents. Under the US patent system, the two shares the same template and the INID codes. However, in view of patents as data, there are some notable differences to consider.

- Patent number (code 10): A design patent has a number with a letter prefix, *D* or *Des*. For instance, in US D801.314 S, *US* denotes that it is a US publication and a letter after the number indicates the kind-of-document code, *S*. Note that this *S* mark has been appearing on the face of design patent documents since January 2, 2001.[6] For more symbols of the kind-of-document refer to Table 3.2.

[6]For example, the USPTO began to print official kind-of-document codes from January 2, 2001.

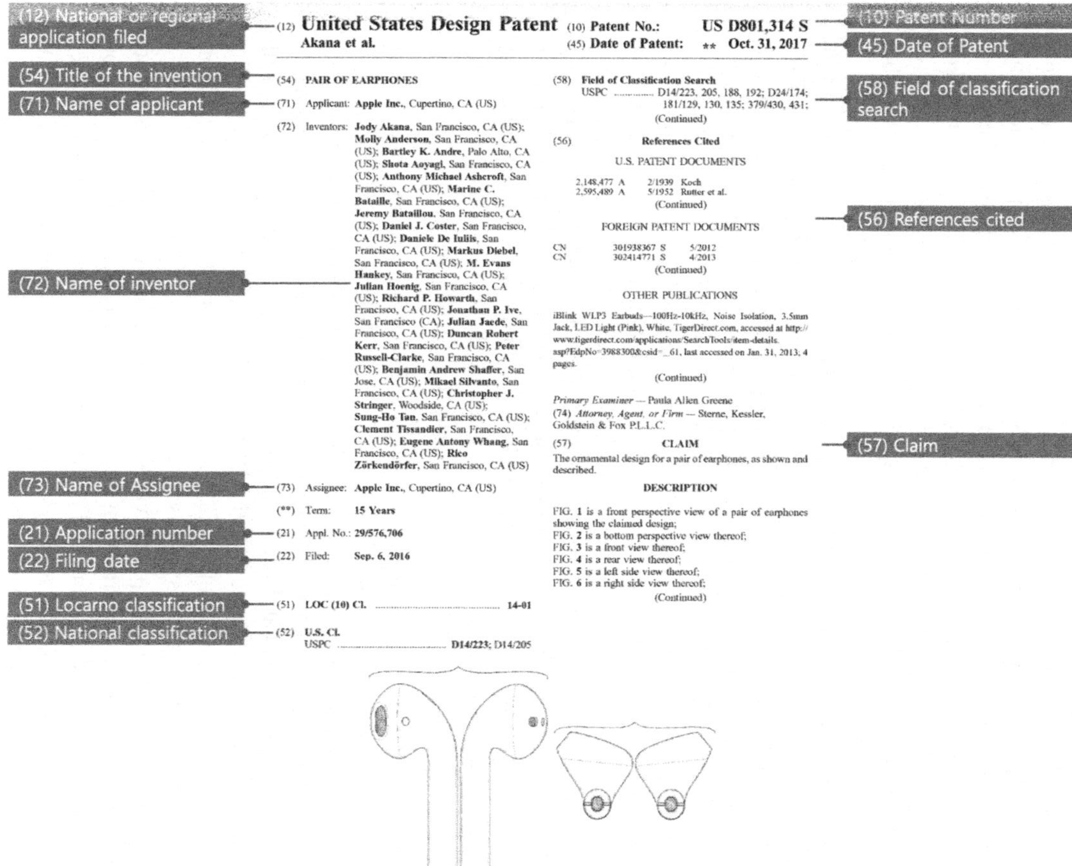

(12) **United States Design Patent**
Akana et al.

(10) **Patent No.: US D801,314 S**
(45) **Date of Patent: ** Oct. 31, 2017**

(54) **PAIR OF EARPHONES**

(71) Applicant: **Apple Inc.**, Cupertino, CA (US)

(72) Inventors: **Jody Akana**, San Francisco, CA (US); **Molly Anderson**, San Francisco, CA (US); **Bartley K. Andre**, Palo Alto, CA (US); **Shota Aoyagi**, San Francisco, CA (US); **Anthony Michael Ashcroft**, San Francisco, CA (US); **Marine C. Bataille**, San Francisco, CA (US); **Jeremy Bataillou**, San Francisco, CA (US); **Daniel J. Coster**, San Francisco, CA (US); **Daniele De Iuliis**, San Francisco, CA (US); **Markus Diebel**, San Francisco, CA (US); **M. Evans Hankey**, San Francisco, CA (US); **Julian Hoenig**, San Francisco, CA (US); **Richard P. Howarth**, San Francisco, CA (US); **Jonathan P. Ive**, San Francisco (CA); **Julian Jaede**, San Francisco, CA (US); **Duncan Robert Kerr**, San Francisco, CA (US); **Peter Russell-Clarke**, San Francisco, CA (US); **Benjamin Andrew Shaffer**, San Jose, CA (US); **Mikael Silvanto**, San Francisco, CA (US); **Christopher J. Stringer**, Woodside, CA (US); **Sung-Ho Tan**, San Francisco, CA (US); **Clement Tissandier**, San Francisco, CA (US); **Eugene Antony Whang**, San Francisco, CA (US); **Rico Zörkendörfer**, San Francisco, CA (US)

(73) Assignee: **Apple Inc.**, Cupertino, CA (US)

(**) Term: **15 Years**

(21) Appl. No.: **29/576,706**

(22) Filed: **Sep. 6, 2016**

(51) **LOC (10) Cl.** **14-01**

(52) **U.S. Cl.**
USPC **D14/223**; D14/205

(58) **Field of Classification Search**
USPC D14/223, 205, 188, 192; D24/174; 181/129, 130, 135; 379/430, 431;
(Continued)

(56) **References Cited**

U.S. PATENT DOCUMENTS

2,148,477 A 2/1939 Koch
2,595,489 A 5/1952 Rutter et al.
(Continued)

FOREIGN PATENT DOCUMENTS

CN 301938367 S 5/2012
CN 302414771 S 4/2013
(Continued)

OTHER PUBLICATIONS

iBlink WLP3 Earbuds—100Hz-10kHz, Noise Isolation, 3.5mm Jack, LED Light (Pink), White, TigerDirect.com, accessed at http://www.tigerdirect.com/applications/SearchTools/item-details.asp?EdpNo=3988300&csid=_61, last accessed on Jan. 31, 2013, 4 pages.
(Continued)

Primary Examiner — Paula Allen Greene
(74) *Attorney, Agent, or Firm* — Sterne, Kessler, Goldstein & Fox P.L.L.C.

(57) **CLAIM**

The ornamental design for a pair of earphones, as shown and described.

DESCRIPTION

FIG. **1** is a front perspective view of a pair of earphones showing the claimed design;
FIG. **2** is a bottom perspective view thereof;
FIG. **3** is a front view thereof;
FIG. **4** is a rear view thereof;
FIG. **5** is a left side view thereof;
FIG. **6** is a right side view thereof;
(Continued)

Fig. 3.5 Front page of Apple's AirPods design patent (US D801,314)

- Claim (code 57): While multiple claiming is an essential part of a utility patent, a design patent has a single claim. In formal terms, the claim in design patents shall be "*the ornamental design for the article (specifying name) as shown, or as shown and described*." For instance, the claim of the D801,314 states, "the ornamental design for *a pair of earphones* as shown and described." Unlike utility patents, where a *claim* describes the invention in a written explanation, a claim in design patents protects what is visually *described* in the drawings. The drawing disclosure is particularly important when it comes to claim the scope of the design protection—or defend against allegations of infringement—of design patents in litigation. Various visual expressions are employed, such as solid lines or broken lines as well as a combination of color or shadings for the sake of clarity of drawings. This is also related to a partial design claiming system, which is further explained in Chap. 4.
- Classifications (code 51 and code 52): Similar to utility patent documents, design patents assign classification codes upon filing and this information is available under the INID codes 51 and 52. The Locarno International Classification is an international classification used for the purposes of registration of industrial designs (code 52). The Locarno Classification is structured with two depths (32 classes and 223 subclasses). The title of the classes and subclasses provides a general indication about the area to which the goods belong. Some goods may be covered by more than one such title. For instance, Apple's AirPods design patent in Fig. 3.5 is assigned LOC (10) CL. 14–01, where Class 14 refers to reading, communication, or information retrieval equipment, and subclass 14–01 is related to equipment used for recording or reproducing sounds. Note that the number of the class and subclass (CL. 14–01) is preceded by the abbreviation *LOC* for the Locarno Classification and its edition number (e.g., 10th edition).

Historically, the Locarno Classification was established in 1968 and is mainly used by the European member nations. Today many patent offices—the USPTO, KIPO and JPO—are officially adopting the Locarno Classification while maintaining their own classification system in parallel. Their domestic or national classifications for design patents can be found at the INID code 52. Referring to Figure 3.5, along with the Locarno Classification (code 51), the USPC (US design classes) are applied to the design patent, in the format of US Cl. USPC D14/223; D14/205 (code 52). Table 3.6 enlists design classification systems by countries,

As the number of design applications is growing rapidly worldwide, many are concerned that the current Locarno Classification system is not sufficient to support prior art search and data management. For this reason, many patent offices are poised to establish advanced classification systems for design patents instead of ad hoc methods of inputting double classifications by nations.

Table 3.6 Comparison of design classification systems by countries with the example of mobile telephones

Patent offices	Classification system	Number of classes and sub-classes (/)	Example	Hierarchies				
				Level 1	Level 2			Level 3
WIPO EUIPO	Locarno classification	32/223	14–03	14	3			
USPTO	USPC	33/5,631	D14/138AA	D14	138			AA
KIPO	Korean design code	13/75/457/2,559/569	H3-301A	H	3	30	1	A
JPO	Japan design classification	13/76/3,114/1,844	H7-43AA	H	7	4	3	AA

Note that the Locarno Classification was initially developed by the European member nations where substantive examination for design applications is not required. The Locarno system has stressed its practical uses rather than its searchability. Therefore, the Locarno Classification appears very broad without any sophisticated hierarchies associated with ornamental forms of designs, such as shape descriptions

3.4 Comprehending Trademark Data

Trademark registration certificates contain simpler bibliographic information compared to the utility and design patent documents discussed above. A certificate includes a serial number, applicant information, depiction of trademark (specimen), international classifications of goods/services, descriptions of goods/services, and date of first use anywhere and first use in commerce. The international classification of goods and services is so-called the *Nice Classification*, which is administrated by the WIPO. The Nice Classification system groups goods and services into 45 classes (classes 1–34 include goods and classes 35–45 comprise services). The Nice Classification is revised every year and the latest version (11th edition) came into force on January 1, 2021. In some countries, such as China and Japan, the Nice Classification is administered through smaller classes to help applicants understand scope of protection in a clear way.

Figure 3.6 shows an example of Apple's AirPods trademark (TM 5,268,740). The trademark AirPods was filed on September 22, 2015, where its first use was on 7 September, 2015. The date of registration was August 22, 2017 with its number 5,268,740. The trademark is assigned to goods in Class 9 (audiovisual and information technology equipment), because such goods are or will be used with wireless communication devices, digital audio players, and smart watches. Table 3.7 provides the legitimate scope for Class 9 that the applicant selects.

Take another example. Starbucks must designate class 43 (café services) to manufacture and sell coffee at a shop. Yet, if Starbucks wishes to launch a new Starbucks product range comprising coffee capsules, it must additionally designate class 30 (coffee capsules) in its trademark portfolio.

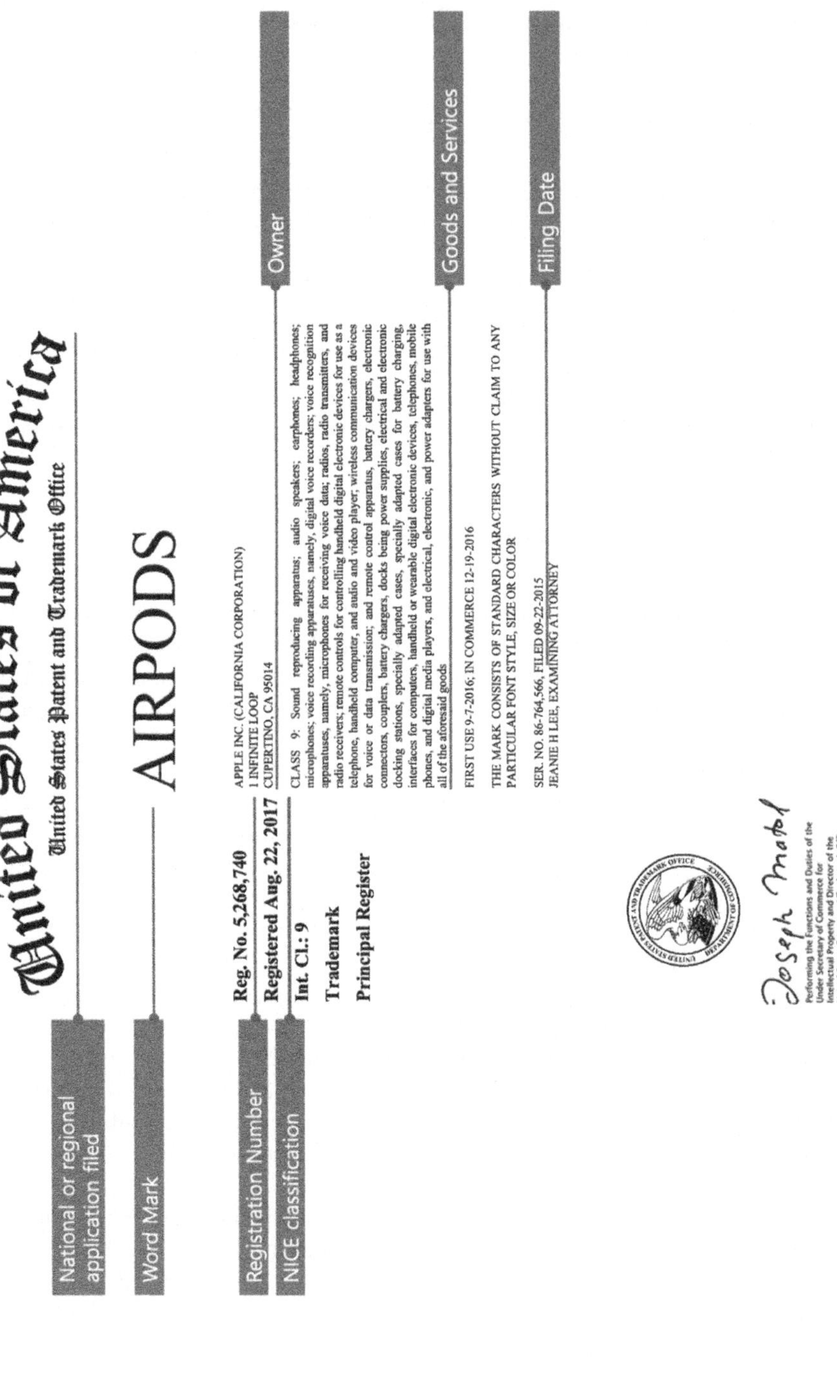
United States of America

United States Patent and Trademark Office

AIRPODS

Reg. No. 5,268,740

Registered Aug. 22, 2017

Int. Cl.: 9

Trademark

Principal Register

APPLE INC. (CALIFORNIA CORPORATION)
1 INFINITE LOOP
CUPERTINO, CA 95014

CLASS 9: Sound reproducing apparatus; audio speakers; earphones; headphones; microphones; voice recording apparatuses, namely, digital voice recorders; voice recognition apparatuses, namely, microphones for receiving voice data; radios, radio transmitters, and radio receivers; remote controls for controlling handheld digital electronic devices for use as a telephone, handheld computer, and audio and video player; wireless communication devices for voice or data transmission; and remote control apparatus, battery chargers, electronic connectors, couplers, battery chargers, docks being power supplies, electrical and electronic docking stations, specially adapted cases, specially adapted cases for battery charging, interfaces for computers, handheld or wearable digital electronic devices, telephones, mobile phones, and digital media players, and electrical, electronic, and power adapters for use with all of the aforesaid goods

FIRST USE 9-7-2016; IN COMMERCE 12-19-2016

THE MARK CONSISTS OF STANDARD CHARACTERS WITHOUT CLAIM TO ANY PARTICULAR FONT STYLE, SIZE OR COLOR

SER. NO. 86-764,566, FILED 09-22-2015
JEANIE H LEE, EXAMINING ATTORNEY

Joseph Matal
Performing the Functions and Duties of the Under Secretary of Commerce for Intellectual Property and Director of the United States Patent and Trademark Office

Fig. 3.6 Front page of Apple's AirPods trademark registration certificate (TM 5,268,740)

Table 3.7 Legitimate scope for Class 9 in the Nice Classification system

Class	Definition
Class 9	Scientific, research, navigation, surveying, photographic, cinematographic, **audiovisual**, optical, weighing, measuring, signaling, detecting, testing, inspecting, life-saving and teaching apparatus and instruments; apparatus and instruments for conducting, switching, transforming, accumulating, regulating or controlling the distribution or use of electricity; **apparatus and instruments for recording, transmitting, reproducing or processing sound**, images or data; recorded and downloadable media, computer software, blank digital or analogue recording and storage media; mechanisms for coin-operated apparatus; cash registers, calculating devices; **computers and computer peripheral devices;** diving suits, divers' masks, ear plugs for divers, nose clips for divers and swimmers, gloves for divers, breathing apparatus for underwater swimming; fire-extinguishing apparatus
Example of goods	smartwatches, wearable activity trackers; eyeglass cases, cases for smartphones, cases especially made for photographic apparatus and instruments; batteries and chargers for electronic cigarettes; **electric and electronic effects units for musical instruments** [...]

An individual may want to include as many classes as possible in order to safeguard a wider protection of trademarks even though they are not actually being used or there is intent-to-use in the near future. However, the scope of protection of trademark is determined by the list of goods or services, so that would be an expensive decision considering that filling and renewal fee for trademarks are calculated on a per class basis. For example, if the Starbucks logo is used in two different classes, such as class 43 and class 30, then the filing fee is doubled (approximately $225 per class in the USPTO). More importantly, if the registered trademark is deferred without being in commerce for a while, it is likely to lose its function of identifying the brands/products to others, and then a third party is eligible to take an invalidation action to invalidate the trademark.

Hence, companies are required to determine strategically which classes of goods or services are worthy of legal protection and the best time to file them. If a company delays the registration until the goods or services are market-ready, it can raise questions of trademark priority. Trademark ownerships are generally determined by a first-to-file basis, where the earliest applicants who register their applications first have the best a priori right for trademarks. This means that if a rival company has filed competing applications beforehand, there is nothing to guarantee the rights for those of who first conceived the trademark with proof of reasonable diligence. On the other hand, if a trademark is registered excessively early, applicants require extra efforts and costs for registration to prove their bona fide intention to use the trademark in commerce. In addition, their new brand identity and concepts are prone to be leaked out.

Apple made the best use of the fragmented trademark system in countries and notoriously deploys secretive trademark filing strategy, namely *foreign trademark filing prior to US*.

Apple first files a trademark application in a nation other than the United States and then files the same trademark in a second nation while claiming the priority. Therefore, the date to judge the requirements for patentability is backdated to the application filing date of the first nation. Consequently, this strategy can maintain the confidentiality of Apple's new product name for at least six months depending on which country is chosen as the first filing country. For example, Apple has chosen Trinidad and Tobago, Jamaica, Liechtenstein, South Africa, and Iceland, where trademark authorities do not maintain easily searchable databases, as a strategic first filing nation.

When filing *Apple TV* trademark in April 2007 in the United States, Apple used a priority claim with its foreign filing date of November 2006 in Trinidad and Tobago. The product was then publicly announced in January 2007. This *foreign trademark filing prior to US* strategy gives Apple five months of secrecy without losing any of the rights they would have had if they would have filed in the United States first. Figure 3.7 lists Apple's major trademarks and the countries in which they were first filed.

Apple's trademarks strategy is applied not only to brand or product names but also technology concepts. When launching Apple iPhone 4 with the first high-resolution screen, Apple registered a trademark, *retina*, for the display. The word *retina* did not directly emphasize its technical specification, but that literally means the human retina and uses as a metaphor of technical superiority that pixels which cannot be seen by human eyes. This clever naming strategy makes consumers perceive Apple's display technology as far more sophisticated than later competitors' in commerce.

3.5 Summary

Intellectual properties seem multifaceted and distributed like a puzzle. To complete the puzzle, strategic use of multiple IP portfolios whereby patents, designs, and trademarks are intertwined is essential. Patent data contains rich information constituting technology, business, and legal applications. However, one of the issues surrounding the use of patents as data is language. As noted above, the use of the INID codes enables us to read bibliographic data on the front page of a patent document. Some remarks on the different meaning and structure of patents, design, and trademarks are of particular interest to readers planning to use the data in interdisciplinary research.

For the last several decades, many regional and national patent offices have made concerted efforts to harmonize patent document formats to make it easier for database providers to compile them for electronic delivery or the generation of databases. However, this does not always get reliably transmitted to the database providers and the coverage for patent-issuing authorities can vary. Therefore, we cannot virtually find patent data needed in one place. Chapter 8 provides a basic roadmap to cope with patent data collection with a list of patent database providers.

Category	2007	2008	2009	2010	2011	2012
Product	Macbook Air(TT) iPhone (TT)		MAGIC MOUSE (TT)	iPad(TT)	SMART COVER (JM)	Macbook Pro(JM), EarPods(JM), iPad Mini(JM)
Service	APPLE TV(TT), iTunes Store(CA)	APP STORE(TT)		iBooks(TT), iCloud (JM)		
Technology	Multi-Touch(TT)	Time Capsule (TT)		FaceTime(TT), AirPlay(TT), Air Print(TT) Retina(TT), Mission Control(JM), Lauch Pad(TT)	AirDrop(JM), iMessage(TT)	Siri(JM) Pass book(JM), Lightining(TT)

Category	2013	2014	2015	2016	2017	2018
Product	iWatch(JM), iPad Air(JM)	Apple Watch, iWatch(JM)	iPad Pro(JM), AirPods(TT)		iMac Pro(LS)	HOMEPOD(JP)
Service		Apple Pay(JM)	Apple Music(JM), Apple News(JM), Apple Wallet(JM)		APPLE PAY CASH(JM), APPLE APP STORE(JM), iBooks STORE (WO), Macos High Sierra(LS)	APPLE BOOKS (JM), APPLE GIVEBACK(JM), HealthKit (JM)
Technology	Carplay (TT)	Touch ID(JM), Tap To Talk(JM), Taptic (JM) Engine(JM), iBeacon(JM), DigitalCrown (JM)	3D Touch(JM), Force Touch (JM), Live Photos(JM), PEEP AND POP (JM)	Touch Bar(JM), Music Memo(JM), Premium Reseller(EU), Apple Handoff (JM), CareKit(EU) Tapback(JM)	Super Retina (LS), True Depth (LS), AIR POWER (LS), AR KIT(LS), ANIMOJI(LS), FACE ID(LS), ProMotion(LS), Vital Signs(JM), Music UP NEXT (JM), Planet of the Apps(JM), Beddit(JM), Live Titles(JM), Expose(WO)	MEMOJI (LS), ProRes(JM), FOUNDATIONDB (JM)
Others				One More Thing(JM)	Think Different(JM), Today at apple(WO)	

Fig. 3.7 Apple's major trademarks and the countries in which they were first filed

References

Adams S (2020) Information sources in patents. De Gruyter, Berlin.

EPO (2011) Patent teaching kit. https://www.epo.org/learning/materials/kit/download.html. Accessed 14 Jan 2021.

Mckenna RJ (2012) Apple, Inc. - A Case Study in Successful Exploitation of Design and Innovation. Design Protection Conference White Paper 1–10.

Oldham P (2016) The WIPO Manual on Open Source Patent Analytics. https://wipo-analytics.github.io/open-refine.html. Accessed 18 Nov 2020.

Trippe A (2015) Guidelines for preparing patent landscape reports. Patent landscape reports. https://www.ompi.org/edocs/pubdocs/en/wipo_pub_946.pdf. Accessed 04 Jan 2021.

WIPO ST.3 (2019) Standard ST.3:Recommended standard on two-letter codes for the representation of states, other entities and intergovernmental organizations. https://www.wipo.int/export/sites/www/standards/en/pdf/03-03-01.pdf. Accessed 15 Jan 2020.
WIPO ST.9 (2013) Standard ST.9: Recommendation concerning bibliographic data on and relating to patents and spcs. https://www.wipo.int/export/sites/www/standards/en/pdf/03-09-01.pdf. Accessed 15 Jan 2020.
WIPO ST.16 (2016) Standard ST.16: Recommended standard code for the identification of different kinds of patent documents. https://www.wipo.int/export/sites/www/standards/en/pdf/03-16-01.pdf. Accessed 15 Jan 2020.

Chapter 4
Claims, "Legally, Less is More!"

Abstract A patent claim is indisputably the most important part of a patent document by which the scope of protection is conferred. However, comprehending a patent claim is notoriously difficult. It is often meticulously written to attain the broad protection scope while using limited wording, thus foreshadowing the doctrine of "*Legally, Less is More.*" This chapter elaborates on the anatomy of patent claims in a step-by-step manner to guide readers to figure out key claim elements and their structural and functional relationships. In addition, given that the protection scope of design patents is primally determined by ornamental shape, the chapter further explains how to define claims in design patents without a wordsmith and practical uses of partial design claiming system.

4.1 Disentangling Patent Claims

In Episode 15 of *The Walking Dead*, Joe explains his group's rules to Daryl, a new member. He says, "If you want something—a rabbit or a bed—you have to *claim it*!" Coincidently, Joe's line underscores the key principle of patent *claims.*

A patent claim is incontestably the most important part of a patent specification, which defines the legal scope of patent protection. In drafting claims, patent professionals walk a fine line between achieving the greatest possible protection scope for the patent while avoiding prior art. Words used in claims are transformed to the terms that have a structural and functional terminology to cover the disclosed embodiments (i.e., means-plus-function). On the one hand, the general terms used in the claims should be fully supported by the detailed descriptions of the invention without too many narrow interpretations. For instance, in patent claims, the term *battery* is replaced by the *electrical power source for electronic circuits* to obtain a broader protection. On the other hand, too little detail about the elements may trap prior arts to invalidate the patents (e.g., *a remote-control method vs a remote-control method and system based on electromagnetic induction*).

Claims are structured to include both broader or *independent claims* and more specific or *dependent claims.* An independent claim usually describes the invention in very general terms to allow a broad interpretation in infringement lawsuits. In

J. Kim et al., *Patent Analytics*,
https://doi.org/10.1007/978-981-16-2930-3_4

contrast, dependent claims usually describe specific ways of realizing the invention that the inventor regards as economically attractive. Structurally, independent claims are stand-alone and do not recite other claims, whereas dependent claims refer to other independent or dependent claims either by incorporating additional elements or further limitations. In any given patent application, the allowable claim categories include claims to physical entities (product, device, apparatus) or activities (process, use, method). A patent referring to more than one category must include at least one independent claim per category.

Figure 4.1 exemplifies the structure of the claims extracted from the US 10,182,282, which relates to Apple's AirPods case (earbud case with charging system). The claim information is available at INID code 57 in the patent document. The number of claims is a sum of both independent and dependent claims. The US 10,182,282 patent consists of 20 claims (three independent and 17 dependent claims). For example, the first independent claim could be read as *a case for an earbud, comprising a housing, a lid [...].* The following dependent claim refers to the previous claim and further limits the invention: *the case of claim 1 where in the housing [...].*

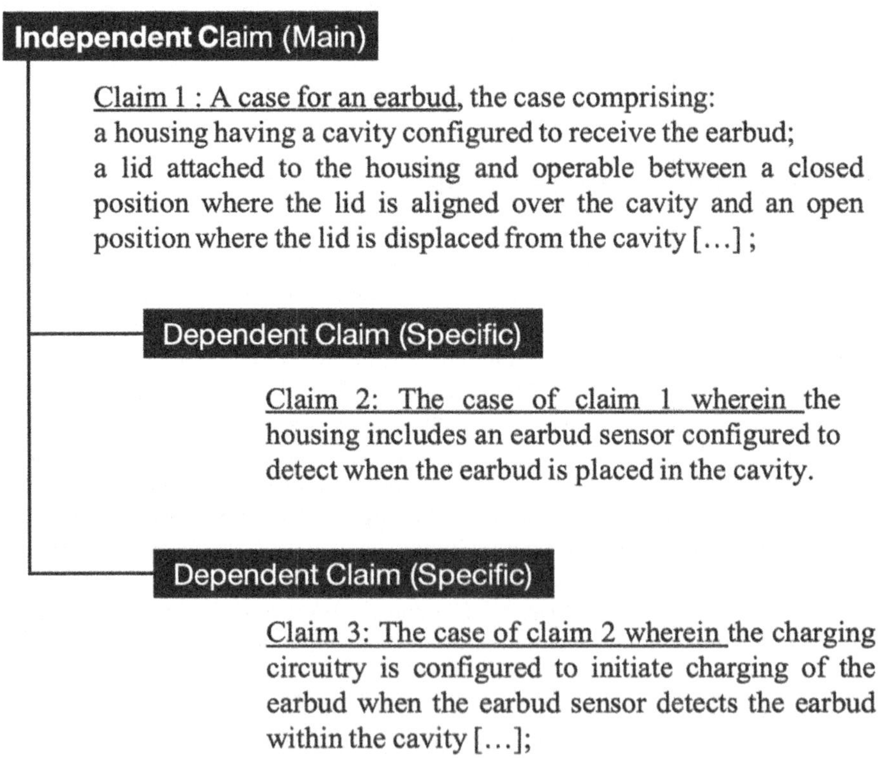

Fig. 4.1 Use of independent and dependent claims to improve protection

The real benefit of structuring claims hierarchically is that if a broad independent claim is later found to be invalid, for example because there is prior art, then the narrower dependent claims may be still be valid.[1] Section 4.2 continues to explain how patent claims changes in examination and litigation process and their potential implications for future patent analytics.

4.2 Broad or Narrow: All-Elements Rule

Economists and other researchers have long used a claim as a proxy for patent values. The typical approaches include: (1) counting the number of claims in the patent (e.g., Lanjouw and Schankerman 2004; Frakes and Wasserman 2013; Kuhn and Thompson 2019); (2) comparing claim counts and technology classes (Novelli 2015); and (3) claim lengths and counts between patent applications and issued patents (e.g., changes in the scope of protection, Macro et al. 2019).

Marco et al. (2019) focus on the patent examination process at the Patent Cooperation Treaty (PCT) system[2] using independent claim counts and word length before and after the examination. The examination process itself tends to narrow the scope of patents relative to the scope at filing, resulting in increasing the claim length. Another approach is to employ patent claim lengths to indicate the degree of fierce competition between the technology field and other industries (Novelli 2015). As technology fields get more crowded, more complex patent structures are required to distinguish between the claimed invention and the nearest prior art.

The process of claim narrowing almost always involves adding words to the claim, such as modifiers, qualifiers, or other details. Moreover, on the other side of it, it makes sense that using lesser number of words per claim helps to pursue the broad claim scope. In drafting patent claims, many experienced IP practitioners state this as "*legally, less is more.*" Figure 4.2 provides an example. Suppose the initial independent claim of a patent is claim 1 (A + B). During prosecution, if an examiner conjectures that the claimed invention lacks non-obviousness against the prior art A + B + C, then an amendment is directed towards narrowing the protection scope. In the example, claim 1 is the added new element D. Amended claim 1 (A + B + D) and new dependent claim 2 (A + B + D + C) are finally granted. First, it is important to note that when more claim elements are included, protection becomes narrower; second, the newly added element D would be considered as the patent's unique feature to distinguish the invention from the nearest prior art.

[1] According to the all-elements rule—a legal test used in US patent law—infringement in a utility patent is defined based on whether a third party's product contains every element in *at least one claim* of the patent.

[2] The Patent Cooperation Treaty (PCT) is administrated by WIPO, where applicants file international applications to seek patent protection across multiple countries.

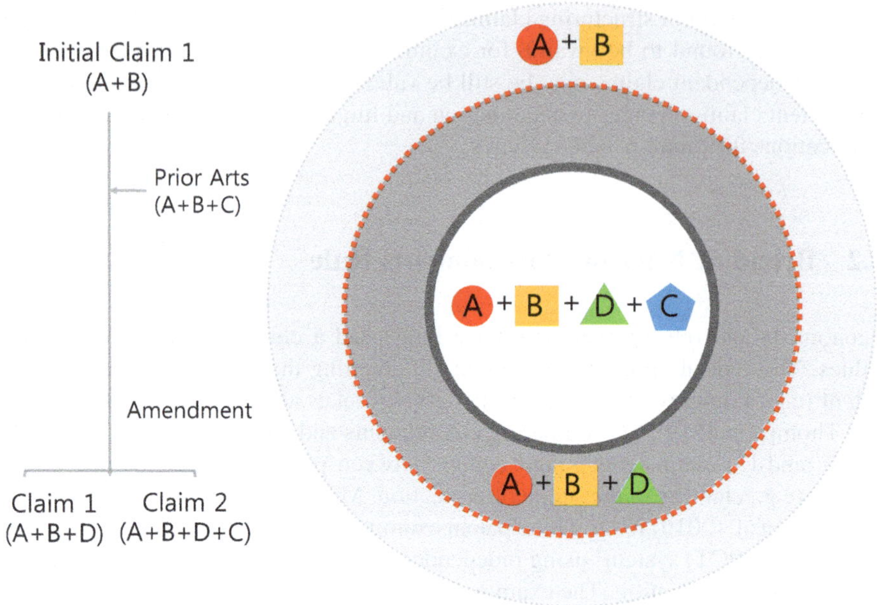

Fig. 4.2 Changes in elements of patent claims after enforcing amendments

In respect of patent infringement, the principles of claim construction suggest that a large number of claims broaden a patent's scope while potential overlapping is allowed. This is the so-called *all-elements rule.*

According to the all-elements rule, if some of the elements in the claims are omitted or changed into another element in the embodiment, it is not regarded as patent infringement in principle. This is somehow deemed a different interpretation from the infringement decision of the copyright of a music or literary work. Instead, in order to infringe a patent, an accused patent must contain every single element in *at least one claim* of the patent.

Question: Company X holds a patent with three claims: independent claim 1 (A + B + D), dependent claim 2 (A + B + D + C), and independent claim 3 (A + B + E). If Company Y is planning to file a patent with a combination of the claim elements shown from ① to ⑧ in Fig. 4.3, does Company Y infringe Company X's patent?

Answers: As each claim is presumed valid independently, the *all-elements rule* is applied to each claim. ① (A + B + D) obviously infringes the patent as it is the same as claim 1 (A + B + D). ② (A + B + D + E) and ③ (A + B + D + C) have unique elements E and C, respectively, compared to the claim 1, but all elements of claim 1 are included. Thus, ② and ③ are infringed. In the case of ④ (A + B + C + E), it does not infringe claim 1, but does infringe claim 3 (A + B + E). In comparison, ⑤ to ⑧ do not constitute infringements as they do not include all elements of claim 1, claim 2 or claim 3.

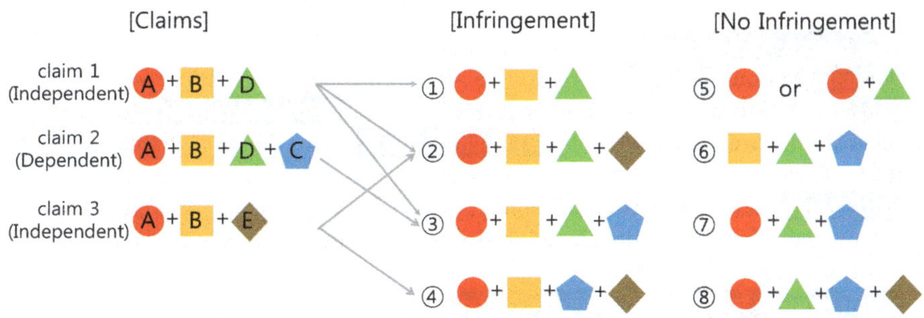

Fig. 4.3 How to apply all-elements rule with examples of accused claims ①–⑧

Although the protection scope of the claims overlaps to some extent, a set of claims can have multifold beneficial effects. First, various design-around possibilities can be prevented in advance. Second, the ability to defend the patent can be strengthened even if some claims may be invalidated during patent infringement litigation. For instance, even if claims ①–④ are invalidated by third parties, claims ⑤–⑧ are judged independently and remain valid.

From the patentee's standpoint, it is better to secure a core invention with as many claims as possible. However, multiple claims engender high costs as examination request and maintenance fees are calculated based on the number of claims. Thus, the number of claims to be filed should be strategically determined according to the relative importance of the patent.

4.3 Anatomy of Patent Claims

Patent claims are written by meticulously selecting and refining the essential elements while seeking maximum scope of invention protection. A stray use of terms and phrases in the claims can easily lead to unintended consequences of limiting the scope of the invention. As a result, reading patent claims seems to resemble learning a foreign language. The claim seems complex to follow as it involves more superordinate concepts than ordinarily used terms, and the words are arranged in a hierarchical structure like a train of thought.

This section elaborates on the anatomy of patent claims systematically. Figure 4.4 shows a three-step guide to figure out the key elements of a claim and their structural

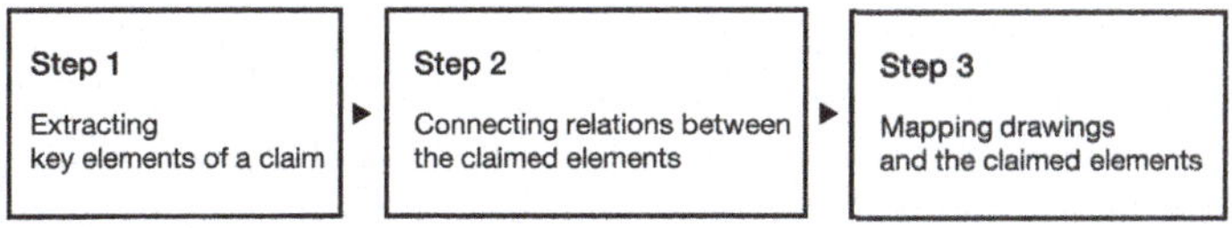

Fig. 4.4 Anatomy of patent claims

1. A case for an earbud, the case *comprising:*
a housing having a cavity configured to receive the earbud;
a lid attached to the housing and operable between *a closed position* where the lid is aligned over the cavity and an open position where the lid is displaced from the cavity;
a lid sensor, at least a portion of which is affixed to the housing, configured to detect when the lid is in the closed position and when the lid is in the open position; and
a charging system including a case battery, and
charging circuitry configured to charge the earbud when the earbud is positioned in the cavity; and
circuitry coupled to the lid sensor and configured to turn off a wireless radio contained within the earbud when the lid sensor detects the lid is moved from the open position to the closed position.

2. The case of claim 1 wherein the housing includes an earbud sensor configured to detect when the earbud is placed in the cavity.
3. The case of claim 2 wherein the charging circuitry is configured to initiate charging of the earbud when the earbud sensor detects the earbud within the cavity [...]

Fig. 4.5 Example of patent claims: a guide to reading

and functional relationships. It consists of step 1: extracting key claim elements; step 2: connecting relations between the claimed elements; and step 3: mapping drawings and the claimed elements. Again, the patent claims excerpted from US 10,182,282 (Apple's AirPods case, *earbud case with charging system)* is used for illustrative purposes (Fig. 4.5).

Step 1. Extracting key elements of a claim

According to the Patent Office's guide to patent claim drafting, the antecedent basis imposes formalities to avoid any stray use of terms and phrases that can easily cause ambiguity and unintended consequences of limiting the scope of invention. For example, the antecedent basis rules compel the use of *a/an* preceding the first introduction of an element and no article in the case of plural nouns or uncountable nouns. Thus, scrutinizing only nouns with indefinite articles in the claims saves hours of laborious investigation.

Figure 4.5 highlights in black nouns with an indefinite article. By reading them in order, we can broadly understand the key elements of the claim. The claim is such that "*a case for an earbud* which comprises of a *housing (cavity), lid, lid sensor, charging system (case battery and charging circuitry),* and *wireless radio circuitry.*" Subsequently, the use of *the*, *said*, or *the said* precede the aforementioned elements.

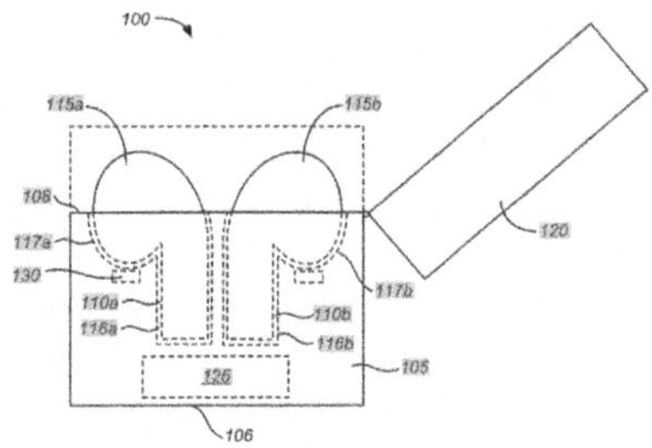

FIG. 1

FIG. **1** depicts a simplified plan view of a case **100** for a pair of wireless earbuds according to some embodiments of the disclosure. As shown in FIG. **1**, case **100** includes a housing **105**, also called a body, having one or more cavities **110***a*, **110***b* configured to receive a pair of earbuds **115***a*, **115***b*. In some embodiments, cavities **110***a*, **110***b* can be positioned adjacent to each other on opposite sides of a center plane of case **100**. Each cavity **110***a*, **110***b* can be sized and shaped to match that of its respective earbud **115***a*, **115***b*. Each cavity can include a stem section **116***a*, **116***b* and a bud section **117***a*, **117***b*. Each stem section **116***a*, **116***b* can be an elongated generally cylindrical cavity that extends

Fig. 4.6 Elements in drawings and their corresponding labels

Step 2. Connecting relations between the claimed elements

The next step is to examine how to connect relations between the comprising elements (or limiting claims). It is important to examine the claims focusing on the interrelationships between comprising elements, operating events, or their control methods. Specifically, *where* or *wherein* are used to limit comprising elements in the claims. The phrases after where or wherein often pertain to claim amendment, which may contain the unique features of the invention.

Wherein is also employed to make the transition for a dependent claim, such as claim 2: "*The case of claim 1 wherein* the housing [...] in the cavity." In the case of claim 3, it does not depend from claim 1, but claim 2, such that claim 3: "*The case of claim 2 wherein* the charging circuitry [...] within the cavity." This is how claims are chained together.

In addition, *comprising* and *consisting of* are referred to as open claim and closed claim, respectively. Referring to Fig. 4.5, claim 1 starts with "a case for an earbud, the case *comprising,*" which means the invention includes but is not limited to the element identified in the claim. The expression *comprising* is by far most common, as it results in broader protection, whereas *consisting of* indicates that the invention is only what is described. The latter defines the boundary of the projection. This is often found in a claim for a chemical compound, such as *consisting of components A, B, and C*, meaning that all three components are required to draw a specific outcome; the presence of any additional component shall be excluded.

Step 3. Mapping drawings and the claimed elements.

A picture is worth a thousand words. Many patent professionals would argue that a drawing is the most important part of a patent document alongside claims. The drawings communicate every feature of the invention specified in the claims.[3]

Consider a drawing and its detailed description taken from US 10,182,282 (Fig. 4.6). The elements shown in the drawing are typically accompanied by reference

[3]Most claims do not insert the drawing numbers/legends in the claim section because it may be interpreted that the invention is limited to only the embodiment in the drawings. Remember that every word counts in a claim.

numerals. Manual mapping of reference numbers and the corresponding description enables understanding of the subject matter of the patent, such as a case (100), housing (105), cavity (110), and a pair of earbuds (115). The detailed description must be read with caution if new comprising elements are defined in claims or functional terms are used.

The anatomy of claims hints at a set of rules for developing intelligent IP solutions, such as an automatic claim tree chart, a drawing tagging system with reference numbers, a claim text analyser based on the antecedent basis writing, dual viewer for comparing claims before and after examination, and more. For example, WIPS Global, a Korea-based IP analytics solution provider, offers claim tree charts that show hierarchy and cites relations between claims to enable easy review on subject matters with different depth levels (Fig. 4.7). Most recently, the company released a drawing-based patent search function based on a drawing tagging system (Fig. 4.8). Furthermore, we expect that the use of natural language processing techniques is likely to produce a more sophisticated measure of patent claims, particularly for examining subject specific terminologies (Alderucci and Ashley 2020).

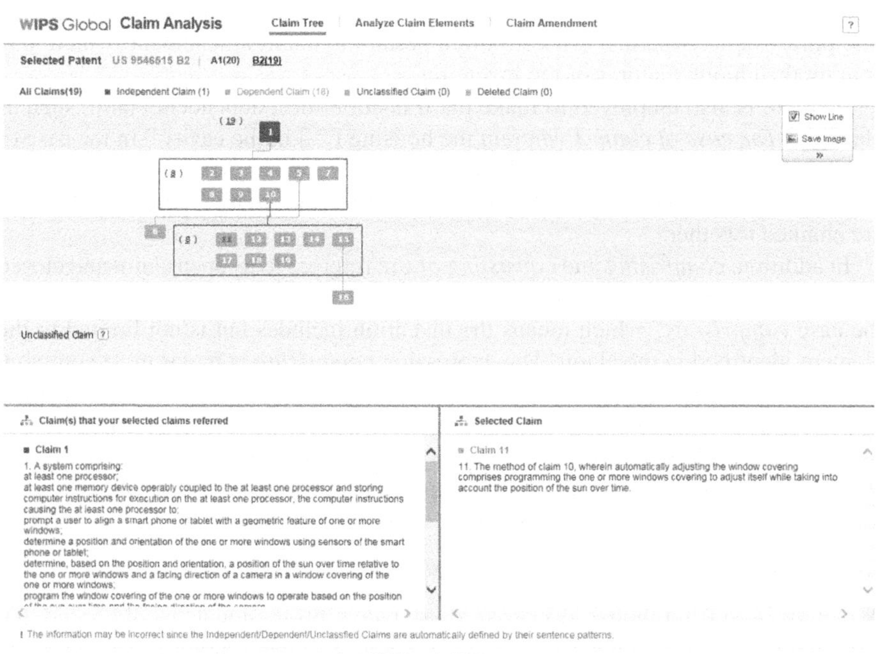

Fig. 4.7 WIPS Global claim chart

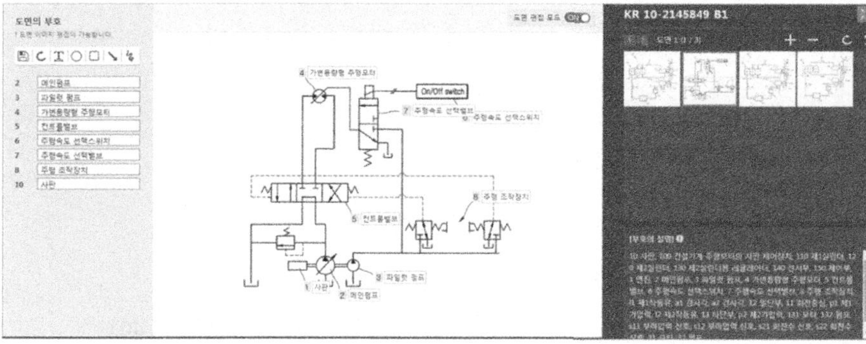

Fig. 4.8 WIPS Global drawing tagging system

4.4 The Butterfly Effect of Design Patents

In the case of utility patents, while drawings are often broad compared to claims and used for practical purposes to aid understandings of the invention, design patents are heavily leveraged on drawings.

Each design patent has a single claim thereby constituting the entire visual disclosure depicted in the drawings. Thus, the protection scope of design patents is primarily determined by the drawings. Yet, as design patents protect only the overall appearance of what is drawn, design-arounds are considered fairly easier than utility patents. Small design changes can be legally valid without infringing the prior art.

Such practices narrow the extent for design protection and become an obstacle in invalidation and infringement determination. To overcome these limitations, design patents allow *partial claiming* whereby applicants can fragment their design into multiple design patents. Compared to claiming an article's design as a whole, partial claiming system can safeguard a wider protection scope, resulting in stronger rights for the applicant.

Any claimed or disclaimed part of the design is generally represented by using solid lines and dotted lines.[4] Solid lines are used to illustrate the essential part of the design and dotted lines are used to outline design parts other than those shown using solid lines. In an infringement litigation, designs can be accused of infringing if the parts of the design with solid lines are substantially similar even though the remaining parts with dotted lines create distinct appearances. Figure 4.9 illustrates how Apple's AirPods designs are protected by multiple partial design claims.

Historically, the first speculative account of a partial design claim dates to the late nineteenth century when dotted lines first emerged in the drawings of US 22,320. The design embodied in the handle of what appears to be a spoon or fork accompanied the bowl, or a tiny portion marked in dotted lines (Fig. 4.10).

On the legal front, the partial design system has stemmed from a 1980 the US Court of Customs & Patent Appeals, *In re Zahn* (*In re Zahn*, 617 F.2d 261, C.C.P.A

[4]Broken lines under the U.S. patent law.

US D801,314
(Pair of earphones)

US D806,388
(Case)

US D849,401
(Case with earphones)

Fig. 4.9 Examples of partial design claiming associated with Apple's AirPods

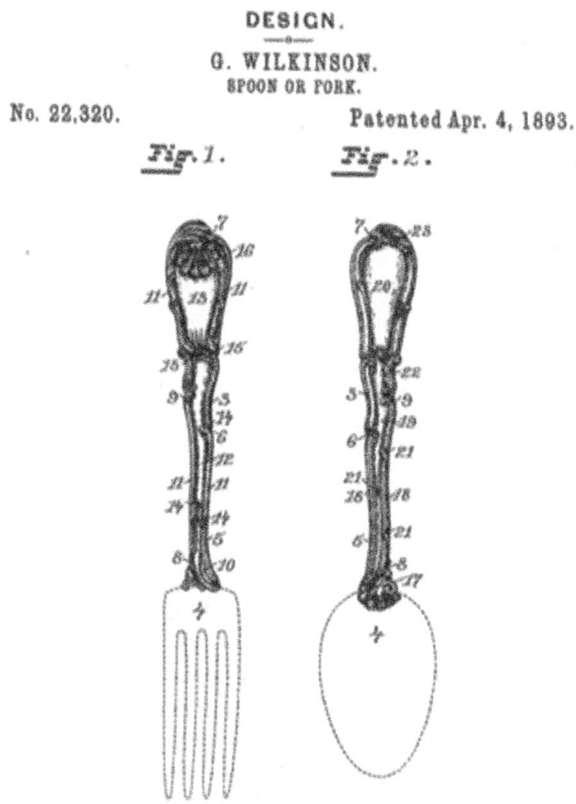

Fig. 4.10 The first speculative dotted lines in drawings (US 22,320)

1980). In 1975, the USPTO initially rejected Zahn's drill bit design application (US D257,511), in which the shank of a drill bit in solid lines is claimed for protection, while the disclaimed section, a blade, is expressed by dotted lines (Fig. 4.11). Later on appeal to the board, the court ruled in favor of Zahn by recognizing a partial claim of the design as a patentable subject matter.

The onset of Zahn's drill bit case profoundly changed the structure of design protection regimes. The implementation of partial design protections enables companies to safeguard both the essential and ornamental components of a design to ensure that competitors cannot use or mimic them. Since then, the USPTO revised the definition of design in §1502 Guidelines of Patent Examination (US) as that "*visual ornamental characteristics embodied in, or applied to, an article of manufacture.*" and "*ornamental design may be embodied in an entire article or only a portion of an article.*"

The partial design claims that Samsung and Apple filed against each other became more important once the design patent infringement trials began. The ramification of those trials determined that infringed designs can constitute even a small portion of an end-product. That being said, a company can launch a partial design claim if any part or piece of their protected design is replicated in another company's design, even when the overall appearance of the product looks nothing like the original. Some companies have started to abuse this legal standard in cases that appear quite frivolous. Furthermore, if a partially claimed design and a "copy" of that design appear too similar, the institution of a design infringement claim is inevitable. For example, Apple's US D618,677, a flat planar surface with round bezel, sparked Samsung and Apple's design litigation. Apple's original patent for the D618,677 capitalized on the flexibility of the application of partial design claims to guarantee the exclusion of other competitors from the market as it was simply impossible to design a smartphone that is neither rectangular with rounded corners nor an object with a flat surface (Fig. 4.12).

Figure 4.13 shows that Apple's early design applications rendered the entire designs in solid lines, which narrowed the scope of future protections that the company could make. As a result, it was easy for competitors to design around them. However, since 2005, dotted lines began to be used in the early design patents related to the Mac mini (US D526,648) and iPod (US D548,747). Since then Apple has continued to obtain elaborate design claims by manipulating the partial design protection system. Only two years after Apple first started to make use of the partial design protection system, Apple slapped Samsung with a lawsuit and claimed that the company was guilty of infringing on three design patents and three utility patents associated with the iPhone. If Apple was limited to only be able to make claims based on the entirety of the iPhone and its major components, competitors would have much more leeway for designing around it.

The partial design system has become a relatively mature system for design protection in many countries and regions, such as the United States (since 1980), Japan (1988), Europe (2001), and the Republic of Korea (2001). In China, the partial design system came into effect in June 2021 in pursuit of promotion and enforcement of design rights.

United States Patent [19]
Zahn

[11] **Des. 257,511**
[45] ** **Nov. 11, 1980**

[54] **DRILL TOOL OR THE LIKE**

[75] Inventor: **Hajo Zahn,** Guilford, Conn.

[73] Assignee: **Olin Corporation,** New Haven, Conn.

[**] Term: **14 Years**

[21] Appl. No.: **611,034**

[22] Filed: **Sep. 8, 1975**

[51] **Int. Cl.** .... **D8—01**
[52] **U.S. Cl.** **D15/139**
[58] **Field of Search** D54/4; 408/226

[56] **References Cited**

U.S. PATENT DOCUMENTS

2,390,950	12/1945	Lanfranconi	408/226
2,570,945	10/1951	Hawkins	408/226 X
2,740,974	4/1956	Lewis	408/226 X

Primary Examiner—Alan P. Douglas
Attorney, Agent, or Firm—Donald R. Motsko

[57] **CLAIM**

The ornamental design for a drill tool or the like, as shown and described.

DESCRIPTION

FIG. **1** is a side elevational view of the drill tool or the like illustrating one embodiment of the new design and showing the cutting portion of the tool in phantom;
FIG. **2** is a top end view of the tool of FIG. **1**;
FIG. **3** is a sectional view taken along the lines **3—3** of FIG. **1**;
FIG. **4** is a partial elevational view of the right side of the tool of FIG. **1**;
FIG. **5** is a side elevational view of the tool illustrating a second embodiment of the new design and showing the cutting portion of the tool of the type shown in FIG. **1** partially in phantom;
FIG. **6** is a top end view of the tool of FIG. **5**;
FIG. **7** is a sectional view taken along the line **7—7** of FIG. **5**; and
FIG. **8** is a partial elevational view of the left side of the tool of FIG. **5**.
The phantom representation of the cutting portion of a drill bit is made in the drawings merely for the purpose of illustrating the environment in which this invention is used. The structure shown in broken lines is not part of the design sought to be patented.

Fig. 4.11 *In Re Zahn* case, US D257,511 Drill bit design

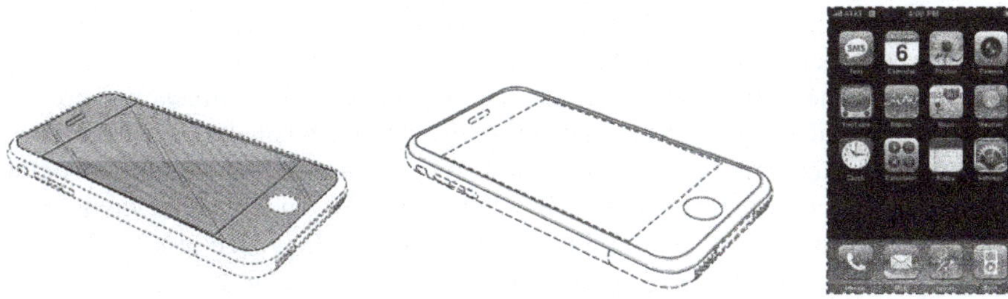

Fig. 4.12 Apple's elaborate partial claiming strategies for iPhone design

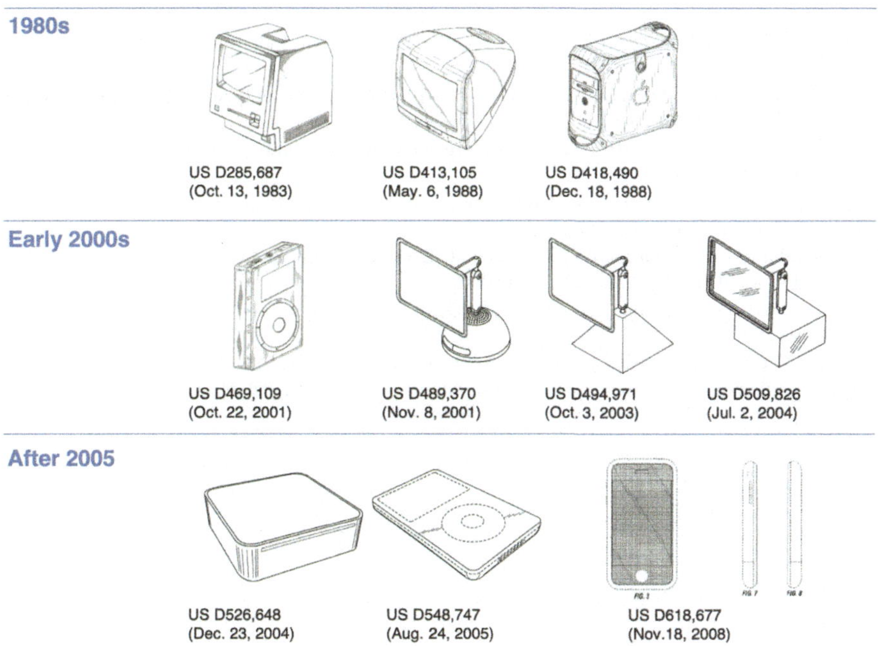

Fig. 4.13 History of Apple's partial design claims

4.5 Summary

There are several attempts to understand a claim as a proxy for patent scope. The breadth of a patent scope is often measured by counting the number of claims in a patent, number of independent and dependent claims per patent, or number of words per claim. However, simple counts of claims or words do not capture complex relationships between patent claim language and the technology space that the language circumscribes. In this regard, this chapter elaborated on the anatomy of patent claims in a step-by-step manner to guide readers to determine key elements of a claim and their structural and functional relationships.

Recently, some pioneers have sparked the use of artificial intelligence to process a claim text and identify information that is relevant to patent analytics. For instance, Google (Stegmaier 2018) demonstrated how to create a machine learning model to estimate the scope of patent claims using claim structure and syntactic complexity which was elucidated in Sect. 4.2. Furthermore, natural language processing techniques endeavor a more sophisticated measure of patent claims, particularly for examining subject specific terminologies.

References

Alderucci D, Ashley K (2020) Using AI to Analyze Patent Claim Indefiniteness. IP Theory 9(1):2 2.

Frakes M, Wasserman MF (2013) Does agency funding affect decision-making?:an empirical assessment of the PTO's granting patterns. Vanderbilt Law Rev 66:67–149.

Kuhn JM, Thompson NC (2019) How to measure and draw causal inferences with patent scope. Int J Econ Bus 26(1):5–38.

Lanjouw JO, Schankerman M (2004) Patent quality and research productivity: measuring innovation with multiple indicators. Econ J 114:441–465.

Marco AC, Sarnoff JD, Charles AW (2019) Patent claims and patent scope. Res Policy 48(9):103790. https://doi.org/10.1016/j.respol.2019.04.014.

Novelli E (2015) An examination of the antecedents and implications of patent scope. Res Policy 44(2):493–507.

Stegmaier O (2018) Measuring patent claim breadth using Google Patents Public Datasetshttps:// cloud.google.com/blog/products/ai-machine-learning/measuring-patent-claim-breadth-using-google-patents-public-datasets. Accessed 14 Jan 2021 .

Part II
Network Analytics

Chapter 5
Basic Network Concepts

Abstract This chapter provides a few basic building blocks for understanding network concepts, terms, and statistics. In addition, it offers a brief primer on the use of patent networks to discover a firm's hidden innovation activities and knowledge flows. Finally, the chapter incites contemplations about patent bibliometrics, such as patent citations and co-inventor information, relevant to formulating networks by selecting their structural properties and relations.

5.1 Why Does Patent Network Analysis Matter?

Network analysis has been widely used for interpreting complex systems from multiple perspectives, ranging from social systems to shared knowledge networks (Kadushin 2012; Prell 2012). With the growing importance of patent data, bibliometric studies based on patents, such as co-inventor and citation links, has been extensively applied to network analysis and provides insights into the efforts promoting innovation and the knowledge flows (Jaffe and Trajtenberg 2002).

A patent citation network is of great relevance to network analysis, specifically for forecasting emerging technologies and innovation trajectories (Pereira et al. 2018). Collaboration networks among applicants or inventors are also useful in formulating networks, which represent knowledge flows and inventive relationships among them (Choi and Park 2016).

Figure 5.1 illustrates the inventor networks of Intrexon (genetic engineering, now Precigen) and Facebook (social networking service). Each *node* reflects an inventor. The size of a node indicates the number of patents the inventor has created for the company. The *edges* connecting the inventor nodes represent co-inventorship. Node colors denote the *attributes* of nodes that relate to the corresponding technology fields.

A glimpse of the inventor network clearly shows that the collaboration structures of Intrexon and Facebook are not identical. At Intrexon, there are distributed, miniature teams where the number of *connections* relative to nodes is low. Contrastingly, Facebook shows a large and cohesive collaboration team at the center of the network, which is sparsely connected to peripheral teams.

J. Kim et al., *Patent Analytics*,
https://doi.org/10.1007/978-981-16-2930-3_5

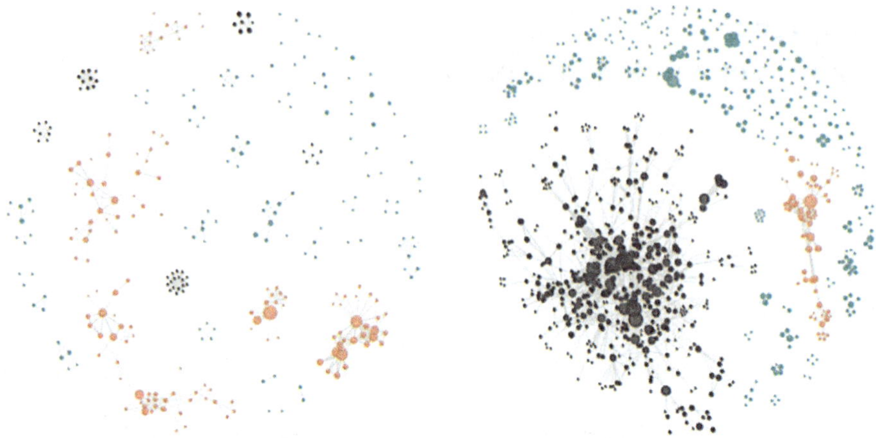

Fig. 5.1 **a** Inventor networks of Intrexon. **b** Facebook (Periscopic 2020)

These simple pictures raise several questions: "How do inventors team up," "who are core inventors," "why are some of the inventors grouped into dyads or triads," "are they new inventors after an acquisition," or "are they grouped for any moon-shot projects?"

The patent network perspective is powerful to comprehend a firm's hidden innovation activities, collaboration patterns, or even knowledge flows across companies. Section 5.2 continues to explicate key terms, concepts, and mathematic foundations of network theory for further advanced analysis.

5.2 Basic Concept of Network and Graph Theory

Network analysis provides a deeper understanding of complex systems that focus on the relationship between the entities that make up the system (Borgatti et al. 2018). Many terms and concepts of network analysis are taken from *graph theory*. The term *graph* here does not refer to a visual representation but rather a branch of mathematics that focuses on the quantification of networks.

5.2.1 Node, Edges, and Attributes

A graph is composed of a set of *nodes* (also called *vertices* or *actors*) that is connected through a set of *edges* (i.e., *links, ties,* or *arcs*). Referring to Fig. 5.1, *nodes* represent inventors, and *edges* represent the relations among inventors who co-worked.

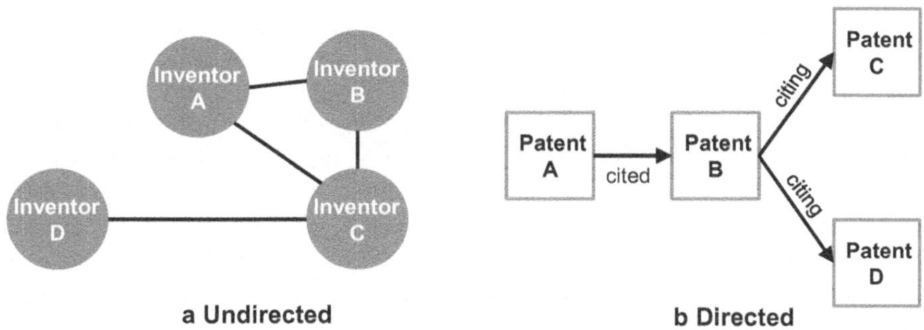

Fig. 5.2 **a** Co-inventor network (undirected). **b** patent citation network (directed)

Each node can have additional information, which refers to *attributes.* In Fig. 5.1, technology fields are considered *node attributes* that distinguish inventors from each other.

5.2.2 *Undirected and Directed Network*

A network can be classified based on the direction of edges in a network. Figure 5.2 shows a topology of different network types.

- In an *undirected network*, the edges are undirected. An example of an undirect patent network is a co-inventor network. Suppose that there are three co-inventors (inventors A, B, and C) for patent A and two co-inventors (inventors C and D) for patent B. As the co-inventor network can be drawn in an undirected way, there is no difference between the statements "inventor A is worked with inventor B" and "inventor B is worked with inventor A" (Fig. 5.2a).
- *Directed networks* have edges that are directed. A patent citation relationship is a good example. Suppose that patent B had cited patent A (i.e., *backward citation*) and is further cited by patents C and D (i.e., *forward citation*). The edges with the arrowheads depict the cited and citing relations of patents (Fig. 5.2b).

5.2.3 *One-Mode and Two-Mode Networks*

In classic network studies, most patent analyses are performed based on one type of data where all the nodes are tied to one another according to one type of relationship (i.e., co-inventors, patent citations in Fig. 5.2). This type of network is referred to as a *one-mode network.*

However, in some large real-world practices, a two-mode nature can exist. This is called a *two-mode network (i.e., bipartite network, affiliation network).* A *two-mode network* includes two types of nodes, and all the edges connect between the different nodes and not within. Figure 5.3a is an example of a two-mode network consisting of inventors and International Patent Classification (IPC) data as nodes. Inventors are tied to one another via technology classifications where they contributed. Similarly, technology classifications can be linked together via inventors who worked in similar technology fields.

A two-mode network can be analyzed in several ways. The most common method is to convert a two-mode network into a one-mode type (Fig. 5.3b). For example, in their recent study of technological convergence, Lee et al. (2016) initially collected co-classifications of patents with respect to the overlap of inventors, as illustrated in Fig. 5.3. The two datasets are then transformed into a one-mode network in order to explore the patterns of convergence among a variety of technologies.

Although converting into a one-mode network is conventional wisdom in many studies on patent networks, an alternative approach aids understanding of two-mode data by considering its bipartite structure. Readers who are interested in exploring more approaches and techniques on two-mode networks may find these readings useful: Faust (1997) and Borgatti et al. (2018).

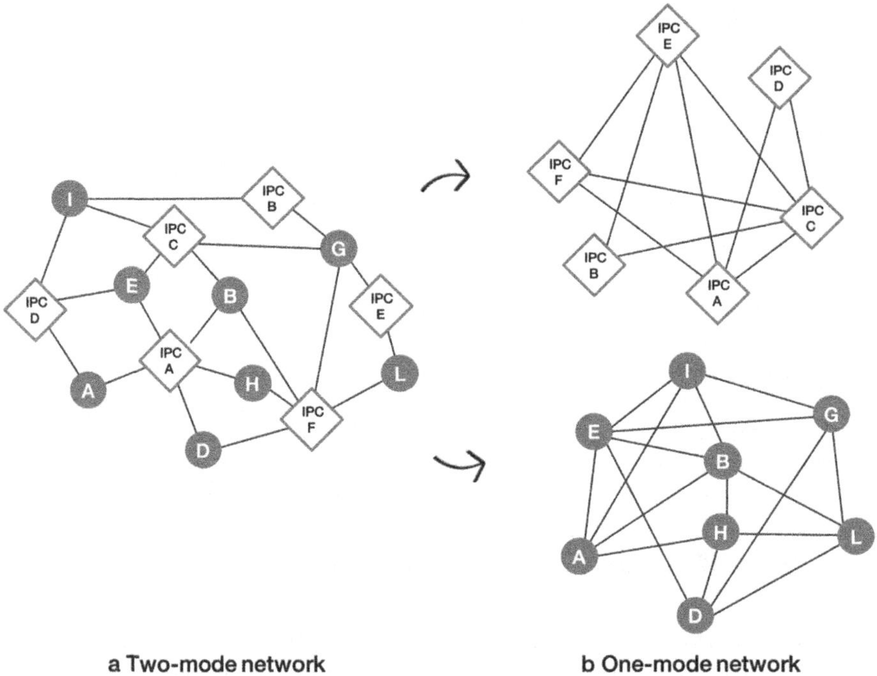

Fig. 5.3 **a** Two-mode network (inventor-IPC technology classifications). **b** converting a two-mode network into a one-mode network

5.2.4 Ego Networks and Complete Networks

Another important terminology that serves to determine the level of network analysis is an *ego network* and a *complete network* (Ahuja et al. 2012). *Ego networks* (also called *personal networks*) comprise a focal node (called *ego*) and other nodes that ego is directly connected with. Nodes that are connected to the ego are referred to as *alters*. In Fig. 5.4a, suppose that each node and edge represent one inventor and co-inventorship. In inventor A's ego network, inventor A is the *ego,* and *alters* are the rest of the inventors that are directly connected to ego.

Complete networks are also called *whole networks*. Many scholars already have an understanding of complete-level network analysis, which measures a fully connected network with direct links between all pairs of nodes (Fig. 5.4b).

Ego-level network analysis can be used to raise questions such as "how many co-inventors is inventor A connected to," "to what extent are the co-inventors of inventor A connected to one another," or "how strongly is inventor A connected to his/her co-inventors?" At a complete network level, many studies are interested in examining the central nodes in a network, network density (e.g., whether a network is tightly or sparsely connected to others), and clustering patterns.

Different network structures and positions may imply differential advantages or constraints for the nodes embedded in the network. For instance, understanding how and why some fields of technology networks emerge, grow, and converge over time may contribute to capturing developments in technological trajectories.

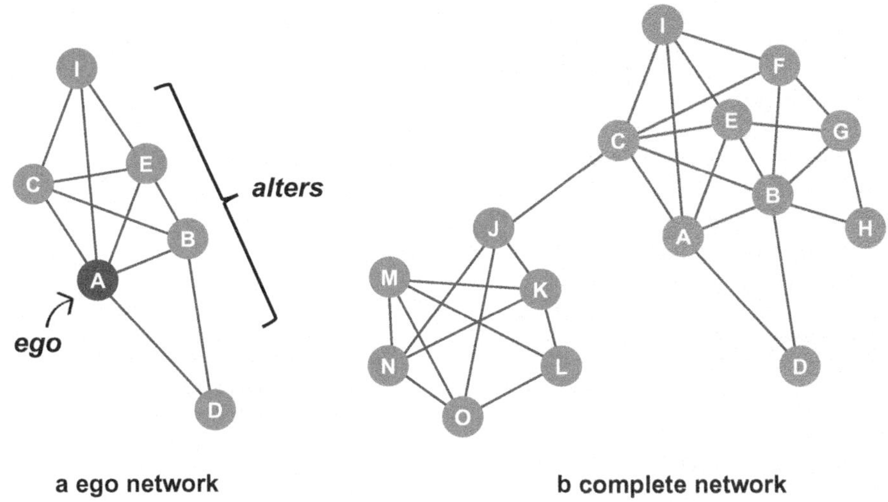

Fig. 5.4 **a** Ego network. **b** complete network

5.3 Network Metrics

Network analysis uses mathematical structures from graph theory to calculate values representing power and placement of nodes, edges, or a network. While much of the work related to network analysis is visually oriented, it is important to understand the mathematical assumptions and formulas used for each metric to make accurate interpretations of the statistical outcomes.

5.3.1 Centrality

Centrality is perhaps the most popular and widely used measure to identify central positions and power in a network (Freeman 1979; Faust 1997; Borgatti 2005). It can be examined with a variety of vantage points, such as "does a node show the highest number of connections to others," or "is a node frequently interposed between other nodes," or "is there a node that has the shortest path length to all other nodes?" Each question offers a unique perspective on centrality—*degree centrality, betweenness centrality*, and *closeness centrality*. Figure 5.5 illustrates the differences between the types of questions centrality metrics can answer.

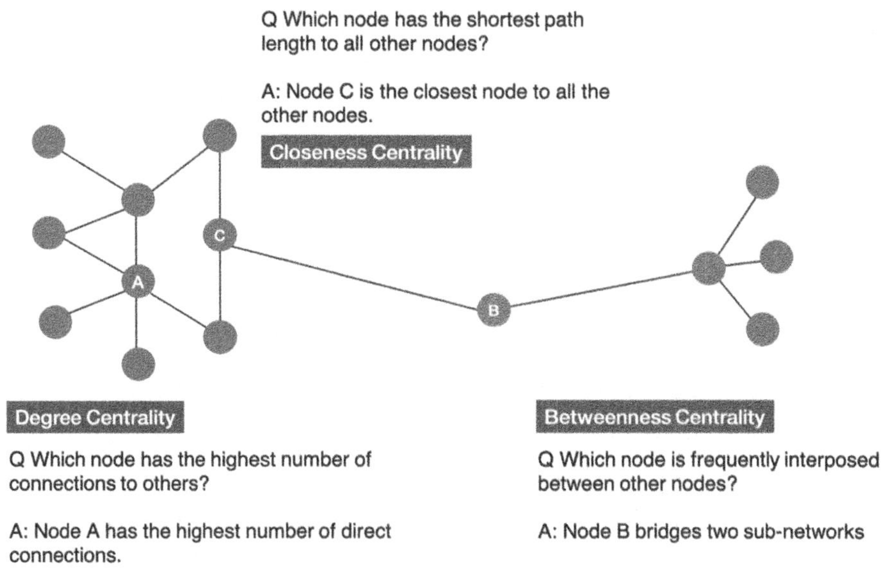

Fig. 5.5 Degree, betweenness and closeness centrality

5.3.1.1 Degree, Indegree, and Outdegree centrality

Degree centrality is a baseline metric of connectedness, which refers to the number of direct edges a node has. The assumption with degree centrality is that the number of connections is a key measure of importance within a network (Eq. 5.1). For instance, in Fig. 5.5, node A has the highest degree centrality as this node has a total of five direct edges with other nodes. In comparison, node B and node C have two-degree and three-degree centrality, respectively. Node A is thus seen as being involved in more activities than nodes B and C. Degree centrality emphasizes the various levels of activities in a network.

Formula for degree centrality, for node *i*:

$$C_D(i) = \sum_{j=1}^{n} G_{ij} = \sum_{i=1}^{n} G_{ji} \quad (5.1)$$

G_{ij}: represents the value of the link between node *i* and node *j* (the value being either 0 or 1); and
n: represents the number of nodes in the network.

If a network has directed edges, then there are two separate measures of degree centrality: *in-degree* and *out-degree. In-degree centrality* refers to the number of edges received by a node from others, and *out-degree centrality* is the number of edges flowing from a node to others (Eqs. 5.2 and 5.3).

Formula for in-degree centrality, for node *i*:

$$C_I(i) = \sum_{j=1}^{n} G_{ji} \quad (5.2)$$

Formular for out-degree centrality, for node *i*:

$$C_O(i) = \sum_{j=1}^{n} G_{ij} \quad (5.3)$$

G_{ji}: represents the value of the link from node *j* and node *i* (the value being either 0 or 1); and
n: represents the number of nodes in the network.

Referring to Fig. 5.2b, the patent citation network is a directed network, where patents can cite other patents as prior art (i.e., backward citations) or are cited by subsequent patents (i.e., forward citations). Based on the different citation directions, the number of backward citations can be regarded as the in-degree centrality, while the number of forward citations can be regarded as the out-degree centrality.

Figure 5.6 shows two ego patent citation networks of Dyson's design patents. One is the first design patent granted to a bladeless fan, US D602,143 in 2008, and

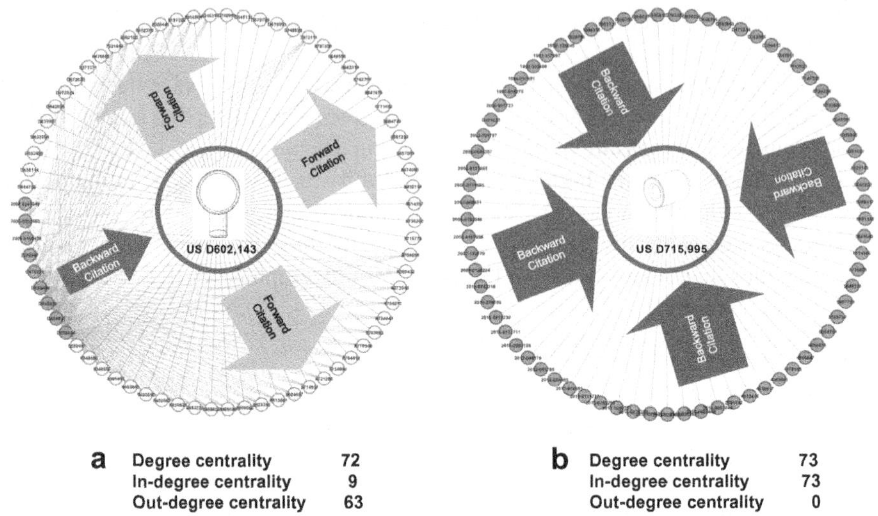

Fig. 5.6 **a** Ego network of US D602,143. **b** ego network of US D715,995

the other is to a hairdryer, US D715,995 in 2014. Both design patents have a degree centrality of 72 and 73 respectively and were considered core patents in terms of their active connections. However, considering the in-degree and out-degree centralities, there are significant differences between them.

The bladeless fan design patent (US D602,143) has an in-degree of 9 and out-degree of 63, while the hairdryer design patent (US D715,995) has an in-degree of 73 but zero out-degree. The bladeless fan design was undoubtedly a big forward leap in fan design and highlighted its influence on other following innovations. Juxtaposing the bladeless fan, the hairdryer design was improved based on already-existing bladeless product design series, such as bladeless fans, heaters, and air purifiers. No other patents cite the hairdryer design patent (US D715,995) as a reference, thus reflecting its diluted influence.

The only word of caution when analyzing out-degree centrality in patent citation networks is that new patents rarely earn many forward citations because it takes time for a patent to be recognized and cited by subsequent patents. Time lag effects must be considered to document patent citation networks. Chapter 6 continues to explain the structure and characteristics of a patent citation network and its values as innovation indicators.

5.3.1.2 Betweenness and Closeness Centrality

Power and placement are fundamental to network analysis. Degree centrality quantifies the total connectivity of a node, that is, power. However, it does not specify a node's location in a network (i.e., placement). In other words, when computing degrees in an ego network, degree centrality focuses on the focal nodes and ignores all the other nodes in the network. Contrastingly, *betweenness* and *closeness centrality* consider the complete network.

Betweenness centrality measures the number of shortest paths that pass through a node (Eq. 5.4), that is, how often a node rests between two other nodes (Brandes 2001). Betweenness centrality is regarded as indicating how much potential control a node has over the flow of information. Betweenness centrality relates to questions such as "who is critical for information flow" or "who plays the role of intermediary or broker in a network?" Refer to the example of Fig. 5.5. Node B has only a degree centrality of two, but it can influence the entire network by connecting two distinctive sub-networks. Remove node B, and the network falls apart.

Formula for betweenness centrality, for node *i*:

$$C_B(i) = \sum_{j<k} \frac{G_{jk}(i)}{G_{jk}} \quad i \neq j \neq k; \tag{5.4}$$

G_{jk}: represents the number of shortest paths linking nodes *j* and *k*; and
$G_{jk}(i)$: represents the number of the shortest paths linking nodes *j* and *k* that pass through node *i*.

While betweenness centrality focuses on the role of a brokerage or gatekeeper of information flow in a network, closeness centrality is considered a global metric.

Closeness centrality scores each node based on its closeness to all other nodes in the network (Eq. 5.5). For example, node C in Fig. 5.5 is relatively close to all the other nodes in the network. A node with high closeness centrality can quickly reach out to other nodes without relying much on intermediaries in the network. In addition, the node would most likely hear about new information early on and quickly diffuse information through the entire network. Overall, closeness centrality can be considered as a measure of a node's independency and a means for uncovering how a network can quickly and efficiently spread information through the entire node network (Prell 2012).

Formular for closeness centrality, for node *i*:

$$C_c(N_i) = \frac{1}{\left[\sum_{j=1}^{n} d(N_i, N_j)\right]} \quad i \neq j; \tag{5.5}$$

$\left[\sum_{j=1}^{n} d(N_i, N_j)\right]$: represents the sum of the shortest distance connecting node *i* and *j*; and
n: represents the number of nodes in the network.

Figure 5.7 compares ego networks of two designers at Samsung Electronics: One with the highest degree centrality and the other with the highest betweenness centrality. These ego networks are formed by the ego (a core inventor, marked in red),

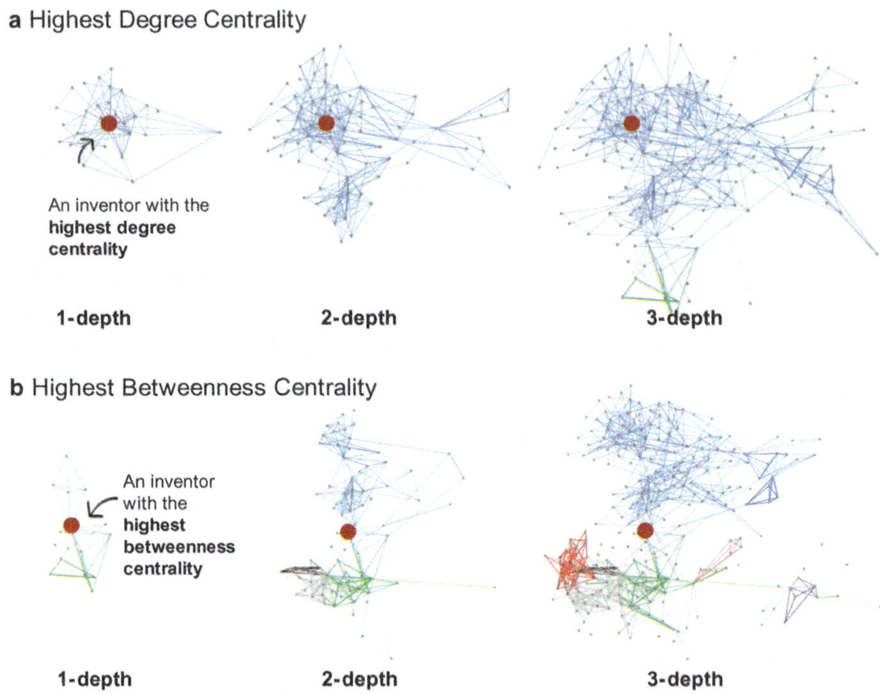

Fig. 5.7 **a** Ego networks of an inventor with the highest degree centrality. **b** ego networks of an inventor with the highest betweenness centrality

alters (the remaining gray dots, who have co-worked with the core inventor), and alters of the alters (indirectly connected inventor group) according to the number of depths of networks. Each colored cluster denotes different design areas where the ego and alters are involved, for instance, graphical user interface (GUI) in blue, washing machine in green, air conditioner in gray, and refrigerator in red.

A glimpse of the two ego networks clearly shows that the designer with the highest degree centrality has many connections with other designers in the same team of GUIs (i.e., intra-collaboration) (Fig. 5.7a). In juxtaposition, the other designer with the highest betweenness centrality has a wide breadth of knowledge by making inter collaborations of different design teams, starting from GUIs and washing machine to several home appliances, such as air conditioner and refrigerator (Fig. 5.7b). The results infer that the designer with the highest betweenness plays a pivotal role in controlling or diffusing design knowledge by reaching out to diverse design teams.

5.3.2 Network Diameter and Density

Network-level metrics provide many statistics to assess the overall structure of a network. A simple metric to understand a complete network is a *diameter*. This measures the distance between the most distant nodes in the network. If the diameter of a network is relatively large, then the network is considered big, and the nodes in the networks are not close to one another.

A more sophisticated idea of calculating network cohesion is *density*. Density is defined as the sum of actual connections divided by the number of possible connections (Eq. 5.6). If the density of a network is relatively large, all the nodes in the network are fairly close to each another, and the network is regarded as cohesive (Fig. 5.8). Such phenomena imply the speed at which information diffuses between the various nodes in a network.

The formula for network density (d) is calculated as follows:

$$d = \frac{L}{n(n-1)/2} \tag{5.6}$$

L: represents the number of actual connections in the network; and
n: represents the number of nodes in the network.

Although *network density* is a simple means for conceptualizing and measuring network-level structure, we need to be wary of its use. When comparing two or more network densities, a pivotal consideration is the size of the network. For instance, the density of inventor network was 0.0002 and 0.001 in Samsung Electronics and Adobe, respectively (Choi and Park 2016; Kim and Kim 2019). In fact, Samsung Electronics has collaborated with several other R&D departments for business units, such as mobile phones, home appliances, digital televisions, semiconductors, and memory, with around four times greater number of inventors compared to Adobe.

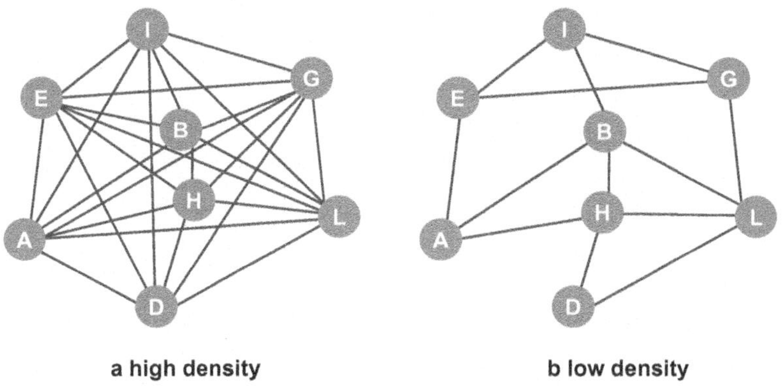

Fig. 5.8 **a** Network with a high-density. **b** network with a low-density

Chapter 11 further examines the measures of inventor networks using Adobe's case study.

5.3.3 *Clustering and Modularity*

Another critical concept in understanding knowledge flow and diffusion at a complete network level is *clustering* and *modularity*. *Clustering* refers to a group of individuals (or entities) linked by some common attribute (or multiple attributes). *Homophily* is one of the key concepts in helping us understand the levels of *clustering*. The term *homophily*, colloquially referring to the *birds of a feather* phenomenon represents the likelihood that people with similar backgrounds, beliefs, or social status (McPherson et al. 2001; Cherven 2015).

Figure 5.9 shows an illustrative example to compare different degrees of homophily in a network. One network where a significant majority of nodes are homogenous represents low levels of homophily (Fig. 5.9a). The other network where many diverse groups coexist shows high levels of homophily, resulting in several self-segregated clusters. In Fig. 5.9b, the nodes in local clusters tend to be connected densely within their own neighborhoods but have little in the way of an external connection.

Given that information sharing tends to happen within the clusters rather than between the clusters, a network with a high degree of homophily may impede the diffusion of ideas and information due to its segregated clusters.

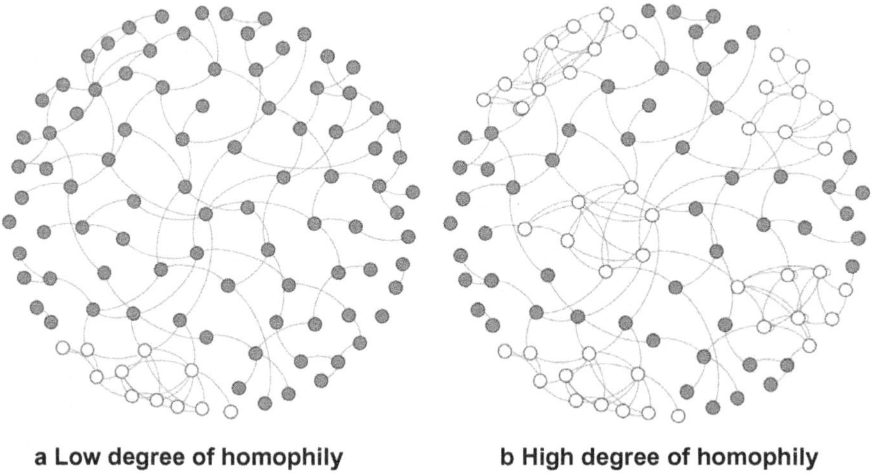

Fig. 5.9 **a** Network with a low degree of homophily. **b** network with a high degree of homophily (Cherven 2015)

Recent research on homophily in patent citation networks reveals that there is a strong inclination to cite patents with respect to the same country and the same language (Chakraborty et al. 2020). This implies that much higher friction exists in knowledge flow and innovation adoption. Since many nodes within specific clusters have little exposure beyond the local cluster due to geographic constraints and language barriers, there is an increased probability that they will not have access to all the latest information, and they may be more reluctant to adopt new technologies, at least until others in their cluster do so.

Furthermore, Chakraborty et al. (2020) highlighted that top companies are encamped in a bubble where communication between companies is achieved with little effort. This results in the formation of *prestige* clusters that limit the outer circles accessing information.

Measuring clustering and homophily are relevant to innovation studies examining subjects, such as innovation adoption, knowledge flows, technology convergence, and collaborations across technology classes, companies, and countries. Figure 5.10 shows Bose's patent citation network regarding the proximity of technology classification. A large and dense cluster in the middle represents Bose's core sound technologies, while several peripherical clusters that are loosely connected with the sound cluster are likely to serve as potential pivoting points for the company. An in-depth case study of Bose's patent citation network is presented in Chap. 10.

Finally, modularity is widely used as a metric to estimate the extent to which the network is clustered within sub-groups or communities. It is based on the strength of the division of a network into clusters. A node with high modularity has dense connections between the nodes within the subject clusters but sparse connections between the nodes in different clusters.

There are several algorithms to calculate network modularity, such as the Louvain method (Blondel et al. 2008) and Valente et al. (2015) community detection algorithm. Valent et al. (2015) suggest a measure of modularity called Q values that vary from zero to one. A helpful guide would be to consider values below 0.30 as low and, depending on the context, amenable to be increased. Values greater than 0.30 indicate a reasonably strong group structure, and those above 0.50 are perhaps overly high in many situations and may impede knowledge diffusion and collaboration between other clusters.

Even this suggestion must be tentative; however, with a higher value of network clustering, both homophily and modularity are posited to be deleterious for information flow but beneficial for forming cohesive teams.

5.4 Summary

Network analysis uses mathematical structures from graph theory to calculate values representing a power, position, and structure of nodes, edges, and a network. This chapter provided basic building blocks for understanding the concepts and terms of a network from foundational elements to complex structures: nodes, edges, one mode

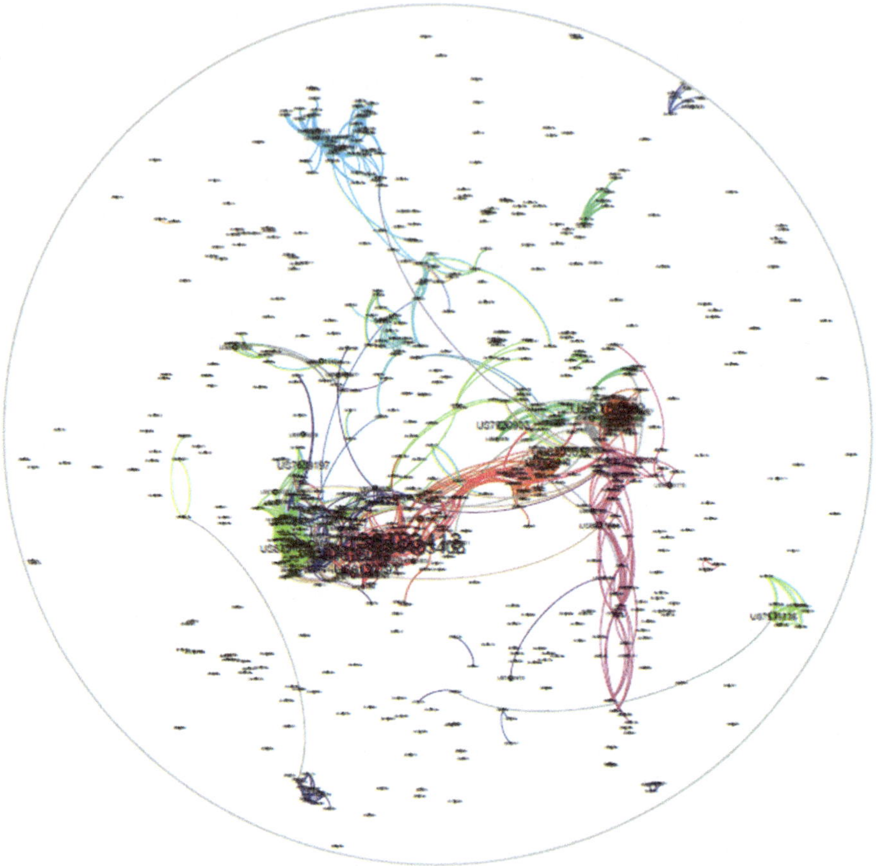

Fig. 5.10 Technology clusters based on the proximity of IPC classifications in Bose's patent citation network

versus two-mode networks, ego networks versus complete networks. We also walked through a brief primer on network metrics focusing on centrality measures (degree centrality, betweenness centrality, and closeness centrality), network measures (network diameter and density), and cluster and neighborhood measures (clustering and modularity) while exploring many ways in which these statistical metrics can be used to address real-world network analysis.

Yet, it falls short of conveying all the information. Critical to successful network analysis is the *goldilocks principle* that has just the context-specific amount of centralities, densities, and clustering involved in its interpretation. Chaps. 9–13 in Part III provide how to interpret and apply network metrics by incorporating case studies, those of Apple, Dyson, Bose, Adobe, Samsung, and LG electronics.

References

Ahuja G, Soda G, Zaheer A (2012) The genesis and dynamics of organizational networks. Organ Sci 23(2):434–448.

Borgatti SP (2005) Centrality and network flow. Soc Networks 27(1): 55–71.

Borgatti SP, Everett MG, Johnson JC (2018) Analyzing social networks. Sage, London.

Brandes U (2001) A faster algorithm for betweenness centrality. J Math Sociol 25(2):163–177.

Blondel VD, Guillaume JL, Lambiotte R, Lefebvre E (2008) Fast unfolding of communities in large networks. J Stat Mech Theory Exp 2008(10):P10008. https://doi.org/10.1088/1742-5468/2008/10/p10008.

Chakraborty M, Byshkin M, Crestani F (2020) Patent citation network analysis: A perspective from descriptive statistics and ERGMs. Plos one 15(12): e0241797. https://doi.org/10.1371/journal.pone.0241797.

Cherven K (2015) Mastering Gephi network visualization. Packt, Birmingham.

Choi S, Park H (2016) Investigation of strategic changes using patent co-inventor network analysis: The case of Samsung electronics. Sustainability 8(12): 1315.

Faust K (1997) Centrality in affiliation networks. Soc Networks 19(2):157–191.

Freeman L (1979) Centrality in social networks conceptual clarification. Soc Networks 1(3):215–239.

Jaffe AB, Trajtenberg M (2002) Patents, citations, and innovations: A window on the knowledge economy. MIT Press, Cambridge, MA.

Kadushin C (2012) Understanding social networks: Theories, concepts, and findings. Oxford University Press, New York.

Kim D, Kim J (2019) Measure of design M&As:Exploratory investigations of ip analysis in design. Strateg Des Res J, 12(1): 43–61.

Lee WJ, Lee WK, Sohn SY (2016). Patent network analysis and quadratic assignment procedures to identify the convergence of robot technologies. PloS one, 11(10): e0165091. https://doi.org/10.1371/journal.pone.0165091.

McPherson M, Smith-Lovin L, Cook JM (2001) Birds of a feather: Homophily in social networks. Annual review of sociology. Annu. Rev. Sociol 27(1):415-444.

Pereira CG, Picanco-Castro V, Covas DT, Porto GS (2018). Patent mining and landscaping of emerging recombinant factor VIII through network analysis. Nat Biotechnol 36(7):585–590.

Periscopic (2020) Exploring Innovation Signatures in Patent Data. https://periscopic.com/#!/articles/Exploring-Patent-Data. Accessed 18 Nov 2020.

Prell C. (2012). Social network analysis: History, theory and methodology. Sage, London.

Valente TW, Palinkas LA, Czaja S, Chu KH, Brown CH (2015). Social network analysis for program implementation. PloS one. 10(6):e0131712. https://doi.org/10.1371/journal.pone.0131712.

Chapter 6
Patent Citations Analysis

Abstract The use of patent citations as indicators of innovation has increased dramatically in the last decade. As patents constitute intellectual and economic value, patent citation analysis makes it possible to reveal the hidden innovation activities and knowledge flows between technologies, individuals, firms, industries, or countries. This chapter describes the meaning of the use and analysis of citations in patents and examines how to structure multi-depth patent citations through a network lens. In addition, this chapter recounts the story of the Apple–Samsung lawsuit using the citation network of iPhone's design patent. Finally, common pitfalls and best practices for using citation data are discussed.

6.1 The Meaning of Patent Citations

In bibliometrics, citation data have been critical in measuring the impact of scientific and technological activities (Okubo 1997). There are several citation-based indicators where a citation count serves to measure the scientific impact of scholarly articles or journals, such as Web of Science, Scopus, and Science Citation Index (SCI) (Wang et al. 2019). The H-index (Hirsch 2005) and g-index (Egghe 2006) have been widely used to measure researchers' and universities' impact. Moreover, for the sake of international comparison of university research quality, the Quacquarelli Symonds (QS) world university rankings adopt a citation per faculty member as a key measure, accounting for 20% of the overall ranking score.

While the analogy with the broader field of bibliometric approaches seems practical to understand citations in patent analytics, patent citations differ from scientific citations in substantial ways (Jaffe and de Rassenfosse 2019). Patents indicate a transfer of knowledge to industrial innovation and constitute intellectual and economic values (Okubo 1997). Many studies have acknowledged that patent citations are a useful metric for measuring knowledge flows and impacts of technology and forecasting potential innovation activities (e.g., Jeff and Trajtenberg 2002; van Raan 2017; Wang et al. 2019; Kim and Kim 2021). Unlike citations for scholarly articles, patent citations perform an important legal function of identifying prior art

J. Kim et al., *Patent Analytics*,
https://doi.org/10.1007/978-981-16-2930-3_6

(56) **References Cited**

U.S. PATENT DOCUMENTS

1,767,060	A		6/1930	Ferguson	
D103,476	S		3/1937	Weber	
D115,344	S	*	6/1939	Chapman	D23/411
2,433,795	A		12/1947	Stokes	
2,488,467	A		11/1949	De Lisio	
D206,973	S		2/1967	De Lisio	
5,881,685	A		3/1999	Foss et al.	
D415,271	S	*	10/1999	Feer	D23/411
6,073,881	A		6/2000	Chen	
D429,808	S	*	8/2000	Krauss et al.	D23/411
6,123,618	A		9/2000	Day	
D435,899	S	*	1/2001	Melwani	D23/382
D485,895	S	*	1/2004	Melwani	D23/370
D539,414	S		3/2007	Russak et al.	
2009/0060710	A1		3/2009	Gammack et al.	
2009/0060711	A1		3/2009	Gammack et al.	

FOREIGN PATENT DOCUMENTS

DE	1 291 090	3/1969
DE	195 10 397	9/1996
GB	1 501 473	2/1978
GB	2 236 804	4/1991
GB	2 242 935	10/1991
JP	56-167897	12/1981

OTHER PUBLICATIONS

GB Search Report directed to related application GB0717151.5 mailed on Dec. 17, 2007; (2 pages).
GB Search Report directed to related application GB0717155.6 mailed on Dec. 19, 2007; (2 pages).
GB Search Report directed to related application GB0717154.9 mailed on Dec. 17, 2007; (2 pages).
GB Search Report directed to related application GB0717148.1 mailed on Dec. 20, 2007; (1 page).
International Search Report and Written Opinion mailed Oct. 29, 2008, directed to related International Patent Application No. PCT/GB2008/002891; (11 pages).
International Search Report and Written Opinion mailed Oct. 31, 2008, directed to related International Patent Application No. PCT/GB2008/002874; (9 pages).

* cited by examiner

Primary Examiner—Lisa P Lichtenstein

Fig. 6.1 Reference cited (INID code 56) section in the front page of patent document

upon which the current invention builds (Jaffe and Trajtenberg 2002). Patent citations are not only added by inventors (e.g., authors in a research paper), but also by a patent attorney, a patent examiner, or even third parties (e.g., during opposition proceedings) (Meyer 2000).

Patent citations or references are available at INID code[1] 56 (*references cited*) on the front page of patent documents (Fig. 6.1). Patent citations constitute the US and foreign patent documents and other publications (i.e., non-patent literature). The references cited by examiners are prefixed with an asterisk symbol (*) in the corresponding literature information. Names of primary examiners can also be identified.

Patent citations are mainly divided into two classes: *backward citations* and *forward citations*. The citations listed in Fig. 6.1 are referred to as backward citations, indicating prior literature cited by a patent at the time of the invention or examinations. Forward citations refer to those obtained by subsequent patents after publication (Fig. 6.2).

Citation analysis is based on the principle that the number and nature of backward and forward citations are indicators of patent values. In general, higher numbers of citations indicate a greater value.

Backward citations have been used to measure the technical knowledge acquired by the patented entities studied (Hall et al. 2001). In contrast, forward citations have been interpreted as a measure of the diffused knowledge to others and the importance or impact of technology. Moreover, the number of forward citations is associated with increases in market value. For instance, Hall et al. (2001) empirically reported that one extra forward citation per patent boosts the market value by 3%.

[1]The Internationally agreed Numbers for the Identification of Data (INID) code is drawn from WIPO's ST.9 recommendation concerning bibliographic data on and relating to patents and SPCs. The recommendation covers a list of approximately 60 distinct bibliographic data widely used on the first page of patent documents (see Chap. 3).

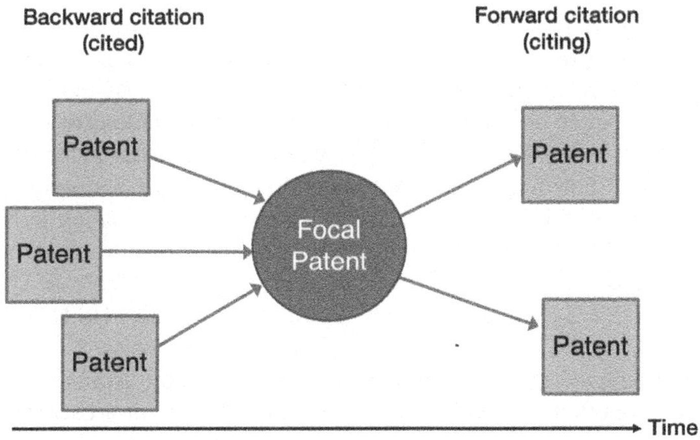

Fig. 6.2 Forward and backward citations

What if citation information is applied to design patents? Figure 6.3 illustrates a patent citation network's snapshot of Apple's iPhone 4 design (US D627,778, 2010). The graphic nodes represent the thumbnails of design patents, and the arrows (directed edges) indicate the cited and citing directions. This design patent network

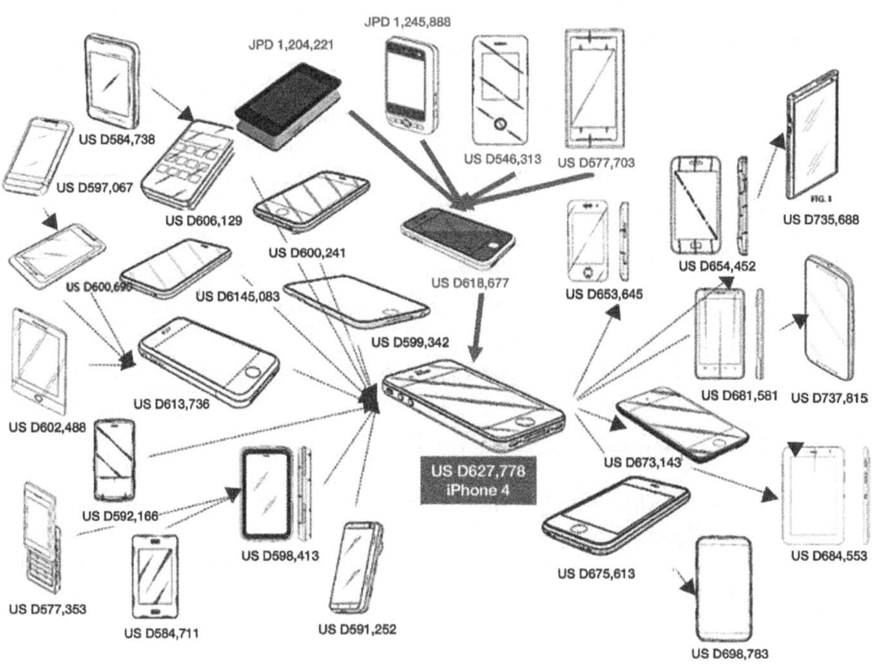

Fig. 6.3 Cited and citing the network of Apple's US design patent D627,778

allows us to explore morphological design changes before and after the iPhone 4 release. More interestingly, it may hint at how to cope with patent litigation.

The design patents connected by the thick arrows in Fig. 6.3 are the patents related to the Samsung–Apple design war. One of the backward citations of US D627,778 (iPhone 4, 2010) is US D618,677 (2007), which claims a flat planr surface with round bezel. This patent gained a lot of media attention as Samsung and Apple accused each other of infringements. In the ex-parte reexamination in the United States, Apple's US D618,677 (priority date, January 2007) was at risk of invalidation due to its obviousness combined with several prior arts: Toshiba's JP D1,204,221 (May 2004), LG's US D546,313 (March 2006), and Samsung's US D577,703 (July 2007).

This could be a reconstruction in hindsight. However, the Apple–Samsung trial addresses the importance of a citation-based approach in prior art search and prosecution processes. A multi-depth citation analysis ensures informed examination and filing processes to mitigate the risk of design infringement, preemptively. Additionally, it would help with a legal action to prove patent infringement in court, particularly to raise potential issues of patent validity.

The next section explains how to build patent citation networks by considering multiple depths of backward and forward citations in time for advanced patent analytics.

6.2 How to Scale up Patent Citation Networks

The expansion of patent citations on a large scale enables the discovery of hidden roles, relations, and clusters among patents. A natural way of representing multi-depth citations is in the form of a network. Figure 6.4 shows the four steps of expanding patent citation networks.

Step 1. Collection of backward citations

The first step is to collect prior arts from a reference-cited section, often catalogued on the first page of patent documents. Citation analysis starts with a focal patent (or a set of focal patents) as a root and directly connected cited documents (backward citations).

Step 2. Direct connections with backward and forward citations (Depth 1)

The prior arts (backward citations) and subsequent references (forward citations) in time are collated in the form of a network, called a *Depth 1 network*. The focal patent has two sets of direct citation relationships: backward and forward citations. Each node in the network represents citation documents, and links with arrows indicate the directionality of backward and forward citations.

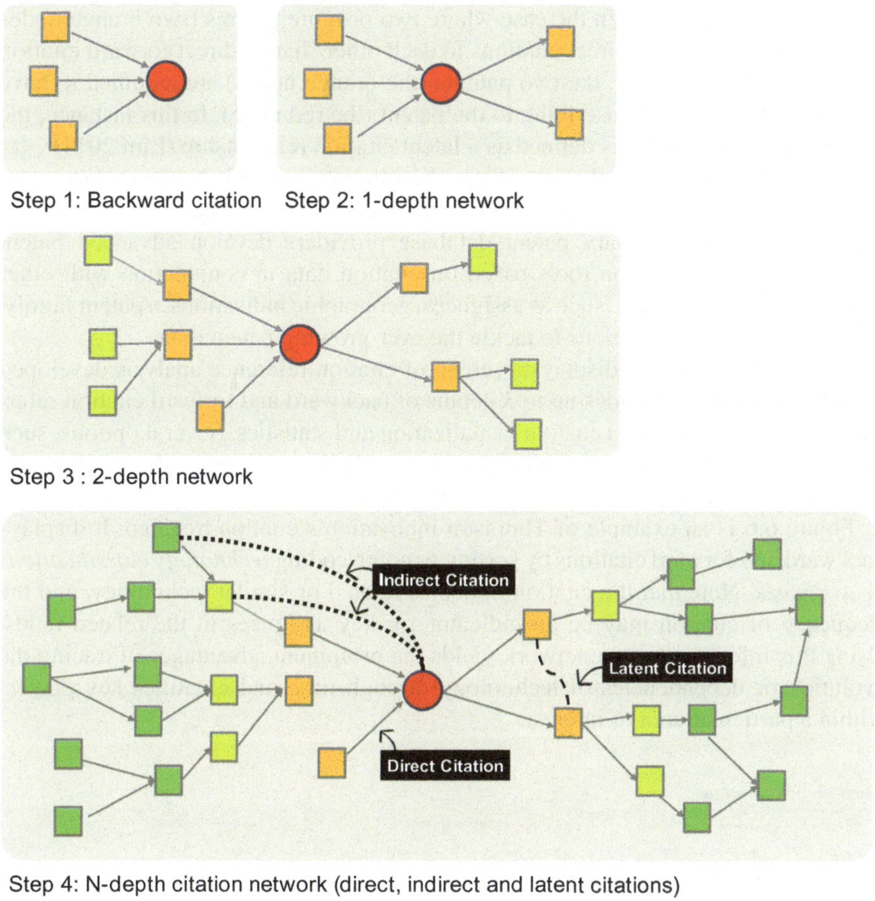

Fig. 6.4 An illustration of N-depth citation networks

Step 3. Generation of both indirect and direct citations (Depth 2)

Forward and backward citations can be expanded over Depth 2 using transitivity between patents that are not directly cited by each other. If the patent A-B and patent B-C citation relationship exist, then patent A-C obtains an indirect citation relationship due to the relationship in patent B with patents A and C. An example of direct and indirect citation relationships is illustrated in the step 4 of Fig. 6.4.

Step 4. Expansion of patent citation networks with latent citation relations (Depth N)

Citation networks continue to grow over multiple depth N. Taking an extra one depth of citations into account embraces a large collection of patent citation data. In addition to direct and indirect citation relationships, it is important to note the term *latent citation relationship*. This refers to the potential or hidden relationship between the two patents. In the case where two or more patents (two orange nodes in Fig. 6.3) that have no direct citations to each other share a direct forward citation to a patent (the red node), the two patents (the orange nodes) are assumed to have a significant relationship ascribing to the patent (the red node). In this instance, the two patents' relationship is defined as a latent citation relationship (Lim 2014).

As the number of depths increases, the citation network becomes large and complex. Too many nodes and connections may hinder the interpretation of the network. Several secondary patent database providers develop advanced patent analytics and visualization tools based on citation data in conjunction with other bibliographic information, such as assignees, geographic indications, a patent family, and technology classifications to tackle the ever-growing patent data.

For instance, Fig. 6.5 displays a screen of citation reference analysis developed by WIPS Global. It provides up to 3 depths of backward and forward citation references of a given patent via custom visualization and statistics. Several options, such as highlighting specific geographic origins, displaying citation with timeline, and excluding or including self-citations, are functional.

Figure 6.6 is an example of Thomson innovation's citation treemap. It displays backward and forward citations by sorting or color-coding *technology classifications* or *assignees*. Note that the citation indicates related or similar technology, and the frequency of citation may be an indicator for key assignees in the related fields. Using this information in a network yields the prominent advantages of tracing the evolution or dependencies of technology through time and identifies key players within a particular area of interest.

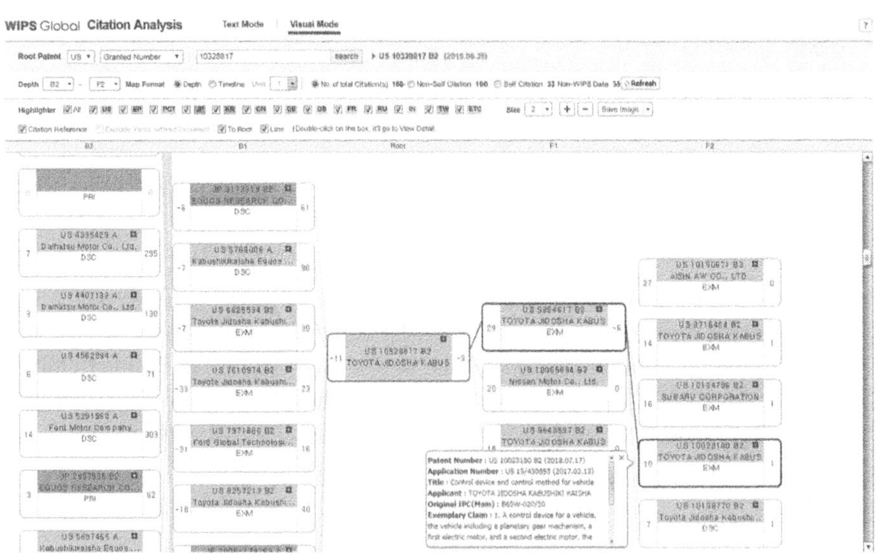

Fig. 6.5 Example of WIPS Global Citation Reference Analysis

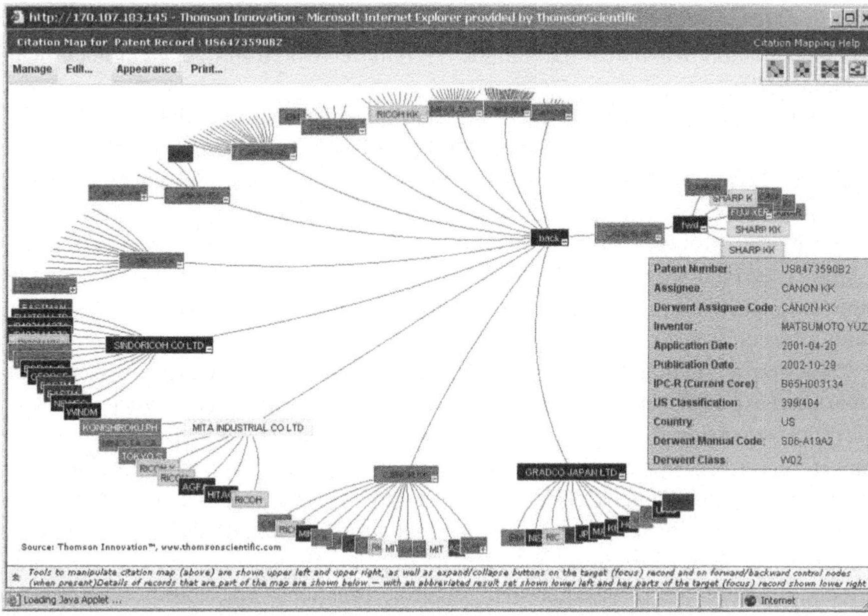

Fig. 6.6 Example of Thomson Citation Treemap

Furthermore, we envision many new features of the next patent analytics tools to exploit patent citation data. For instance, if an initial patent application was amended in response to an official action (OA), newly added references are more likely to contain key elements of the invention. Additionally, examiner citations can complement the selection of prominent citation documents. Finally, this information can be further collated with patent family[2] or technology classification data and filter out weakly relevant citation data. Such techniques can be used to highlight the nodes for major contributors in a network and conduct more pertinent patent analytics.

6.3 Pitfalls and Best Practices in Using Patent Citation Data

Patent citations have long been used for various purposes, including prior art search, litigation, and a measure of innovation activities. Yet, there are several pitfalls to consider citation-based patent analytics, such as citation quality, citation patterns by technology fields, and time lags (Aristodemou and Tietz 2018, Jaffe and de Rassenfosse 2019).

First, citation data quality is an important prerequisite to conduct citation-based patent studies. However, the heterogeneous global patent system may raise concerns

[2] A patent family is a collection of patent applications covering the same or similar technical content, which are related to each other through priority claims or by one common priority filings.

regarding the accuracy and reliability of the citation data in question. This is particularly questionable when dealing with the *references cited* from US patent documents (Adams 2020).

Under US patent law, applicants (and their attorneys) have a "duty of candor" to disclose any prior art "material to patentability" of an invention, implying all relevant background art and information of an invention have to be submitted during the patent prosecution process. This unique requirement in the United States is referred to as an information disclosure statement (IDS). A list of references cited in the US grants is largely derived from the IDS. IDS are treated as applicant-given references or applicant citations to distinguish them from references added by examiners during patent prosecution (i.e., examiner citations).[3]

Critics point out that the enforcement of information disclosure results in a consequent increase in the number of citations in the US grants in the absence of much relevance regarding the subject matter of an invention. Historically, this has been true. However, recent statistics demonstrate that examiners play an important role in adding citations to patents. Criscuolo and Verspagen (2008) found that the examiner's share of citations was 63% on the average patents. Additionally, examiner citations accounted for 74% of foreign applicants on average, higher than the US applicants, reflecting differences in international patenting practices. The volume of examiner citations suggests it may be problematic to discount how much the citations are worth for patent citation analytics.

Reliability concerns in citation data can be driven by specific characteristics of applicants and patent offices. Suppose an applicant is not meticulous in informing the prior art pertinent to an application, or examiners do not have an in-depth understanding of the invention or enough time to search relevant prior arts. In that case, it leads to superfluous or irrelevant references being cited, hindering subsequent analysis.

Second, the counts of citation considerably vary by technological field or maturity of the technology. If a technological field cites less but is cited more, it could indicate that the technological field is related to emerging domains. In addition, computing citation lag (the time difference between the cited and the citing patents) helps measure the cycle of innovation. For instance, citation lag is generally shorter in semiconductors than in the shipbuilding industry, as the cycle of innovation in semiconductor technology is growing rapidly. Moreover, in the case where a specific technology field is in fierce competition, it is likely that the citation list increases (Aristodemou and Tietz 2018).

Therefore, it is important to note that the number of citations received by a patent increases as time passes such that there are strong cohort effects. This leads to the third pitfall regarding the use of patent citation data in innovation studies. Unlike backward citation, the number of forward citations emerges and accumulates over time. Generally, they can be analyzed within five to ten years of the publication date to leave sufficient time for patents to have a reasonable chance of being cited. For

[3] A third party may suggest prior arts during the course of reexaminations or trials for invalidation of granted patents.

those interested in investigating forward citation data in a short space of time, Lee and Sohn (2017) suggested a proxy of patent value, named *the first citation lag*, which measures the time taken until the first citation.

6.4 Summary

The digitalization of patent bibliographic data and increasing computer power allow us to access patent citation data with ease and analyze the complex patent citation analysis. Identifying indirect and latent citations in patent networks can be regarded as one of the leading indicators for predicting the next innovation trajectories and potential convergences, as well as potential patent litigation.

Although patent citation data are the widely used and empirically supported proxy of innovation indicators, we addressed several common issues that might arise with patent citation analysis and proposed best practices to cope with them. This chapter would be useful to readers interested in conducting patent citation analysis in future research. The next chapter introduces how to use visualization techniques to make patent analysis effective and meaningful and to be intrigued by visualizing patent data.

References

Adams S (2020) Information sources in patents. De Gruyter, Berlin.

Aristodemou L, Tietze F (2018) Citations as a measure of technological impact: A review of forward citation-based measures. World Pat Inf 53:39–44.

Criscuolo P, Verspagen B (2008) Does it matter where patent citations come from? Inventor vs. examiner citations in European patents. Res. Policy 37(10):1892-1908.

Egghe L. (2006) Theory and practice of the g-index. Scientometrics 69(1):131–152.

Hall BH, Jaffe AB, Trajtenberg M (2001) The NBER patent citation data file: Lessons, insights and methodological tools (No. w8498). National Bureau of Economic Research https://doi.org/10.1186/1471-2164-12-148.

Hirsch JE (2005) An index to quantify an individual's scientific research output. Proceedings of the National academy of Sciences 102(46):16569–16572. https://www.ncbi.nlm.nih.gov/pmc/articles/PMC1283832/.

Jaffe AB, Trajtenberg M (2002) Patents, citations, and innovations: A window on the knowledge economy. MIT Press. edition 1, volume 1, number 026260065x, September.

Jaffe AB, de Rassenfosse G (2019) Patent citation data in social science research: Overview and best practices. In Research handbook on the economics of intellectual property law. Edward Elgar Publishing https://doi.org/10.4337/9781789903997.00043.

Kim D, Kim J (2021) Is innovation design-or technology-driven? Citation as a measure of innovation pollination. World Pat Inf 64: 102010. https://doi.org/10.1016/j.wpi.2020.102010.

Lee J, Sohn SY (2017) What makes the first forward citation of a patent occur earlier? Scientometrics 113(1):279–298.

Lim J (2014) Analysis of the relationship between patent litigation and citation: Subdivision of citations. Appl Math Inf Sci 8(5):2515. http://dx.doi.org/10.12785/amis/080549.

Meyer M (2000) What is special about patent citations? Differences between scientific and patent citations. Scientometrics 49(1):93–123. https://doi.org/10.1023/a:1005613325648.
Okubo Y (1997) Bibliometric indicators and analysis of research systems: methods and examples. https://doi.org/10.1787/18151965.
van Raan AF (2017) Patent citations analysis and its value in research evaluation: A review and a new approach to map technology-relevant research. J Data Info Sci 2(1):13–50. https://doi.org/10.1515/jdis-2017-0002.
Wang M, Zhang J, Jiao S, Zhang T (2019) Evaluating the impact of citations of articles based on knowledge flow patterns hidden in the citations. PloS one 14(11):e0225276. https://doi.org/10.1371/journal.pone.0225276.

Chapter 7
Patent Data Through a Visual Lens

Abstract This chapter starts with an anecdote of a patent attorney coping with an increasing amount of patent data and reimagining legal service provisions with the emergence of data analytics and visualization tools. This chapter serves to inspire the disentanglement of the complex nature of patent data armed with greater flexibility in data visualization techniques from basic charts to elaborate network visualization.

7.1 Unexpected Encounters

Patent data contains a treasure trove of information that is of great value to present and future innovators, business leaders, and policy makers. Over the years, the quantum of patent data has increased at a tremendous speed. Diverse types of data are being accumulated throughout the lifecycle of patents. With this high volume, variety, and velocity of patent data, the use of new technologies, such as big data analytics and visualization tools have the promise of greater benefits. However, their implementation, though headed in the right direction, is still in its infancy.

Patent analytics starts with gathering relevant data from patent databases owned by national or international patent offices, such as the US Patent and Trademark Office (USPTO) and World Intellectual Property Organization (WIPO), or a few free secondary sources, like Google Patents and The Lens. These search engines allow users to access their databases for patent searches and export the query results. Rudimentary statistical analysis and visualization are also available for some cases.

Patent data can be exported in several ways but has predominantly been done using a simple spreadsheet program, such as MS Excel. Excel is an excellent tool for data cleaning, but it has several drawbacks. Figure 7.1 is an example of the technology roadmap for hair irons made using MS Excel. It needs to show core patents in the target technology field on a time series. However, in Excel, with the sheer amount of data, the reader cannot read the screen or print information. The current large, static form of visualization does not allow readers to explore the data independently.

J. Kim et al., *Patent Analytics*,
https://doi.org/10.1007/978-981-16-2930-3_7

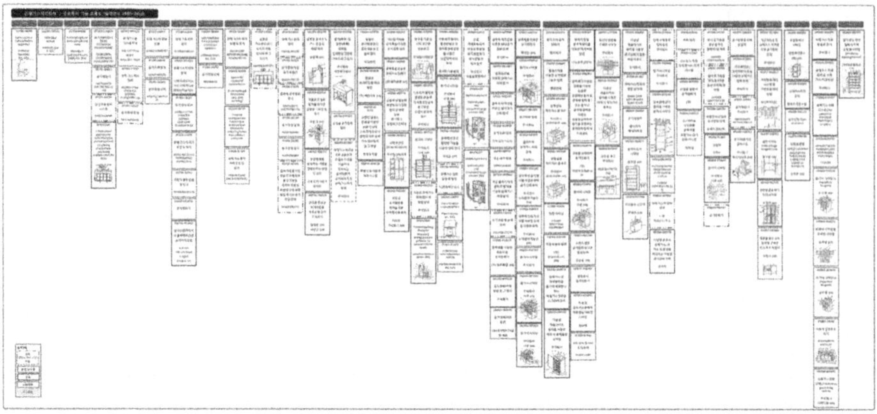

Fig. 7.1 Technology roadmap for hair irons using MS Excel

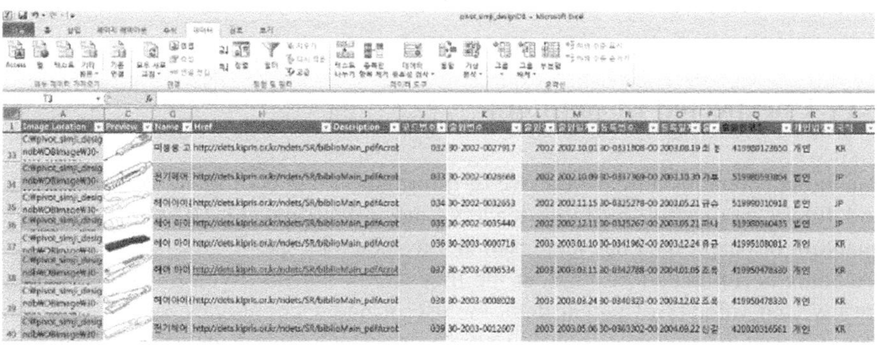

Fig. 7.2 Screen of database creation in Excel (Step 1)

In the 2010 TED talk,[1] Gary Flake unveiled *Microsoft Live Labs Pivot*, an interactive pivoting application with Excel add-ins. The Pivot incorporates a large number of images and data online, enabling smooth zoom and pan effects. It was a light-bulb moment for me, and I asked myself, "*what if these images were the drawings of design patents*?" The Pivot had many defects at that time. However, the interface was intuitive enough, and I relentlessly experimented with the application using iron hair patent data in the following steps. A video demonstration is also available at this link: http://youtu.be/YYU27tF9JxM.

First, preload a patent datasheet in Excel, including the drawing image files and basic patent information, such as publication year, applicants, application number, and a hyperlink of the URL corresponding to the patent (Step 1 in Fig. 7.2). Second,

[1] In the 2010 TED talk, entitled "Is Pivot a turning point for web exploration?", Gary Flake, then the Director of Microsoft Live Labs, demos Pivot, a new way to browse and arrange massive amounts of images and data online.

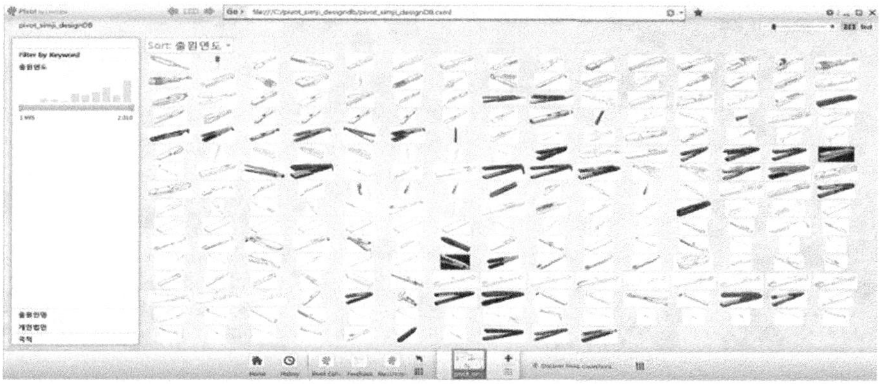

Fig. 7.3 Initial screen of MS Live Labs Pivot (Step 2)

activate a pivot viewer. Figure 7.3 shows the initial screen of the pivot viewer in Step 2. In the left menu of the pivot viewer, there is a field separator value for a pivot. For instance, if the publication date is selected, the application sorts thumbnails of patents by year, as illustrated in Step 3 (Fig. 7.4). The drawing images move directly and gather to form a bar graph.

Additionally, zoom-in and zoom-out images can be viewed simultaneously by scrolling the mouse, as shown in Step 4 (Fig. 7.5). We see the 60-year history of hair flat iron design from its early days to the present. Zoom-in and zoom-out satellite images might not seem surprising today, but this unprecedented level of scaling changes in patent data gave a novel analytic perspective. Furthermore, mapping the spatio-temporal trajectory of each drawing is particularly intriguing as this helps me see the morphological changes, as shown in Fig. 7.6.

The uptick in visualization tools eliminates the hassle of manipulating a large volume of patent data and the subsequent search for the corresponding details.

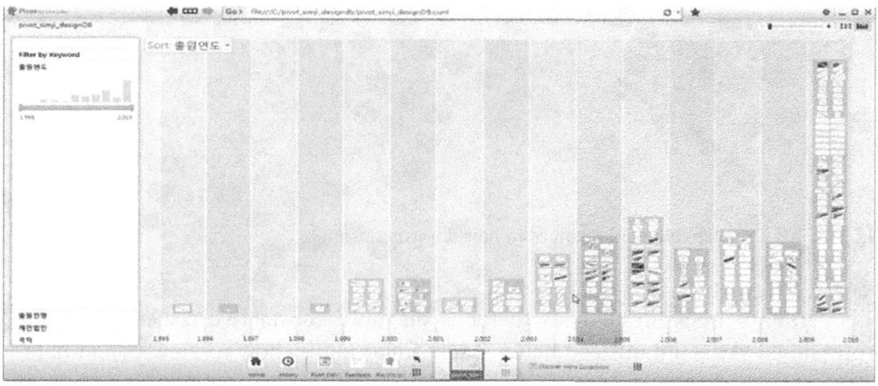

Fig. 7.4 Screen of arranged design drawings by year (Step 3)

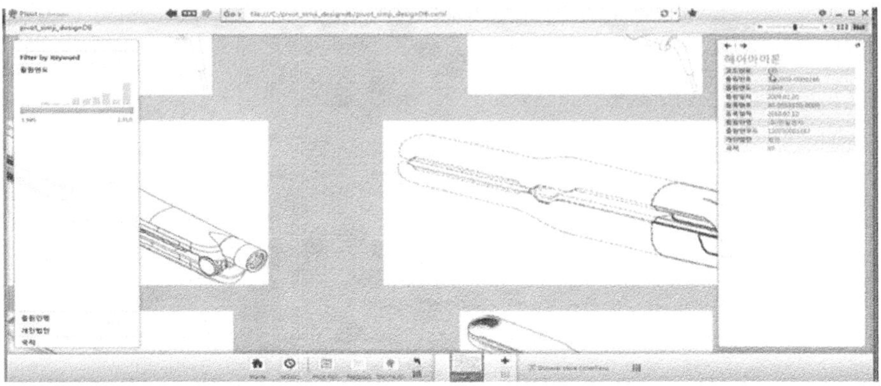

Fig. 7.5 Zoom-in and zoom-out screenshots of thumbnail images of drawings (Step 4)

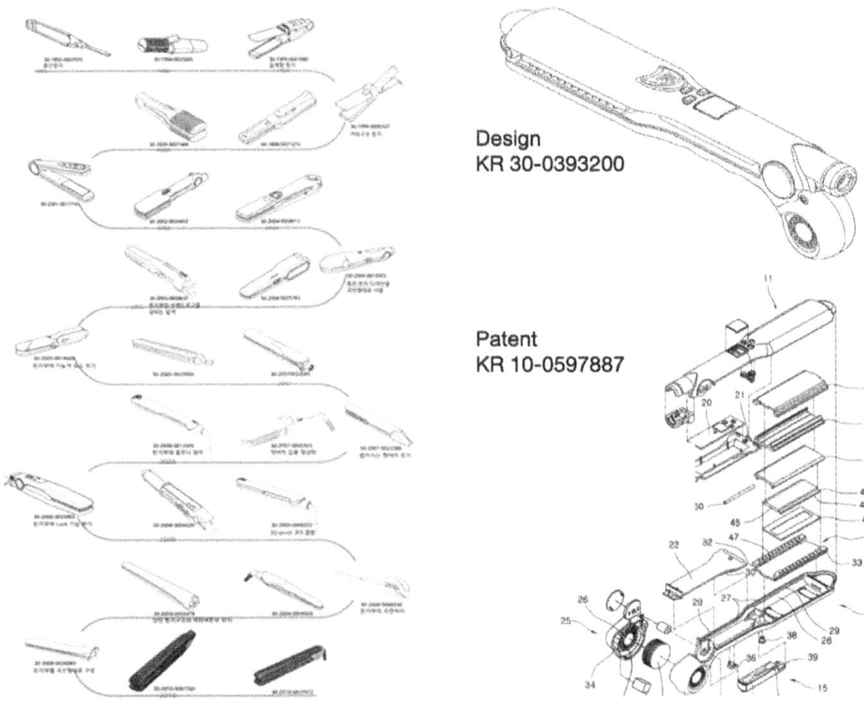

Fig. 7.6 Major morphological changes in hair flat iron design

This certainty frees up analysts to focus on more substantive issues where their professional skills are utilized better. Most importantly, how to view patent data is a crucial part of patent analytics processes, providing new opportunities to see the data through a different lens.

The next sections review several data visualization tools and techniques to analyse patent data effectively and in a meaningful way. Section 7.1 focuses on simple one or two-dimensional views of patent data with real-world examples; Sect. 7.2 highlights complex patent network data and its way to create compelling visualizations.

7.2 Six Basic Charts

This section introduces six types of charts in patent data visualizations, extracted from various sources of patent analytics studies: patent landscape reports, annual reports of patent offices, and secondary IP analytics solutions. We analyze their application scenarios to help select the type of chart to convey the patent data's compelling story. The six are bar, line, and pie charts, geospatial visualizations, bubble charts, and treemaps.

7.2.1 Bar, Line, and Pie Charts

Bar and line graphs and pie charts are the most popular ways to show simple patent statistics—number of applications, inventors, and claims. The use of lines, shading, and color, incorporating the elements of labels and basic visual elements, have had no appreciable improvement since they were first used two centuries ago. William Playfair (1759–1823), a businessperson, engineer, and economist from Scotland, is credited with inventing four types of charts: line, bar, pie, and circle. Playfair communicated numerical data on the economy and trade using statistical graphs effectively (Playfair 2005). His works form the basis of current charts available in Excel and other office programs.

The WIPO Intellectual Property (IP) Statistics Data Center collects a vast amount of information from the databases of national and regional IP offices worldwide and displays them in basic interactive charts and tables. WIPO IP Facts and Figures section serves as a quick overview of annual IP activity using various interactive charts. Figure 7.7 shows the shares of IP filing activity by region using a pie chart and bar charts. The number of applications in Asia for all IPs is relatively higher than those of other regions. Additionally, patents, utility models, trademarks, and designs in Asia are over two-thirds of worldwide applications. This simple visualization not only communicates key data clearly but also stimulates viewers' curiosity and attention.

A series of visualizations powered by Tableau and USPTO data is a good example. Figure 7.8 shows Patents Statanalyzer, a Tableau public visualization solution aiming to reveal new cancer research and treatment insights. Based on the USPTO's dataset consisting of 269,353 patents published between 1976 and 2016, patent activities can be examined by the selected years and patent filing categories. Parameter filters can be updated to focus on certain sections of the data.

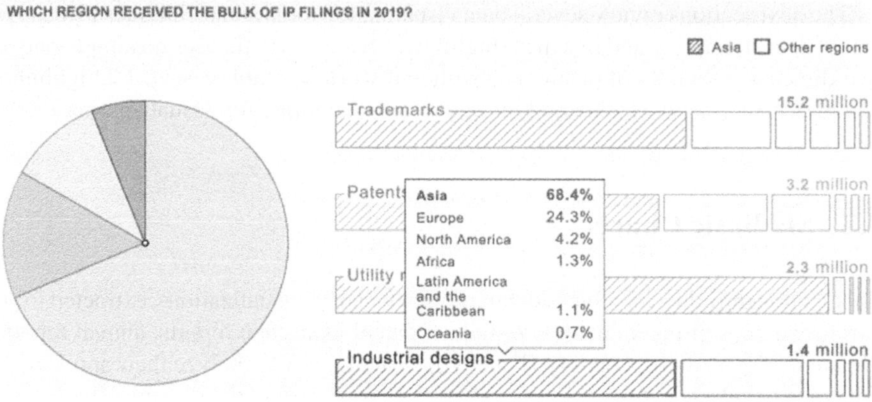

Fig. 7.7 WIPO's interactive charts regarding IP filing activity by region (WIPO 2020)

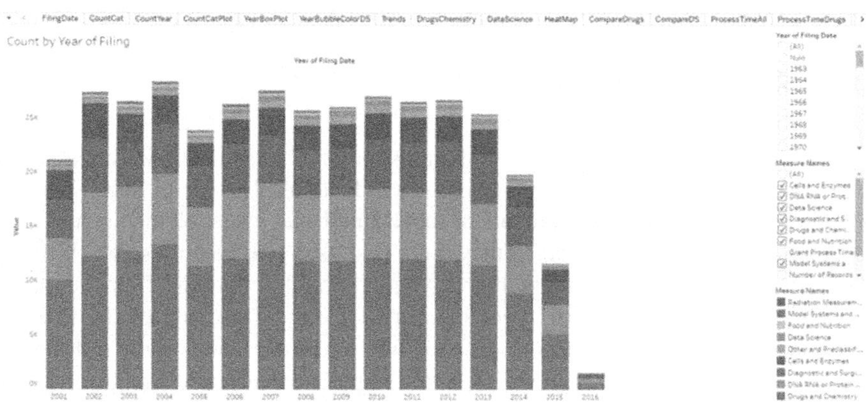

Fig. 7.8 Screen of the USPTO's Patents Statanalyzer

Tableau public, a free, interactive data visualization platform, has attracted significant attention in patent offices and across patent analytics research communities. With a drag-and-drop interface, Tableau public supports a variety of custom charts and maps (e.g., line graph with time series, bubble chart, and heatmap). Its built-in geocoding function effectively connects patent data onto geographic maps. Most importantly, the outcome of patent statistics and analysis is easy to make public through an online interactive dashboard. Tableau tutorials with patent data are available in the USPTO's Open Data Portal and the WIPO Manual on Open Source Patent Analytics online.

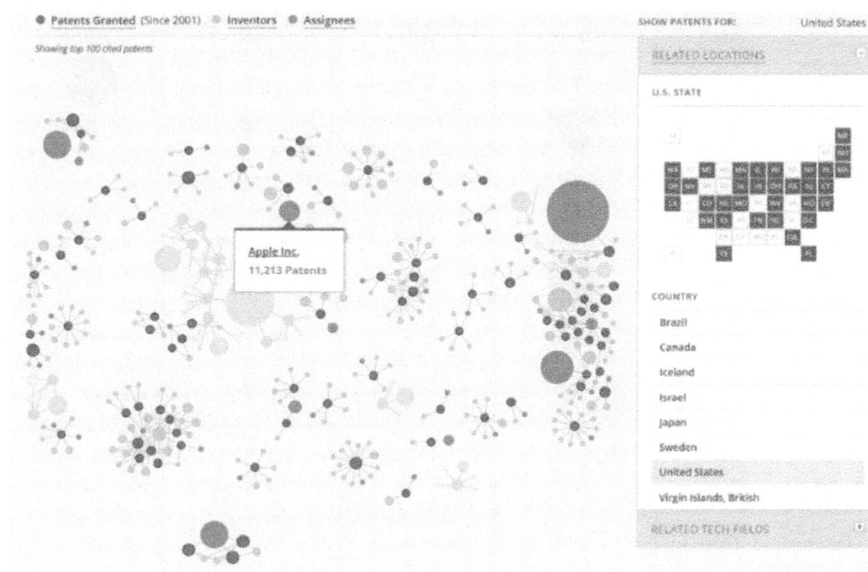

Fig. 7.9 USPTO's PatentsView "where innovation happens"

7.2.2 *Geospatial Visualizations*

Geospatial visualization of patent data is useful in locating where innovation takes place in the world. The analysis focuses on innovation hotspots in general or niche clusters where innovation density is high in one or more fields of patenting. There are many choices in the market for geospatial visualization tools. For instance, the USPTO's *PatentsView* provides an interactive map using patent activities data associated with countries, regions, and cities of applicants. By zooming up to the city level, we can explore the most cited patents, inventors, assignees, and popular technology areas that correspond to the selected geographic area (Fig. 7.9).

7.2.3 *Bubble Charts*

Applicant data can be paired with technology fields of interest. Figure 7.10 illustrates a bubble chart with the top 10 applicants, and their patent counts corresponding to the five key Cooperative Patent Classification (CPC) symbols in the AI fields. The chart clearly shows the technology fields where major applicants have focused and the gaps in a particular technology field (a.k.a. white space analysis). For instance, data recognition (G06K) and digital data processing (G06F) patent filing are competitive, and concentrated computational models (G06N) and image data processing (G06T) are underrepresented in the overall AI patenting activities among the top applicants.

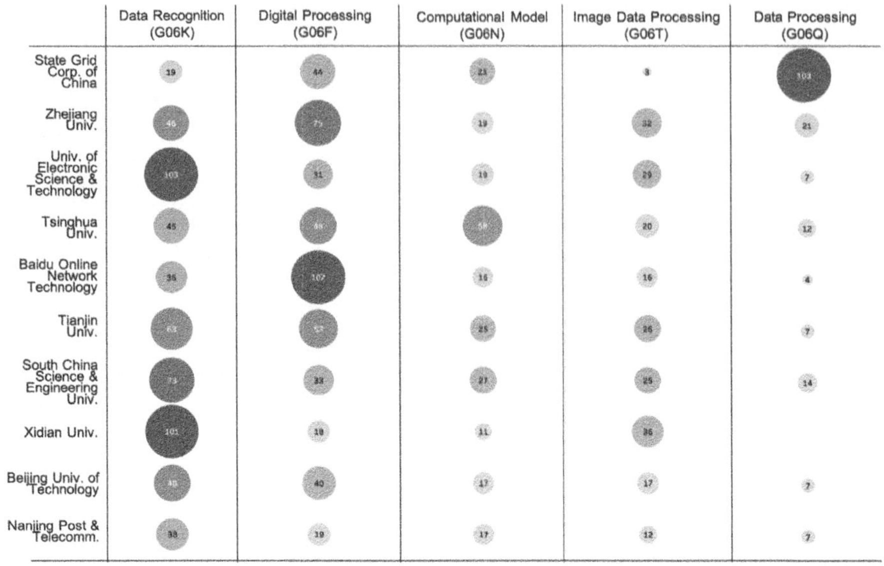

Fig. 7.10 White space analysis using a bubble chart

Particularly, the State Grid Corporation of China outperformed in data processing areas (G06Q).

Patent white space analysis[2] can also be conducted using a paid service, such as Derwent Innovation's *ThemeScape Maps*. Figure 7.11 shows a spatial concept mapping associated with technical classifications and applicant information.

7.2.4 Treemaps

Treemaps are ideal for displaying a hierarchical view of data using nested rectangles of varying sizes and colors. Professor Ben Shneiderman invented the Treemap in the early 1990s. The rectangles are proportionally sized to the corresponding data quantity, while the color-codes add categorical values to the data. This visualization effectively plots the shares of patent technology classes—the International Patent Classification (IPC) and CPC—that support hierarchical, tree-like structures. For instance, CPC is divided into nine sections: A–H and Y, which are sub-divided into classes, sub-classes, groups, and sub-groups (e.g., Section G deals with physics, and its G06 class deals with computing, calculating, and counting.). Figure 7.12 demonstrates how treemaps can be used with technology classification fields to monitor the research and development trends of Samsung Electronics.

[2]White space is the area with little or no patenting activity. White space analysis is designated to identify gaps in a technology landscape that have potential for attending exclusivity.

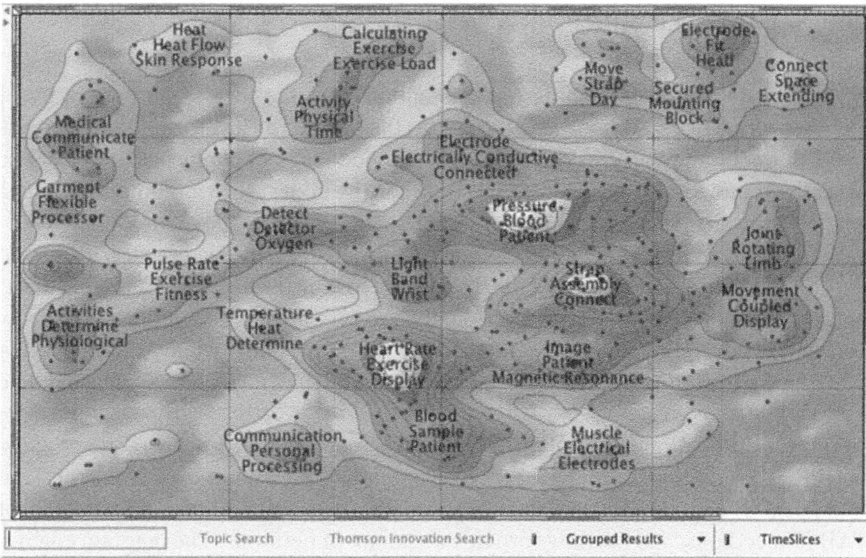

Fig. 7.11 ThemeScape map: example of wearable fitness (Thomson Reuters 2016)

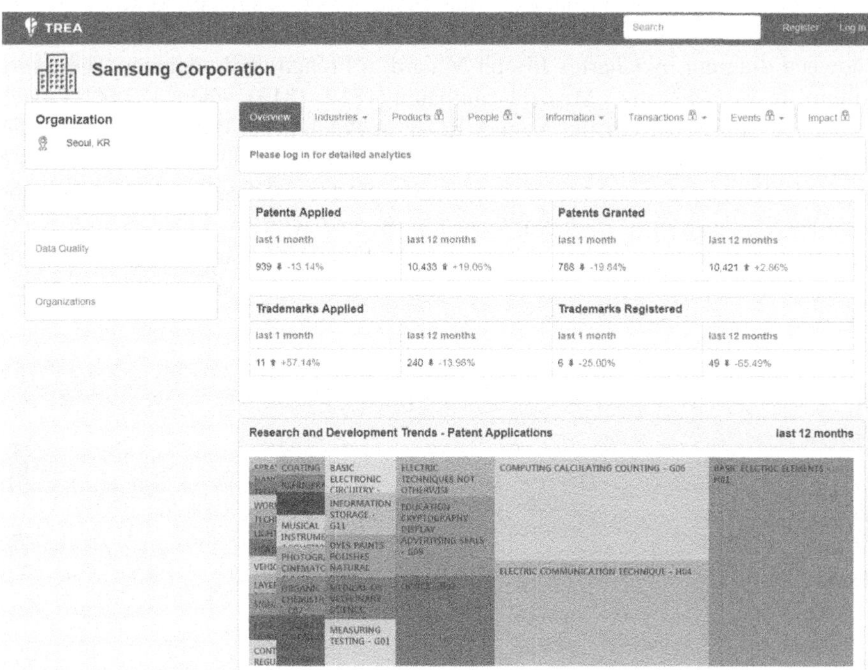

Fig. 7.12 Screen of a treemap in TREA (https://trea.com)

7.3 Network Visualizations

Network visualization is gaining more attention with the increasing popularity of social networks, like Facebook and Twitter. At the most basic level, a network consists of a set of nodes and links. Nodes represent individual actors or physical objects, and links correspond to a type of connection between the nodes, such as common friends, monetary flows, or citations and co-assignments in the case of patent documents.

A *Sankey diagram* is a popular example for visualizing a directed, weighted network. It is useful in visualizing the magnitude of *flow* between nodes in a network. The changes in a network are proportionally expressed using the width of an arrow or arc to represent the quantum of flow. This diagram is also widely utilized when analyzing the evolution between two states or the level of contribution by intermediate steps.

Figure 7.13 illustrates a Sankey diagram of the inter partes review (IPR) process. The IPR is an administrative trial type to challenge patentability at a Patent Trial and Appeal Board (PTAB). In this example, the nodes represent the various states of PTAB proceedings, and the flows provide the count of petitions. The diagram enables tracking the number of petitions passing through at different stages—terminations by settlement, dismissal, or other cases.

The Sankey diagram is named after an Irish-born engineer Matthew H.P.R. Sankey; nevertheless, he was not the first to conceptualize it. Figure 7.14 is a renowned diagram by Charles Joseph Minard, a French civil engineer. The figure exhibits the French army's Moscow campaign (1812–1813), where 422,000 French troops had departed from the Neman River in Poland, but only 10,000 or fewer soldiers survived the retreat from Moscow. To illustrate the flows of troops, Minard invented a Sankey diagram-like representation. Nodes, marked in the text, show the locations of the troops. Their links are represented with sparklines whose width is proportional to the number of troops (10,000 soldiers/mm). The outward and backward directions of the troops' movement are displayed in gold and black,

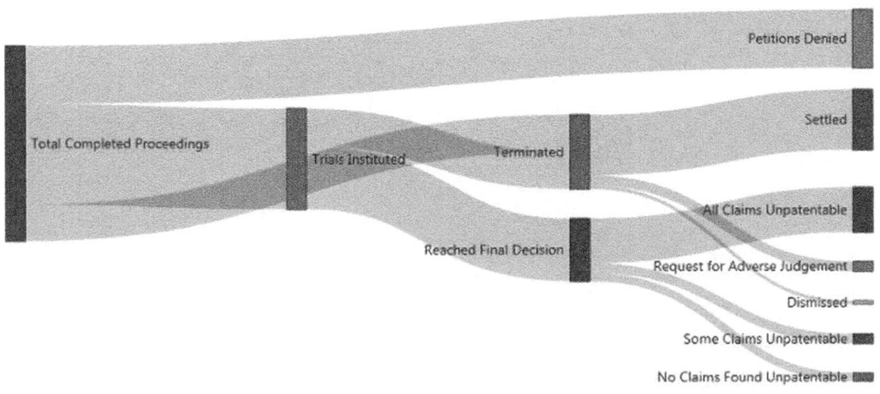

Fig. 7.13 A Sankey diagram of USPTO's Inter Partes Review (USPTO 2017)

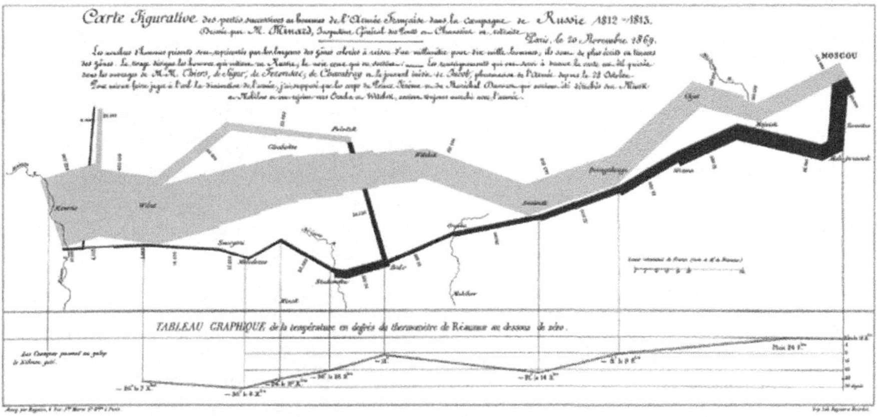

Fig. 7.14 Charles J. Minard, diagram of Napoleon's Russian campaign (1869): a figurative map of the French army's continuous troop losses in the Russian territory (1812–1813)

respectively. He then overlaid the diagram onto a geographical map. This provides details about the troop's main and branching routes with the geographical features, major battles, and the return path's temperatures. The expression of multivariate data (number of troops, direction, latitude, longitude, temperature, and time) in a single diagram effectively conveys multi-faceted data at a glance. More importantly, such visualization chronicles the expected or unforeseen consequences—without inundating the reader.

Let us take more examples from the annual IP filing activity report (WIPO 2017). The table and figure in Fig. 7.15 show an equivalent amount of data on design patent filing activities worldwide. Figure 7.15a displays the raw data by country, whereas Fig. 7.15b focuses on the relationship patterns in the data. In this example, the Sankey diagram illustrates the flow of non-resident design counts between two nodes: the origin of applicants and IP offices. The proportional color-coded flows illustrate the trends of resident status on design filing behavior. Additionally, comparing the width of flows yields a fair idea of inventors' desire, where they plan to commercialize the designs among foreign markets. For instance, the most popular destination for non-resident design filing is the European Union Intellectual Property Office (EUIPO) due to the high numbers of US residents' filings.

Another popular way to visualize networks is to use *centrality measures*, where nodes are sized according to their importance based on centrality levels. Specifically, on the social network Facebook, every individual represents a node and is linked to others in a friendship (referred to as links or edges). Centrality measures define the position of an individual in a network regarding other individuals. It allows us to understand if a particular individual is central to a network in various ways: having the most direct connections, controlling the information flow, and being an influential person (see Chap. 5).

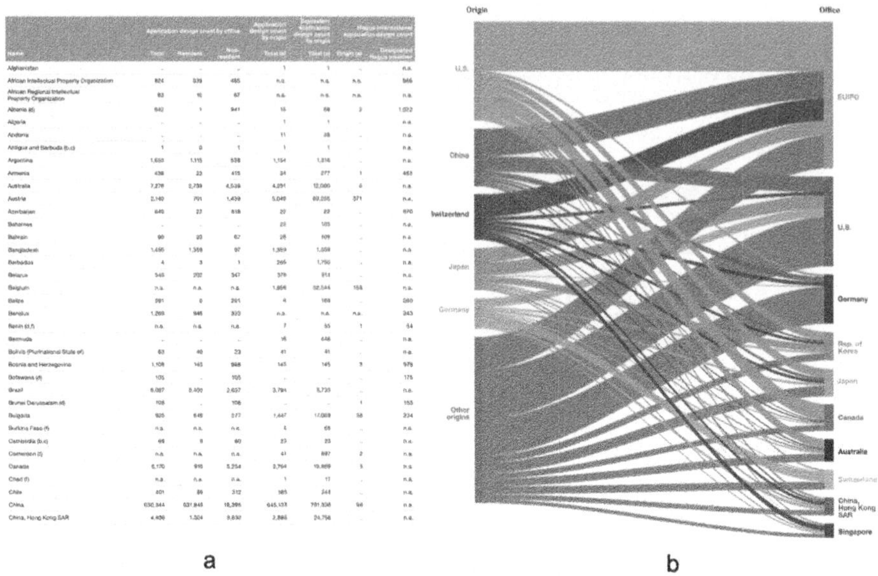

Fig. 7.15 **a** Statistics on design patent filling activities using a table. **b** Sankey diagram excerpted from WIPO annual IP filing activity report (WIPO 2017)

The general principle of social networks applies to patent networks. Bibliographic patent data can be formed in the nodes. Simultaneously, the relationships—co-inventorship, co-assignments, and backward and forward citations—can be used to connect the nodes. This approach is useful to investigate the dynamics of patenting activities while exploring key applicants, co-inventor networks, and citation patterns.

Take an example of Amberscope, a patent specialized citation network (Amberscope 2020). When entering a patent search query (e.g., patent number), it returns an ego patent citation network for the given patent (Fig. 7.16). The citing and cited nodes are color-coded in green and purple, respectively. An arrow is an edge that shows a time-series flow from older to newer patents. Further information is displayed when the cursor hovers over any node—patent number, title, applicant, publication date, and the number of forward and backward citations from the selected node. An important feature of Amberscope is to suggest ghost patents marked with gray nodes. These are not explicitly cited in patent documents but are likely to have a hidden relationship (i.e., latent citations, see Chap. 6) based on their patent families and cross-citation patterns of an examiner and applicant.

Questel Orbit in Fig. 7.17 offers assignment network visualization based on the changes in patent ownership information. Patent assignment information and transactional connections enable a greater vigilance to keep track of competitors' M&A activities and patent transaction information because most M&As are accompanied by patent due diligence and investigation on change in applicant and assignee names over sale and transfer. In this map, color codes can be customized to

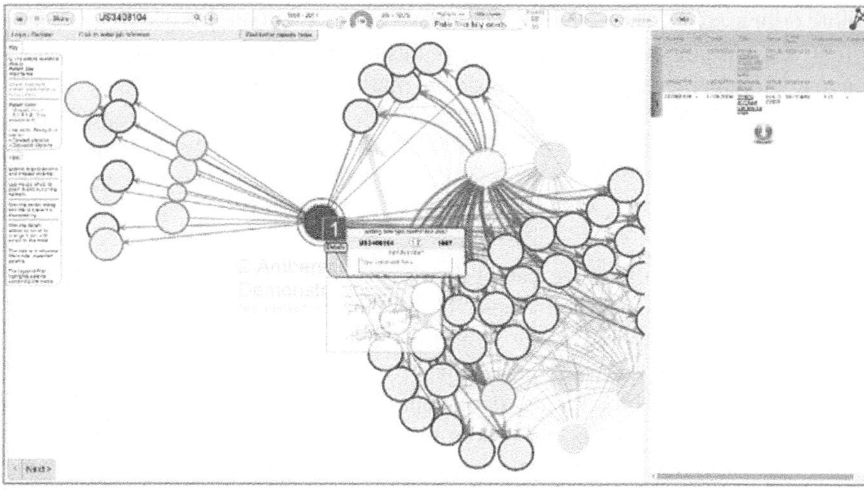

Fig. 7.16 Overview of Amberscope (Amberscope 2020)

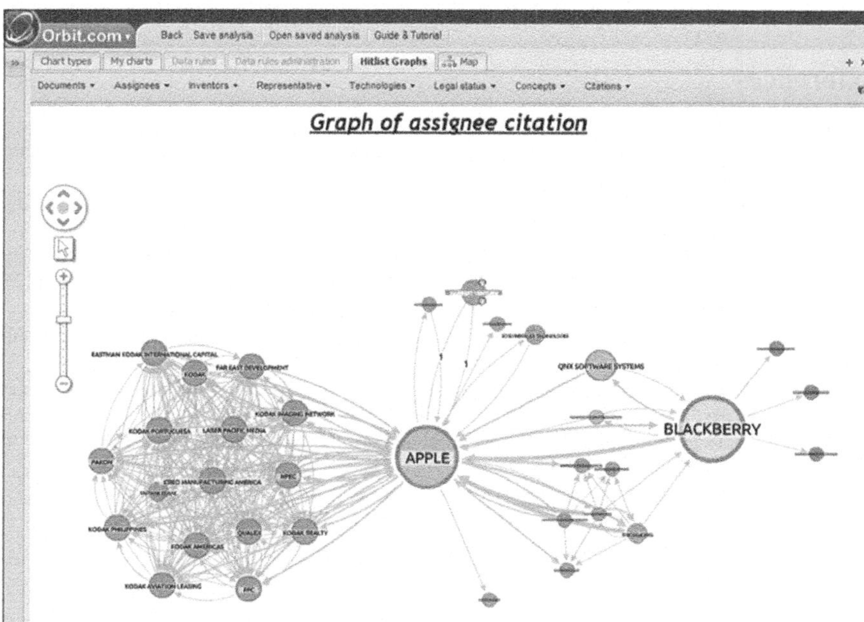

Fig. 7.17 Assignee citation network of Questel Orbit

explore prior assignees or technology domains (e.g., IPC or CPC). An assignee's past, current, and possible future patenting activities indicate a clue about the technology area to complement, reinforce or choose the market for entry.

7.4 Summary

We live in an age with massive patent data easily accessible to the public, but in a format that can easily overwhelm most. The uptake of visualization tools eliminates the hassle of manipulating a large volume of patent data. Most importantly, how we view data, whether it is one-dimensional, two-dimensional, or multidimensional, determines how much breadth and depth can be delved into. Additionally, through a visual lens, hidden trends and patterns can be pinpointed to draw out more sophisticated insights. Chapter. 8 further introduces a handful of software tools that offer different functionalities for network analysis and visualization with a practical guide.

References

Amberscope (2020) https://www.ambercite.com/amberblog/2017/7/11/amberscope-vs-ambercite-ai-which-is-better. Accessed 18 Nov 2020.

Playfair W (2005) Playfair's commercial and political atlas and statistical breviary. Cambridge University Press, London.

Thomson Reuters (2016) Derwent Innovation: Explanation on ThemeScape. In: Thomson Innovation: Thomson Innovation User Guide. https://edisciplinas.usp.br/pluginfile.php/3521125/mod_resource/content/1/thomson%20innovation.pdf. Accessed 18 Nov 2020.

USPTO (2017) Proceedings at PTAB. https://developer.uspto.gov/visualization/proceedings-ptab. Accessed 18 Nov 2020.

WIPO (2017) World Intellectual Property Indicators 2017. p. 167. http://www.wipo.int/publications/en/details.jsp?id=4234&plang=EN. Accessed 18 Nov 2020.

WIPO (2020) Facts and Figures. https://www.wipo.int/edocs/infogdocs/en/ipfactsandfigures2019/. Accessed 18 Nov 2020.

Chapter 8
How to Study Patent Network Analysis

Abstract A guide to aid research design in conducting patent network analysis from the formulation of research questions to patent data collection and subsequent network analysis introduces this chapter. It is designed for those with no programming skills and provides a high-level overview of free, open-source tools that offer different functionalities for network analysis and visualization. Finally, Gephi and Dyson's patent data samples are used to exemplify a four-step patent network analysis—data collection (step 1), data cleaning and mapping (step 2), network analysis (step 3), and network visualization (step 4).

8.1 Research Design

Network analysis is a way of thinking about the complex system that focuses on the relations among the system entities. Patent network analysis is one of the popular areas of social network analysis. Various network-based metrics and graph representations enable researchers to comprehend the patent network structure and its interactions.

This section sets out with three questions to aid research design for network analysis: *What is a research question? What types of nodes and relations will be used? Where is a network boundary?*

It should be noted that this section highlights several topics that are discussed in greater depth in other chapters. Particularly, the reader should refer to Chaps. 3, 6, and 7.

Formulation of research question

The first step in the process of patent network analysis is to formulate a research question or hypothesis. When constructing a research question, it is helpful to consider how a network (as one variable) relates to, affects, or is affected by another variable or set of variables (Prell 2012). Here are a few examples to help researchers get started.

- Do patents with a higher number of forward citations considered radical innovations?

J. Kim et al., *Patent Analytics*,
https://doi.org/10.1007/978-981-16-2930-3_8

- How does radical innovation affect later innovation activities?
- Do patents with a higher share of non-patent literature citations are more valuable than others?

All of the preceding questions are the examples of research questions at a patent-level. If researchers are interested in studying an inventor-level or assignee-level of patent networks, the following research questions are pertinent to formulate.

- How has the global collaboration network been changed during the COVID-19 crisis?
- Where is a company positioned in technological collaboration networks? Who are potential competitors or collaborators?
- Who is the most important inventor in a team? Who is an influencer, gatekeeper, or active team member?
- Can we identify university-industry collaborations in a specific technology field?

The list of possible research questions is endless. Before attempting to formulate a research question, a comprehensive literature review on the subject area of interest is highly recommended. Lessons learned from previous studies offer opportunities to refine the current research question and guide further steps.

Identification of sources of network data (nodes and links)

Many patent network studies have attempted to structure a network with patents (or inventors) as the nodes and co-citations (or co-inventorship) as the links. However, the nodes can be any entity—applicants, geographic origin, technology classifications, among others. Identifying the type of node for the study has a major impact on what types of links are collected and how they are gathered.

Borgatti et al. (2018) state that relations among nodes can be of many different kinds, and each type gives rise to corresponding networks. If we identify co-inventorship links, we have a co-inventor network. If we measure the co-classification of technologies where the inventors are co-worked, we have co-inventor networks in the field of interest. Table 8.1 provides the topology of relation types and their examples, commonly used in patent network studies.

Determination of Network Boundary

After formulating research questions and identifying relevant network data sources, the next step is to determine a network boundary. A network boundary refers to the boundary around a set of nodes that the researcher deems to be a complete set of nodes for the network study (Prell 2012).

As discussed in Chap. 5, there are two fundamental kinds of network research design: *ego networks* and *complete networks*. With egocentric networks, identifying a network boundary is fairly straightforward. An *ego* is the focal point of the network during data collection and analysis and is surrounded by alters. Thus, researchers have to determine a focal node as *ego* (e.g., a focal patent or core inventor) and the *alters* to whom the *ego* is directly connected to the links.

Table 8.1 Types of relations commonly studied in patent networks

Relation type	Example
Co-occurrence	Co-classification of technologies Co-classification of design classes Co-occurring keywords in patent documents
Relations	Co-inventorship Co-citations Patent family Origin of the inventor (spatial locations)
Interactions	Patent transactions (e.g., M&As) Role of assignee interactions (competition, collaboration, or coopetition)
Flows	Backward and forward citations Patent to patent citations Patent to non-patent literature citations

With complete networks, determining the network boundary is more complicated. This is related to the issues of data sampling. If a researcher were to have a research interest in Bose's patenting activities in the United States as a boundary, other patents published outside of the United States should be ignored. In patent bibliometrics studies, it is often possible to use a complete patent dataset, i.e., the full patent information for one or more entities. However, we make the caveat that this is a complete dataset only insofar as it is complete for a particular source such as the USPTO. Other but unpublished or international patent applications usually exist. Ego networks pose fewer data collection problems than complete networks. However, ego network studies often fail to capture the full structural properties of the complete network, such as network density and dimension.

To summarize, the decisions—what to study, what nodes and relations to identify, and where to determine the network boundary—are interlinked and must, to some extent, be considered together.

8.2 Choosing Network Analysis Tools

A handful of free, open-source, or paid tools offer different functionalities for analyzing and visualizing networks. Many of these tools are developed considering particular application domains, such as social network analysis and bibliometrics (Faysal and Arifuzzaman 2018). Recently, they have been gaining considerable traction in patent analytics communities.

Table 8.2 provides an exhaustive list of network analysis tools and a few free, open-source, desktop-based network analysis tools with different graph analytics and visualization features. Additionally, as machine learning techniques for assisting advanced patent analytics are in great demand, a general-purpose programming

Table 8.2 An overview of network analysis tools

Tool	Tool type	Support platform	Programming	Key features
Gephi	Free, Open source	Web, Desktop (Mac, Windows)	N	User-friendly interface, up-to-date plug-ins, Customizable graph visualization, support a large-network analysis (more than 100,000 nodes)
NodeXL	Free (premium version available)	Desktop (Windows)	N	Excel plug-in, familiar interface to MS Excel, major APIs of social networks (e.g., YouTube, Wikipedia)
Pajek	Free (Premium version available)	Desktop (Windows)	N	A high degree of running accuracy and speed on a large-network analysis (more than millions of nodes)
Python with NetworkX and Plotly	Free	Web, Desktop (Mac, Windows)	Y	Access to machine learning packages for advanced patent analytics

language, Python, with developer packages to display network data, is added to the list.

Some tools provide effective visualization along with a suite of network algorithms. Some others provide an interactive and user-friendly interface; researchers use the tools as a means of network statistics and as the tool for supporting the visual thinking process by interacting with data. Moreover, the emergence of patent big data necessitates the development of scalable network analysis tools. We describe four popular network analysis tools in the patent analytics community as follows.

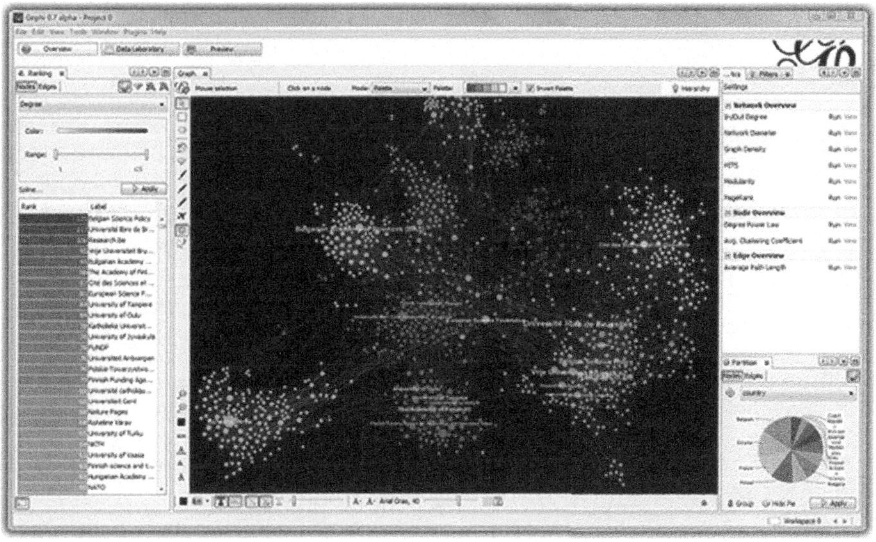

Fig. 8.1 A screen of Gephi (https://gephi.org)

Gephi (https://gephi.org)

Gephi is an open-source software for visualizing and analyzing large network graphs. It is probably the most popular network visualization tool for data analysts and scientists keen to explore patent bibliometrics. Substantial optionality of graph layouts and statistics is free to use and continually fueled by a large set of plug-ins. Gephi can calculate advanced network metrics including centralities, density, clusters, and graph layouts, such as Yifan Hu, Force Atlas, and Fruchterman Reingold.

Gephi does not require any prior coding expertise. Its interface is easy and intuitive enough to interact with patent data and customize high-quality network visualizations (Fig. 8.1). The feature to load and operate on a large network (more than 100,000 nodes) is also significant. However, the runtime can be longer depending on the choice of graph layouts. The accuracy of network statistics comes at the cost of speed.

NodeXL (https://www.smrfoundation.org)

NodeXL (basic version) is a free plugin to Microsoft Excel that structures data for network analysis and visualization. This tool is probably the easiest starter for network analysis as its interface has greater compatibility with Excel spreadsheets' features (Fig. 8.2). As to network metric calculations, NodeXL is able to calculate different centralities, clustering coefficients, and graph density, to name a few. However, comparing Gephi and Pajek, the ranges of network metrics, layouts, and graphical options are limited. NodeXL runs stable with a relatively small-sized network with a few thousands of nodes due to memory and spreadsheet restrictions.

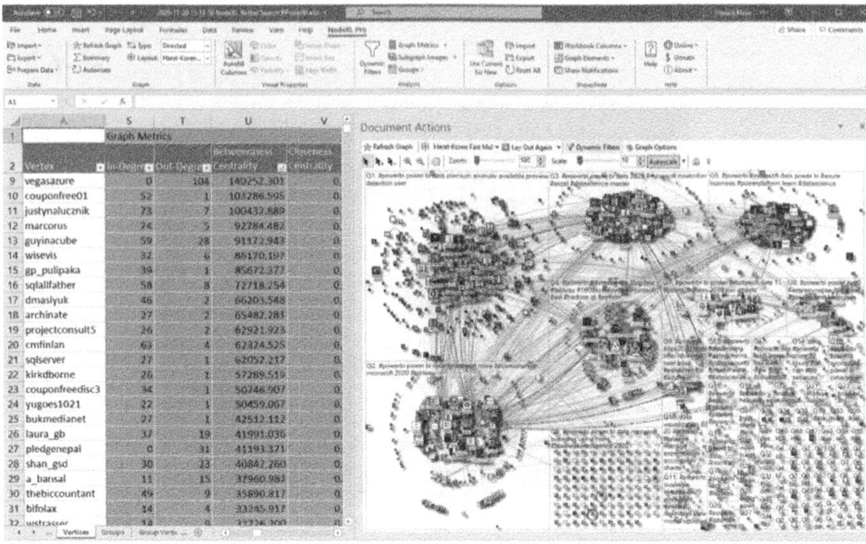

Fig. 8.2 A screen of NodeXL (https://www.smrfoundation.org/)

Nonetheless, NodeXL can be powerful for social network analysis by scraping API data from Twitter, YouTube, Flickr, and Wikipedia (available for annual licenses).

Pajek (http://mrvar.fdv.uni-lj.si/pajek)

Pajek is one of the oldest free tools for large network analysis in continuous development since 1996. It is still the only network analysis tool that can handle a *huge* network containing more than millions of nodes (Fig. 8.3). At the same time, memory consumption and runtime are significantly less compared to Gephi and NodeXL.

In Pajek, analysis and visualization of large networks are performed using six data types: network (graph), partition (nominal or ordinal properties of nodes), vector (numerical properties of nodes), cluster (the subset of nodes), permutation (reordering of nodes, ordinal properties), and hierarchy (general tree structure on nodes) (Mrvar and Batagelj 2016).

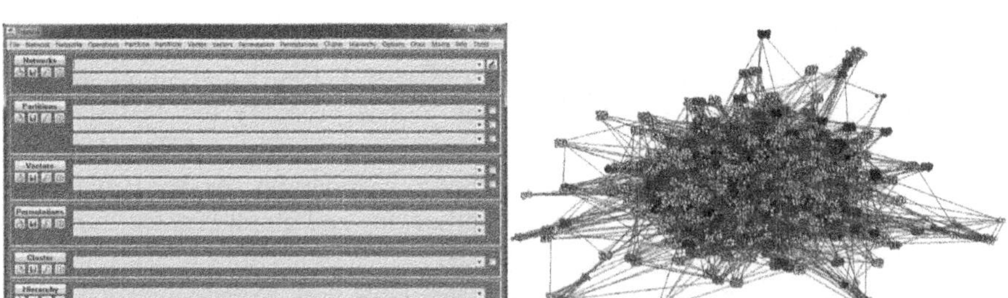

Fig. 8.3 A screen of Pajek (http://mrvar.fdv.uni-lj.si/pajek)

While Pajek excels at large network analysis with a high degree of operation precision, its menu-based interface devalues its excellence. It creates a hindrance when customizing the network graph layout. For those who prefer the visualization layouts and filters offered by Gephi, but have to work with millions of patent data without any prior coding skills, they can choose Pajek to calculate network metrics, and the results obtained from Pajek can be further exported to Gephi.

Python, NetworkX, and Plotly (https://plotly.com/python/network-graphs).

Python is a high-level and general-purpose programming language, which comes with several plotting packages. Plotly is an increasingly popular free graphing package that incorporates a range of API clients for Python, R, MATLAB, and Excel. Plotly's wide variety of graph types and access from various environments are big reasons for its growing success. Plotly's API services for R and Python allow data analysts to share custom graphs with colleges and make publicize them.

While Plotly is not a data processing tool, the integrative use of NetworkX and Plotly packages would be the best way to begin with patent network analysis and visualization on Python (Fig. 8.4). NetworkX is a Python programming software package for the creation and manipulation of graphs and networks. Similar to Pajek, NetworkX is reasonably efficient and scalable for large-sized networks with over 10 million nodes.

Furthermore, with Python libraries for machine learning such as TensorFlow and NLTK, we can exploit several applications of machine learning techniques to patent data (Ladd et al. 2017). However, for those with no prior knowledge of programming language, Python can be a costly choice because a basic programming skill is required.

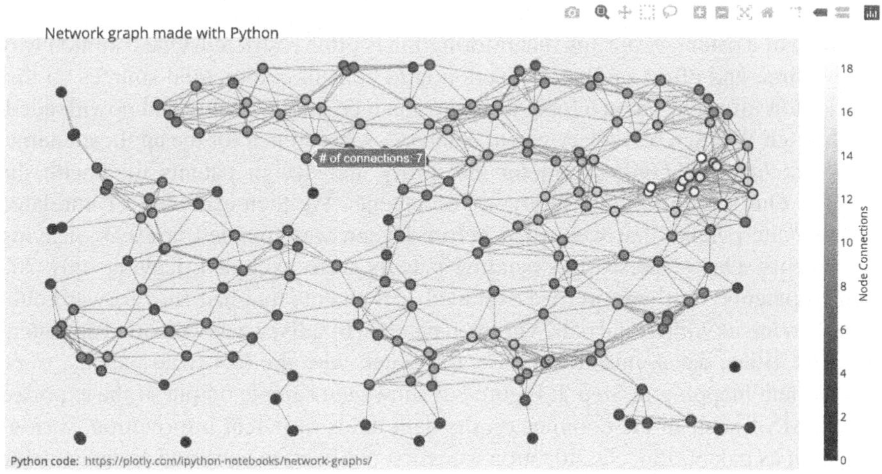

Fig. 8.4 A screen of Python with NetworkX and Plotly (https://plotly.com/python/network-graphs)

8.3 Four Practical Steps for Patent Network Analysis

This section focuses on patent network analysis using the open software Gephi and Dyson's patent dataset. We go through four steps: data collection (step 1), data cleaning and mapping (step 2), network analysis (step 3), and network visualization (step 4).

Step 1 Data Collection

The first step of patent network analysis is to select the source of patent data. Many national and regional patent offices provide patent documents online, most notably, *WIPO's Patentscope, USPTO's Patents view,* and *EPO's Espacenet.* While these primary sources are usually free and enable an easy search of basic bibliographic patent data in a timely manner, the amount of patent data that can be exported is often limited with respect to the range of data fields and country coverage (Adams 2020). Several free or commercial services collect patent databases from various primary sources and make it accessible through a single interface. These secondary services often offer additional enhancements and features associated with the data (e.g., patent family relations, licensing information), or even analysis tools (e.g., word cloud, citation map) (Trippe 2015).

Table 8.3 provides a non-exhaustive list of patent database services. Remember each source has different coverage and exporting options for patent documents. The decision on what patent database service will be used is an important decision for patent analysts with regard to completeness and the cost ofacquiring data.

As for practical demonstrations of data collection, we examined Dyson's product innovation case, which is also a subject of Chap. 9. We collect Dyson's utility and design patents filed with the USPTO during 2001–2008 and their backward and forward citations. While many patent offices allow the search of cited or citing literature of a patent, exporting that information is often restricted. One common way to save time and effort on data collection is to consult commercial sources so that the citation information on a topic of interest can be finely created and downloaded.

Through WIPS, a secondary patent database, we searched for the applicant name, *Dyson Technology Limited*, among the utility and design patents filed with the USPTO. Our search initially returned 966 patents. We then excluded 51 unrelated patents—the patents that were filed before Dyson was founded in 1993—leaving 915 patents. Out of these, 153 pending patents were excluded, leaving only 762 granted patents. Furthermore, we excluded 138 patents that had zero forward citations, leaving us with a total of 624 granted patents. Finally, we downloaded the patent numbers, titles, dates, inventors, IPCs associated with the 624 focal patents, to be used in data mapping in Step 2. Figure 8.5 shows the sample output of the exported data in MS Excel. In the columns on the data fields of patent information, various data such as patent title, classification category, publication year, and assignee name are displayed, while the rows list the searched patents.

Table 8.3 A non-exhaustive list of patent database provider

Producer	Service name	URL
Public Sector databases (Regional offices and IP5)*		
WIPO	Patentscope	http://www.wipo.int/patentscope/search/en
EPO	Esp@cenet	https://worldwide.espacenet.com/
	PASTAT	https://www.epo.org/searching-for-patents/business/patstat.html
JPO	IPDL	http://www.ipdl.inpit.go.jp/homepg_e.ipdl
KIPO	KIPRIS	http://eng.kipris.or.kr/enghome/main.jsp
CNIPA	PSS System	http://pss-system.cnipa.gov.cn/
USPTO	PAIR (Patent Application Information Retrieval	https://portal.uspto.gov/pair/
	TESS (Trademark Electronic Search System)	http://tmsearch.uspto.gov/bin/gate.exe?f=tess&state=4805:pu10xo.1.1
	Bulk data download	https://bulkdata.uspto.gov/
EAPO	Eurasian publication server	https://www.eapo.org/en/publications/publicat/publicat.php
Free-of-charge Private Sector Database Services		
Google	Google Patents	https://patents.google.com/
Cambia	PatentLens	http://www.patentlens.net
Fee-based Private Sector Database Services		
Clarivate	Derwent World Patents Index	https://clarivate.com/derwent/solutions/derwent-world-patent-index-dwpi/
Questel	Orbit	http://www.orbit.com
LexisNexis	TotalPatent	http://www.lexisnexis.com/totalpatent
Minesoft	PatBase	http://www.patbase.com
	PatBaseXpress	http://www.patbaseexpress.com
FIZ Karlsruhe	STN	http://www.stn-international.de

(continued)

Table 8.3 (continued)

Producer	Service name	URL
WIPS	WIPS Global	http://www.wipsglobal.com

* IP5: The European Patent Office (EPO), the Japanese Patent Office (JPO), the Korean Intellectual Property Office (KIPO), China National Intellectual Property Administration (CNIPA), and the United States Patent and Trademark Office (USPTO)

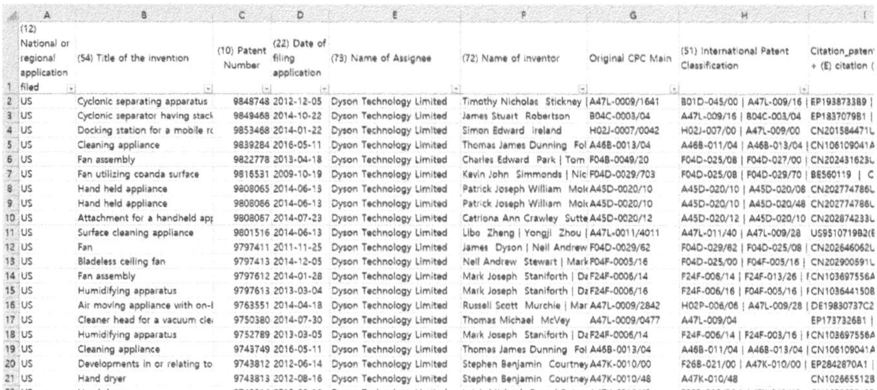

	A	B	C	D	E	F	G	H	I
1	(12) National or regional application filed	(54) Title of the invention	(10) Patent Number	(22) Date of filing application	(73) Name of Assignee	(72) Name of inventor	Original CPC Main	(51) International Patent Classification	Citation_paten + (E) citation (
2	US	Cyclonic separating apparatus	9848748	2012-12-05	Dyson Technology Limited	Timothy Nicholas Stickney |	A47L-0009/1641	B01D-045/00 | A47L-009/16 |	EP1938733B9 |
3	US	Cyclonic separator having stack	9849468	2014-10-22	Dyson Technology Limited	James Stuart Robertson	B04C-0003/04	A47L-009/16 | B04C-003/04	EP1837079B1 |
4	US	Docking station for a mobile rc	9853468	2014-01-22	Dyson Technology Limited	Simon Edward Ireland	H02J-0007/0042	H02J-007/00 | A47L-009/00	CN201584471L
5	US	Cleaning appliance	9839284	2016-05-11	Dyson Technology Limited	Thomas James Dunning Fol	A46B-0013/04	A46B-011/04 | A46B-013/04 |	CN106109041A
6	US	Fan assembly	9822778	2013-04-18	Dyson Technology Limited	Charles Edward Park | Tom	F04B-0049/20	F04D-025/08 | F04D-027/00 |	CN202431623L
7	US	Fan utilizing coanda surface	9816531	2009-10-19	Dyson Technology Limited	Kevin John Simmonds | Nic	F04D-0029/703	F04D-025/08 | F04D-029/70 |	BE560119 | C
8	US	Hand held appliance	9808065	2014-06-13	Dyson Technology Limited	Patrick Joseph William Mok	A45D-0020/10	A45D-020/10 | A45D-020/08	CN202774786L
9	US	Hand held appliance	9808066	2014-06-13	Dyson Technology Limited	Patrick Joseph William Mok	A45D-0020/10	A45D-020/10 | A45D-020/48	CN202774786L
10	US	Attachment for a handheld apr	9808067	2014-07-23	Dyson Technology Limited	Catriona Ann Crawley Sutte	A45D-0020/12	A45D-020/12 | A45D-020/10	CN202874233L
11	US	Surface cleaning appliance	9801516	2014-06-13	Dyson Technology Limited	Libo Zheng | Yongji Zhou |	A47L-0011/4011	A47L-011/40 | A47L-009/28	US9510719B2(E
12	US	Fan	9797411	2011-11-25	Dyson Technology Limited	James Dyson | Neil Andrew	F04D-0029/62	F04D-029/62 | F04D-025/08 |	CN202646062L
13	US	Bladeless ceiling fan	9797413	2014-12-05	Dyson Technology Limited	Neil Andrew Stewart | Mark	F04F-0005/16	F04D-025/00 | F04F-005/16 |	CN202900591L
14	US	Fan assembly	9797612	2014-01-28	Dyson Technology Limited	Mark Joseph Staniforth | Da	F24F-0006/14	F24F-006/14 | F24F-013/26 | f	CN103697556A
15	US	Humidifying apparatus	9797613	2013-03-04	Dyson Technology Limited	Mark Joseph Staniforth | Da	F24F-0006/16	F24F-006/16 | F04F-005/16 | f	CN103644150B
16	US	Air moving appliance with on-l	9763551	2014-04-18	Dyson Technology Limited	Russell Scott Murchie | Mar	A47L-0009/2842	H02P-006/06 | A47L-009/28 |	DE19830737C2
17	US	Cleaner head for a vacuum cle	9750380	2014-07-30	Dyson Technology Limited	Thomas Michael McVey	A47L-0009/0477	A47L-009/04	EP1737326B1 |
18	US	Humidifying apparatus	9752789	2013-03-05	Dyson Technology Limited	Mark Joseph Staniforth | Da	F24F-0006/14	F24F-006/14 | F24F-003/16 | f	CN103697556A
19	US	Cleaning appliance	9743749	2016-05-11	Dyson Technology Limited	Thomas James Dunning Fol	A46B-0013/04	A46B-011/04 | A46B-013/04 |	CN106109041A
20	US	Developments in or relating to	9743812	2012-06-14	Dyson Technology Limited	Stephen Benjamin Courtney	A47K-0010/00	F26B-021/00 | A47K-010/00 |	EP2842870A1 |
21	US	Hand dryer	9743813	2012-08-16	Dyson Technology Limited	Stephen Benjamin Courtney	A47K-0010/48	A47K-010/48	CN102665512B

Fig. 8.5 Export patent search results to MS Excel (step 1: data collection)

Step 2. Data Cleaning and Mapping

Data cleaning is one of the most challenging and time-consuming tasks when dealing with patent data. Raw patent data notoriously contains misspellings, inconsistent data formats, or many terms with the same or similar meanings, which requires cleaning up and standardization to enable accurate analysis. The most common errors can be found in the patent assignee and inventor fields. For example, Dyson has many names in patent documents, such as Dyson Technology Limited, Dyson Ltd., Dyson Technology, or Dyson. This kind of inconsistency should be corrected before analysis. Undesirable patents could also be included, which will exacerbate any noise or problems when moving to the next steps. Perhaps a subject-matter expert or trained patent searcher should be engaged in this step. Or we could use *Open Refine* (previously Google Refine), an open-source tool for data cleaning to deal with the messy patent data. An online tutorial for Open Refine to cope with patent data cleaning is available in *The WIPO Manual on Open Source Patent Analytics* (Chapter 8 Open Refine, Oldham 2016).

The next step is data mapping. We define the nodes and edges of a network and transforms them into two datasheets: a node sheet and an edge sheet. The *node* sheet looks like Fig. 8.6; the first column is named ID for identifying a node. The node ID should be standardized and has a unique name that is used consistently. As a rule of thumb, a patent application number is often set to be a node ID. While

ID

Additional Patent Information

	A	B	C	D	E
1	ID	(12) National or regional application filed	(54) Title of the invention	(22) Date of filing application	(73) Name of Assignee
2	9848748	US	Cyclonic separating apparatus	2012-12-05	Dyson Technology Limited
3	9849468	US	Cyclonic separator having stack	2014-10-22	Dyson Technology Limited
4	9853468	US	Docking station for a mobile rc	2014-01-22	Dyson Technology Limited
5	9839284	US	Cleaning appliance	2016-05-11	Dyson Technology Limited
6	9822778	US	Fan assembly	2013-04-18	Dyson Technology Limited
7	9816531	US	Fan utilizing coanda surface	2009-10-19	Dyson Technology Limited
8	9808065	US	Hand held appliance	2014-06-13	Dyson Technology Limited

Fig. 8.6 Example of a node sheet (step 2: data cleaning and mapping)

all member nations of the Paris Convention comply with the standardized system for patent documentation, supplementary information can be expressly permitted to accommodate regional offices' needs and their management systems. A patent number generally consists of a two-character country code (e.g., US, KR, JP) and a seven-digit serial number. This can be followed by a combination of a letter and a number, known as the kind-code document (e.g., A1, B1, B2). Patent offices vary in their use of kind code, which has changed over time according to the publication status (see Chap. 3). As a rule of thumb, kind codes are eliminated before analysis to avoid any duplication or misinterpretation, particularly when dealing with patents from multiple countries. Except for the node ID, the rest of data fields can be expanded without constraints, like the title of the invention, IPC main and subclass, and origin of the inventors.

Figure 8.7 shows the sample of the *edge* sheet where all the relations between the nodes are expressed as relations between IDs. The two most common uses of relations in patent network analysis are co-inventorship and citations. The edge sheet must have the columns for source and target, where the source is the source node and the target is another node, which has a link between the nodes. Then, it can be followed by attribute columns—type, direction, or weight, where applicable. Note that the relationship between the nodes—directed or undirected—must be clearly determined. For instance, co-inventorship is undirected whereas citations have a forward or backward direction. In the latter case, the edge sheet must be carefully filled with the *source-target* couples corresponding to the directions of relations.

Here, we focus on creating Dyson's patent network with citation relationships between patents. The patent number (as a unique ID) and pertinent patent information, such as technology classification, filing date, invention title, and IPC/CPC codes are entered in the node sheet (Fig. 8.6). In the edge sheet, a patent in the first column

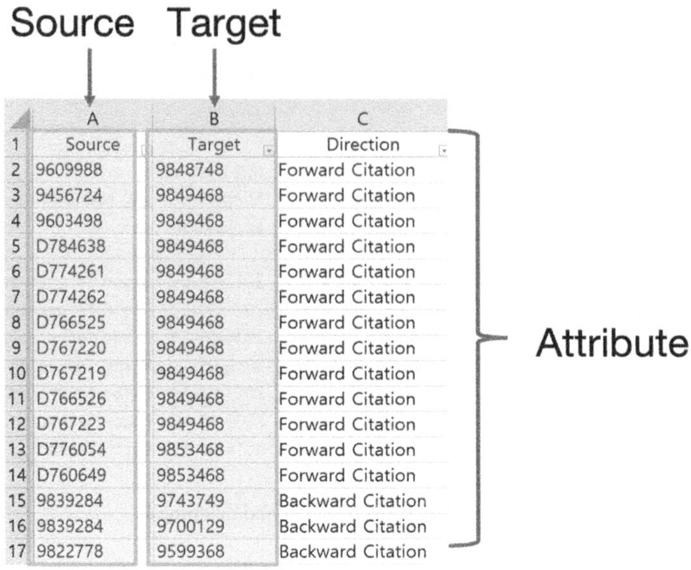

	A	B	C
1	Source	Target	Direction
2	9609988	9848748	Forward Citation
3	9456724	9849468	Forward Citation
4	9603498	9849468	Forward Citation
5	D784638	9849468	Forward Citation
6	D774261	9849468	Forward Citation
7	D774262	9849468	Forward Citation
8	D766525	9849468	Forward Citation
9	D767220	9849468	Forward Citation
10	D767219	9849468	Forward Citation
11	D766526	9849468	Forward Citation
12	D767223	9849468	Forward Citation
13	D776054	9853468	Forward Citation
14	D760649	9853468	Forward Citation
15	9839284	9743749	Backward Citation
16	9839284	9700129	Backward Citation
17	9822778	9599368	Backward Citation

Fig. 8.7 Example of an edge sheet (step 2: data cleaning and mapping)

source is cited in the second column target. Accordingly, data processing is needed to accommodate this source-target couple. In addition, the third column is created to annotate forward or backward citation attributes (Fig. 8.7).

Step 3. Network analysis

Steps 3 and 4 focus on patent network analysis and subsequent visualization using Gephi. As mentioned in Sect. 8.2, there is a handful of free network analysis and visualization tools, such as Gephi, NodeXL, and Pajek. We chose Gephi in this demonstration because it is an easy and efficient tool for large network analysis without significant needs for statistical knowledge or programming skills. Moreover, Gephi plug-ins offers advanced network analysis with a wide array of graph layouts (Cherven 2015).

Figure 8.8 is a basic view of Gephi. It consists of six main components. ① Primary windows: Overview (the main workplace), Data Laboratory (for data import and spreadsheet-like data view), and Preview (for visual rendering and export). Under the overview menu, we can find components ②—⑥: ② Appearance (for partitioning and clustering network graphs), ③ Layouts (a set of layout algorithms and properties), ④ Graphs (for manual configuration of graphs, including the size and color of nodes, edges, or labels), ⑤ Contexts (for a summary of network information), and ⑥ Filter and Statistics (for manipulating the size of a network and for computing mathematical network metric).

A range of statistical analyses on a network graph analysis is available under ⑥ Filter and Statistics (Fig. 8.9). As we learned in Chap. 5, one of the key network metrics is the idea of *centrality* that examines the position of a node in the graph

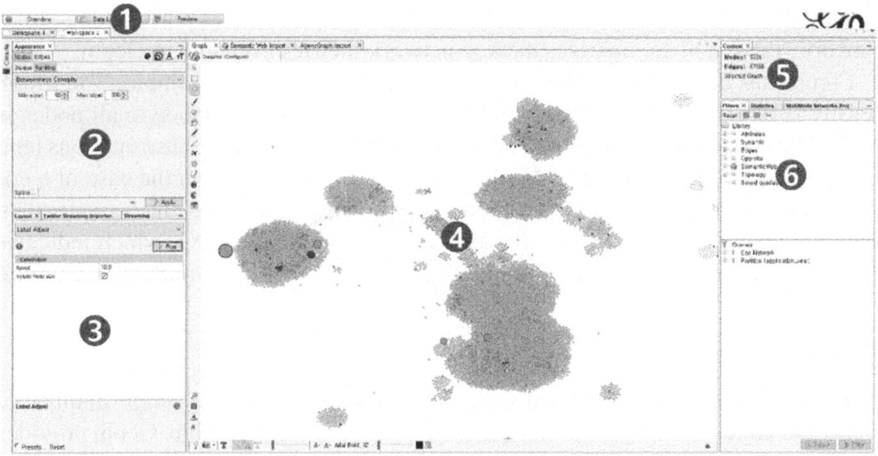

Fig. 8.8 Overviewing Gephi 0.9.2 interface

Fig. 8.9 ⑥ Filters and statistics (step 3: network analysis)

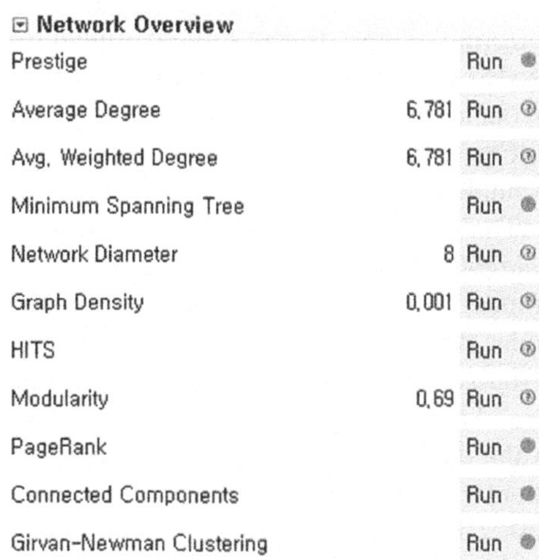

in relation to other nodes. There are several ways we can measure centrality, with each method providing a different definition, and often, very different results. *Degree centrality* measures the number of direct connections to a specific node; *closeness centrality* is a measure of proximity of a specific node to all other nodes within the network. Another centrality measure is *betweenness centrality*, which often returns a very different result, as it counts the frequency with which a node appears on the shortest paths between nodes in the network.

In addition to the centrality measures, *network density and modularity* are also popular metrics in patent network analysis. *Modularity* can be used to detect internal subdivisions or clusters in networks based on the relative strength of connections.

In addition, *network density* is useful for detecting the closeness or broadness of a network. Table 8.4. summarizes the key network metrics available in Gephi.

Figure 8.9 demonstrates the statistical analysis of Dyson's sample. The graph density is 0.001, which means that the connection level of one node to all nodes is 0.1%. The density of patent citation data is generally very low because citations tend to be unidirectional, either backward or forward. In this regard, in the case of a co-inventorship network, which is bi-directional, the density would be much greater than that of the citation network. The average degree centrality is 6.781, which indicates that a single node (a patent) is connected to six or seven other nodes (patents) on average.

Step 4. Network Visualization

Figure 8.10 shows the initial network. This network has a very large number of nodes and edges creating an overly dense graph which is unreadable. Gephi provides a multitude of options to rectify this quickly.

First, move to the bottom left panel to ③ Layouts. There are many network layout options are available in the basic Gephi version, or additional plug-ins can be downloaded and installed to meet analysts' intents. Technically speaking, any layout will perform the basic function of creating a network. However, an iterative approach is needed to best display a network that tells an effective story of the data. Multiple layout algorithms need to be considered to make a holistic network visualization.

Figure 8.11 gives an idea of the appearance of some layouts. Some of the popular examples in layout types are force-based, circular, geographic, and layered layouts.

The *force-directed layout algorithms,* such as *Force Atlas 2*, *Fruchterman-Reingold*, and *Yifan Hu*, are one of the most widely used algorithms for network graphs. These layouts position the linked nodes closer while pushing unrelated nodes farther apart. This is effective to detect behavioral network patterns. *Circular layouts*, such as *circular*, *concentric*, and *dual circles* provide an intuitive structure of networks when there is a limited number of nodes with predefined attributes in the data, for example, degree values or technology classifications. In addition, circular layouts are capable of creating networks with a high degree of connectedness. *Layered layouts* allow the segmenting of dense networks with distinct layering patterns based on clusters or groupings. Some examples of layouts in Gephi are *Isometric layout*, *Layered layout*, and *Network Splitter 3D*. Finally, in cases where the network data has geographical components, geographic layouts, like *Geo layout* and *Maps of Countries layouts*, can be used to place the data with the relevant geographical references. On most patent documents, the physical addresses of both the applicants and the associated inventors can be identified. Perhaps, a patent network for co-inventorship or industry collaboration can be useful by providing geo-layouts. Such that, geocoded patent networks can take advantage of the analyst's innate ability to view and interpret spatial data by overlaying the networks on a geographic foundation.

While visualizing networks, an iterative approach is needed to best display a network that tells an effective story of the data. For demonstrating Dyson's patent network, we selected the Force Atlas 2 layout. In Fig. 8.12, there are several over-

Table 8.4 Example of Gephi's five key network metrics

Measures	Gephi statistics	Description	Diagram
Degree centrality	Network Overview > Average Degree	A count of the number of direct connections to an individual node. Simple, effective metrics highlighting a node's activity and adjacent relationships	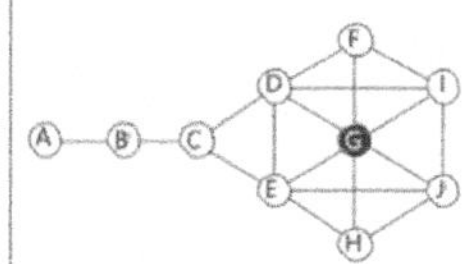
Closeness centrality	Network Overview > Network Diameter	The average distance from a starting node to all other nodes in the network, which includes a count of the number of indirect connections and identifies a node's independence	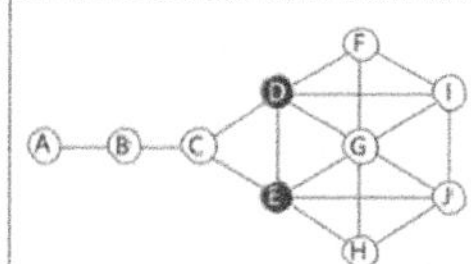
Betweenness centrality		A measure of the frequency with which a node appears on the shortest paths between nodes in the network, reflecting the intermediary level of the structure	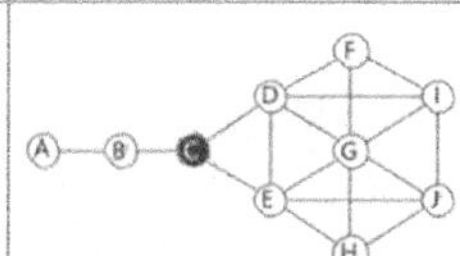
Modularity	Network Overview > Modularity	Similar to clustering methods. The probability of an edge's existence in relation to a specific node that belongs to specific subdivisions	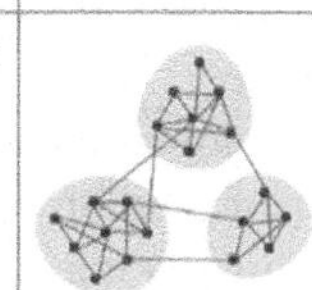
Network density	Network Overview > Graph Density	A measure of how tightly interconnected a network is. Calculated by examining the proportion of edges relative to the possible number of connections	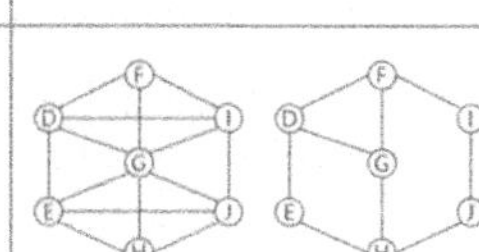

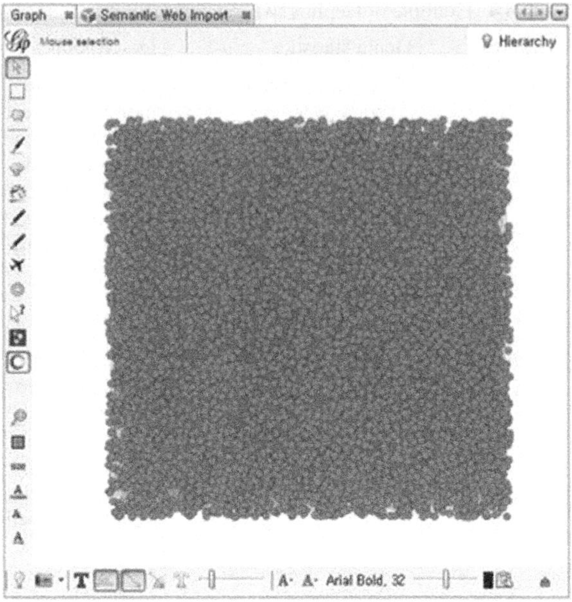

Fig. 8.10 An initial network view before laying out the graph

lapped nodes and edges which are bound to convey the meaning of the network. Regardless of the layout chosen, it is often difficult to completely overcome the cluttered graphs —the so-called *hairball effect*. Hence Gephi entails several data filtering and graphic options to support further network customization. The component ② Appearance on the top left is especially helpful when we have a dense network. Using the *partition* option, we can filter out the data based on degree levels, classifications, or clusters. Resizing and coloring nodes and edges can be done using the *ranking* option.

Figure 8.12 shows a network with patents (nodes) that are sized proportionally to their number of citations (degree centrality). Colors are used to differentiate nodes based on modularity classes, as clusters of closely-linked patents. In general, a layout represents a graph type and a node's size reflects the centrality metrics, such as degree centrality, closeness centrality, or betweenness centrality. The use of color can vary with a greater degree of customization, like color gradient and opacity. This is effective in those cases where a specific patent information—publication year or technology classification—is to be highlighted in the network.

An analyst can use different layouts and graphical appearances depending on data size and types, areas of interest, or visual preferences. It is essential to create a network that incorporates a graph layout and configuration options in a comprehensive manner.

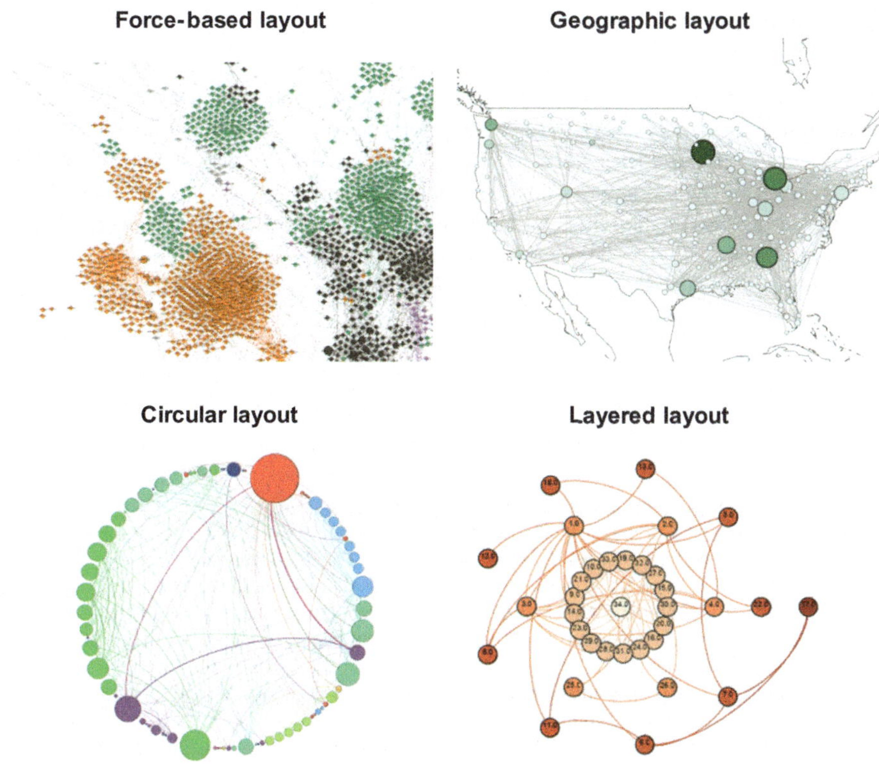

Fig. 8.11 Common layout types available with Gephi plug-ins

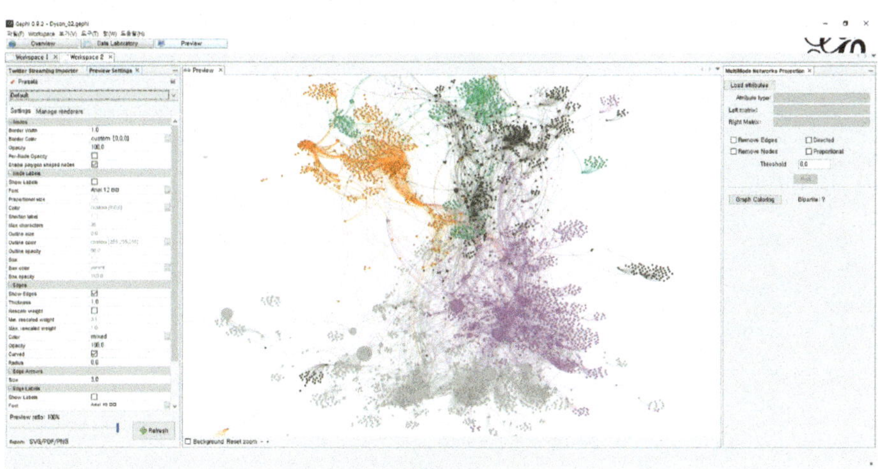

Fig. 8.12 Dyson's patent network visualization using Force Atlas 2 (step 4: network visualization)

8.4 Summary

This chapter covers some of the major free, open-source tools that are readily adapted to patent network analysis. With few exceptions of patent data cleaning steps, patent data is very well suited for network-based analysis. In practice, it is important to identify a set of tools that work best for analysts.

After you have finished this chapter you may want to follow the quick start guide of Gephi (Cherven 2015). There are also a lot of forums and resources online to get help with large-scale patent network analysis, such as the WIPO Manual on Open Source Patent Analytics (Oldham 2016).

References

Adams S (2020) Information sources in patents. De Gruyter, Berlin
Borgatti SP, Everett MG, Johnson JC (2018) Analyzing social networks. Sage, London
Cherven K (2015) Mastering Gephi network visualization. Packt, Birmingham.
Faysal MAM, Arifuzzaman S (2018) A comparative analysis of large-scale network visualization tools. In 2018 IEEE International Conference on Big Data (Big Data), 10 Dec 2018.
Ladd J, Otis J, Warren CN, Weingart S (2017) Exploring and analyzing network data with Python. Programming Historian, 6.
Mrvar A, Batagelj V (2016) Analysis and visualization of large networks with program package Pajek. Complex Adapt Syst Model 4(1):6–14.
Oldham P (2016) The WIPO Manual on Open Source Patent Analytics. https://wipo-analytics.github.io/open-refine.html. Accessed 18 Nov 2020.
Prell C (2012) Social network analysis: History, theory and methodology. Sage, London
Trippe A (2015) Guidelines for preparing patent landscape reports. Patent landscape reports. https://www.ompi.org/edocs/pubdocs/en/wipo_pub_946.pdf. Accessed 04 Jan 2021.

Part III
Uncover Corporate Innovation with Patent Analytics

Chapter 9
Is Innovation Design-or Technology-Driven? Dyson

Abstract Can innovation be cross-pollinated between design and technology? Dyson is known for harnessing new technology and design to revolutionize the household appliance market with innovative products such as bagless vacuum cleaners and bladeless fans. This chapter introduces patent citation networks to both quantitatively and visually assess how Dyson's product innovations grow and are connected, and what these connections mean for its next innovations. Finally, the multi-depth ego-networks of US D602,143, the first Dyson's bladeless fan design patent, allows us to unfold how this ground-breaking innovation cross-pollinates different design and technology.

9.1 Dyson: From Bagless Vacuum Cleaner to Bladeless Hairdryer

When bees fly from one flower to another, collecting pollen, they spread it from plant to plant. This *cross-pollination* plays a vital part in every ecosystem and ultimately leads to species *diversity*. This concept of pollination in innovation is much the same.

Firms' product innovation can come in two different forms: technology innovation and design innovation. Traditional innovation research suggests that either technology innovation or design innovation can enhance firm performance (Talke et al. 2009; Srinivasan et al. 2009). Recent studies repeatedly address that technology and design are closely intertwined. Changes in both technology and design may spur radical innovation (Norman and Verganti 2014; Verganti 2006).

Since its founding in 1991, Dyson has been known for revolutionizing the household appliance market armed with new technology and design. Figure 9.1. illustrates the timeline of Dyson's product innovations from its first design patent of a bagless vacuum cleaner to the latest bladeless hairdryer.

The term of cross-pollination in innovation refers to the recombination of previously unrelated ideas (Fleming 2004). Kim and Kim (2021) explored the effect of cross-pollination on product innovation by examining forward citation patterns of utility and design patents. Their empirical study based on Dyson's patents revealed

J. Kim et al., *Patent Analytics*,
https://doi.org/10.1007/978-981-16-2930-3_9

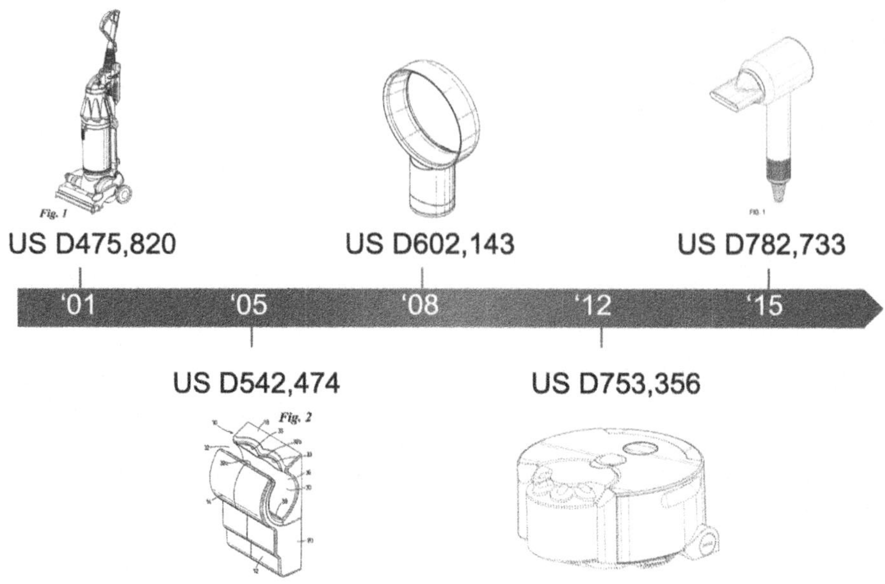

Fig. 9.1 Timeline of Dyson's product innovation and each first design patent

that the first bladeless fan design patent (US D602,143) was highly cited by subsequent design and utility patents, which creates cross-pollination in the next innovation. Bladeless fan influences not only fans and their assembly but also heaters, humidifiers, and hairdryers with the concept of being bladeless. Radical innovation incorporates its cross-citation between design-utility, other than citation within the same category, i.e., design to design or utility to utility.

This chapter extends the previous study of Kim and Kim (2021) with network-based citation analysis. In Sect. 9.2, a complete network of Dyson's backward and forward citations allows us to both quantitatively and visually assess how Dyson's product innovations grow and are connected, and what these connections mean for its next innovations. Six of the product categories—vacuum cleaner, fan, motor, robot vacuum, hairdryer, and hand dryer—were considered. Furthermore, the multi-depth ego-networks of US D602,143, the first Dyson's bladeless fan design patent, allows us to unfold how this ground-breaking innovation cross-pollinates different design and technology and to examine the central question of cross-pollination in innovation (Sect. 9.3).

9.2 Dyson's Patent Citation Analysis: A Complete Network

In 2001, when it entered the US market, Dyson filed its first patent for a vacuum cleaner handle (hose and wand assembly, US 7,000,288, January 8, 2001). A total of 34 patent applications (17 for vacuum cleaners, 10 for washing machines, six for robot cleaners, and one other application) were filed in the United States Patent and Trademark Office (USPTO) in the same year. Dyson now holds 624 patents (432 utility and 192 design patents) that have been granted in the US (Data collected February 1, 2018). Table 9.1 lists Dyson's product category with respect to patent classifications: the International Patent Classification (IPC) for utility patents and the Locarno classifications for design patents. Six product categories were identified: vacuum cleaner, fan, motor, robot vacuum, hairdryer, and hand dryer.

Table 9.2 provides the descriptive analysis of Dyson's patenting activity by product category. The vacuum cleaner category was dominant among Dyson patents, covering 55.9% of the patents (349 patents), followed by the fan (n = 98, 15.7%), motor (n = 33, 5.3%), robot vacuum (n = 31, 5.0%), hairdryer (n = 22, 3.5%), and hand dryer (n = 21, 3.4%). Note that the motor category ranked third (n = 33, 5.3%) is not an end product; it is included in this study because of its considerably high figures and technological effects influencing Dyson's end products.

Let us dive into Dyson's patent citation network. A four-step practical guide to patent network analysis was described in Chap. 8, which uses an open software Gephi and Dyson's patent dataset. Table 9.3 summarizes its stepwise data configurations and visualizations used in the study. A total of 9,964 patents (nodes) and 67,566 connections (edges) were collected.

Table 9.1 Relevant International Patent Classification (IPC) and Locarno symbols by product category

Product category	IPC symbols	Locarno symbols
Vacuum cleaner	A01, A46, A47, A63, B01, B03, D06, F01, F16, G05, H01, H02	13–02, 15–05, 23–04, 30–99
Fan	B05, F01, F04, F24, H02	23–03, 23–04, 28–03
Motor	A47, F26, H01	28–03
Robot vacuum	A47, F04, H01, H02, H03	15–05
Hairdryer	A45, H05	28–03
Hand dryer	A47, F26, H01	28–03

Table 9.2 Dyson's patenting activity by product category

Product category	Utility patent	Design ptent	Total (%)
Vacuum cleaner	230	119	349 (55.9%)
Fan	70	28	98 (15.7%)
Motor	33	0	33 (5.3%)
Robot vacuum	15	16	31 (5.0%)
Hairdryer	16	6	22 (3.5%)
Hand dryer	14	7	21 (3.4%)
Others	53	16	70 (11.1%)
Total (%)	432 (69.2%)	192 (30.8%)	624 (100.0%)

Table 9.3 Overview of Dyson's patent network analysis

Step 1: Data collection	Step 2: Data cleaning and mapping
Assignee: Dyson Corporation Period: 2001–2018 Origin of data: USPTO Number of patent data: 624 (432 utility, 192 design)	Backward citation: 1 depth Forward citation: 1 depth Number of nodes: 9,964 Number of edges: 67,566 Edge Type: direct
Step 3: Network analysis	Step 4: Network visualization
Average degree: 6.781 Network diameter: 8 Network density: 0.001 Modularity: 0.69	Software version: Gephi v.0.9.2 Layout: Yifan Hu Node size: Degree centrality Node color: Product category

Figure 9.2 illustrates Dyson's complete patent citation network in 2001–2018. It comprises the largest cluster in the lower center, and four clusters are loosely connected like islands. The largest and most densely connected cluster refers to the vacuum cleaner category, covering over half of Dyson's total filings. This cluster includes several types of bagless vacuum cleaner design: canister, upright, and cordless as well as Dyson's signature root cyclone technology: Cyclonic separating apparatus (US 6,607,572, 2001) and Cyclonic separating apparatus (US 7,874,040, 2008). These technologies have dramatically improved the performance of vacuum cleaners by dividing a big whirlwind into a few small whirlwinds.

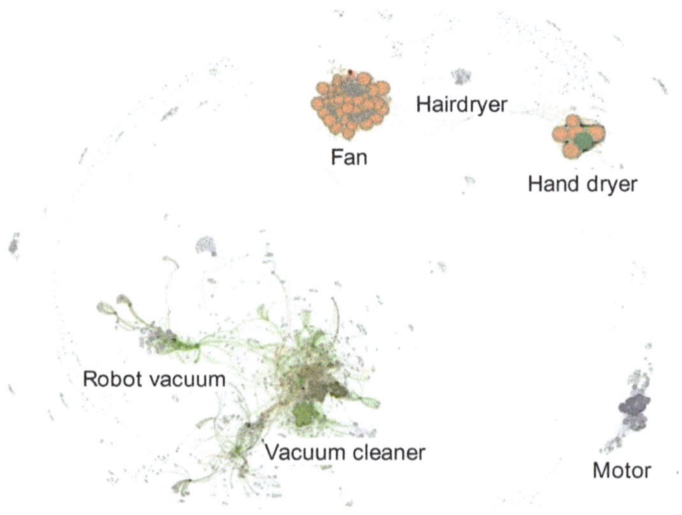

Fig. 9.2 Dyson's patent citation network by product category

Right next to the vacuum cleaner cluster, there is a small-sized cluster relating to robotic vacuum cleaners. This relative position implies that the robot vacuum innovation has evolved by borrowing or improving many designs and technologies derived from the vacuum cleaner cluster. In addition, to introduce the self-operating vacuum, Dyson has expended much effort to investigate robotic technologies, such as self-driving cleaning (US 6,671,592, 2001), dust sensing (US 6,553,612, 2001), and an auto-charging system (US 6,605,156, 2002).

Next, the fan cluster is placed on the top of the network. It is quite disconnected from the vacuum cleaner cluster but closely connected to the hairdryer and hand dryer clusters. A series of bladeless fanlike designs is included in this cluster. For instance, the patents granted to the first bladeless fan (i.e., Dyson Cool™ AM06) were US 8,308,445 (2008), US D602,143 (2008), and US D605,748 (2008). The next generation of a tower-type fan (e.g., US D602,144, US 8,714,937, US 8,873,940) and other multi-functional patents in relation to AM9 Hot + Cool™: US D672,023 (Fan heater, 2011) and US D643,098 (Fan heater, 2011).

Considering the date of patents and their connections, the fan cluster is initially influenced by the hand dryer clusters. In particular, the idea for Dyson's Air Multiplier was borrowed from the hand dryer's airfoil technology, namely a jet airflow circular outlet.

Furthermore, after putting the company's spin on hand dryers and then bladeless fans, one probably guesses which technology most influenced the latest supersonic hairdryer. As shown in Fig. 9.2, the hairdryer cluster is positioned between the fan and hand dryer clusters. This relative position would imply that Dyson's hairdryer technology and design were inspired by the hand dryer's high-velocity controlled technology and the bladeless fan's morphological design, respectively. The next section provides more details on the bladeless fan's innovation paths by employing its multi-depths ego networks.

9.3 Technology or Design First? Ego Networks of the Bladeless Fan

To many of us, a *fan* is simply one of many home appliances that surround us—fans, hairdryers, and refrigerators. Despite its simple structure comprising small motors and propellers, a fan has long been used in many high-tech industries, such as automobiles, aircraft, and satellites, which requires stable operation in extremely demanding environments.

The first fan patent in the United States was US 414,758, a ceiling fan with an electric motor (Fig. 9.3a). It was invented by Phillip Diehl in 1889. At that time, electricity was very expensive. The fan technology was first invented for public areas, such as hotels, restaurants, or factories, rather than in households. A more familiar stand-type fan was invented by Schuyler Wheeler in 1886, three years ahead of the first US fan patent. However, its filing time was delayed until 1893, so the

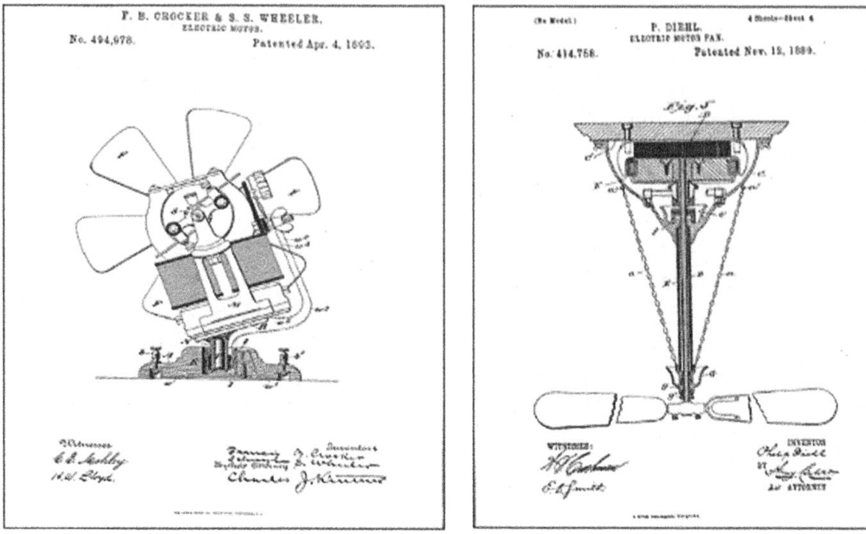

a b

Fig. 9.3 **a** First US electric motor fan patent in 1889 (US 414,758). **b** first US stand-type fan in 1893 (US 494,978)

glory of the first fan patent title was given to Philip Diehl. Wheeler's US 494,978 was equipped with a DC motor and was very large (Fig. 9.3b). As of the late 1920s, General Electric (GE) and Westinghouse dominated the fan market by adopting small-sized AC motors. The fan blades at the time used aluminum or steel, but most of the current ones use plastic.

The first patent of Dyson's bladeless fan was filed in the UK in September 2007 (bladeless fan, GB 2007–017.155). In the United States, the first application in the fan category was a design patent (fan, US D602,143) on December 4, 2018, in which James Dyson participated as one of the inventors along with Peter David Gammack.

A deep dive of ego networks of US D602,143 hints at how the first bladeless fan design was born and spurred to subsequent innovations. Figure 9.4 illustrates one depth of backward and forward citation network of US D602,143. Among the 14 backward citations for US D602,143, 11 referenced fans and fan housing. The remaining three related to aerodynamic and air movement apparatus. In the case of forward citations, the focal bladeless design patent influenced both subsequent fans and their assembly, as well as heaters and humidifiers that were bladeless.

Furthermore, the multi-depth ego-network of US D602,143—in which backward and forward citations were extended to two and three generations, respectively—shows how design and technology are intertwined.

Table 9.4 summarizes the data configurations and visualizations for this extended citation network (Backward 2–Forward 3). This network comprised 687 nodes and 2,372 edges. The ForceAtlas 2 layout was used for visualization. Node size was

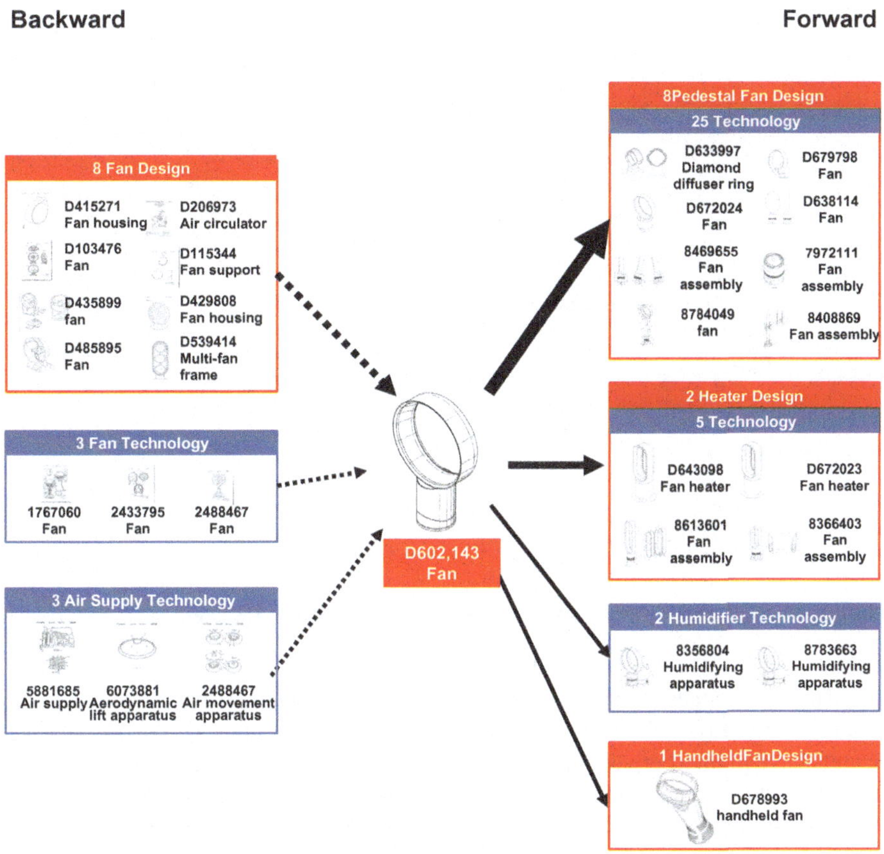

Fig. 9.4 A one-depth ego network of Dyson's bladeless fan design, US D602,143

Table 9.4 Overview of Dyson's multi-depths ego-network of the bladeless fan design, US D602,143

Step 1: Data mining	Step 2: Data cleaning and mapping
Focal patent: US D602,143 Period: 1974–2014 Origin of data: USPTO Number of patent data: 207	Backward citation: 2 depths Forward citation: 3 depths Number of nodes: 687 Number of edges: 2,373 Edge type: Direct
Step 3: Network analysis	Step 4: Network visualization
Average degree: 2.036 Network diameter: 10 Network density: 0.001 Modularity: 0.711	Software version: Gephi v.0.9.2 Layout: ForceAtlas 2 Node size: Betweenness centrality Node color: Product category

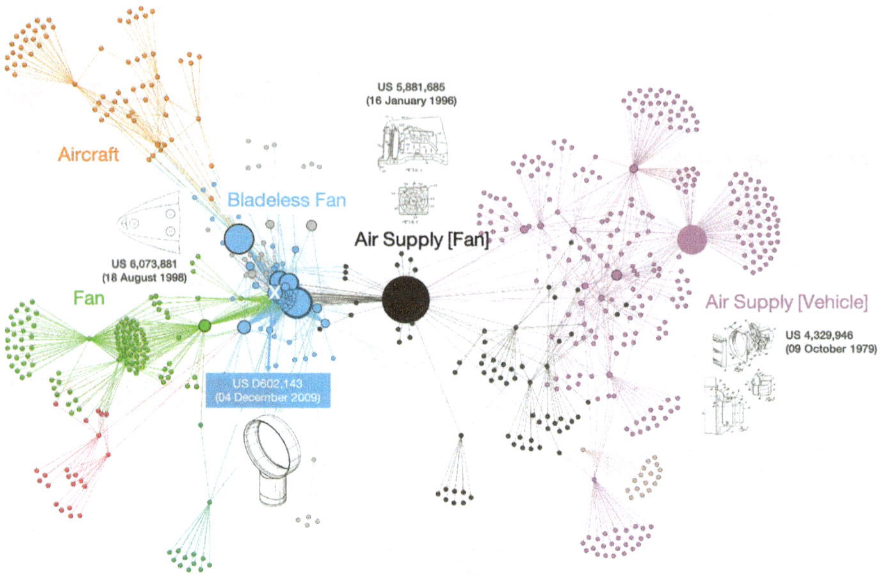

Fig. 9.5 Multi-depths ego network of Dyson's bladeless fan design, US D602,143

based on betweenness centrality, which measures the influence of nodes in a network relative to the flow of information between others (see Chap. 5). For instance, as patents have higher betweenness centrality, they will have more control of information flows over the network and easily acquire information as more information will pass through that node, like a "brokering" or "bridging" role in a network.

Figure 9.5 shows that the bladeless fan design (US D602,143, in sky-blue) is placed between the air supply technology for fans (US 5,881,685, in black) and aircraft technology (US 6,073,881 in orange). In particular, the latter indicates vertical takeoff and landing technology through Bernoulli's Principle, which has come into play to amplify airflow in the bladeless fan's circular ring section.

The extended backward and forward citation map illustrates that the bladeless fan design was deeply influenced by air supply and fan technology from aircraft and vehicle fields. The fan also served as a strong influence in diversifying the product categories, including not only the same product line (e.g., Air Multiplier™ series) but also multi-functionality with heating and cooling air (e.g., Hot + Cool™, AM9), which showed incremental changes in design and technology.

9.4 Forecasting Dyson's Next Innovation

The first Dyson's patent network analysis was conducted in September 2014, and a further thorough analysis was continued in September 2018. With Dyson's first citation map back in 2014, we revealed an increase in the number of patent applications placed between fan and hand dryer clusters—signaling a new invention. At that time, Dyson had not explicitly mentioned hairdryers or handheld devices in any of its patent applications or media. However, our network citation analysis hints at the fact that the company had considered developing small appliances for convenience in single-handling while keeping close connections with noise-reduction and aerodynamics of airfoil technologies.

Taken together, our research team took preemptive patenting, insofar as filing certain patents may involve creating obstacles to prevent competitors from patenting related inventions. A hairdryer patent (KR 10–2016-0,096,888) was filed in Korea in 2015, two years ahead of the Dyson supersonic hairdryer launch. The proposed invention shown in Fig. 9.6a resembles the Dyson bladeless fan design, which became far smaller without a fan blade inside the head of typical hairdryers.

Dyson's first hairdryer patent—US 10,016,040 (handheld appliance, filed on March 28, 2013)—was made public 18 months after our patent application. Dyson's hairdryer patent application claimed the priority of United Kingdom Application No. 1205695.8, filed on March 30, 2012. The initial drawing outlined in Fig. 9.6b was not included in Dyson's latest hairdryer, which was launched in September 2016.

We may not be able to predict exactly what Dyson will do, but we may be able to identify the set of possibilities of the company's next innovation. For instance, what would be the underlying meaning of Dyson's new patent regarding a pair of headphones with a built-in air purifier (GB 1,811,994.1, filed on July 23, 2018, publication date: January 29, 2020). Perhaps, if you were the CEO of Bose Corp., would Dyson be a potential competitor or collaborator in the personal audio equipment market? Is Dyson planning to venture out wearable electronic markets beyond the domestic markets? Can Dyson's new innovations be a complete game-changer?

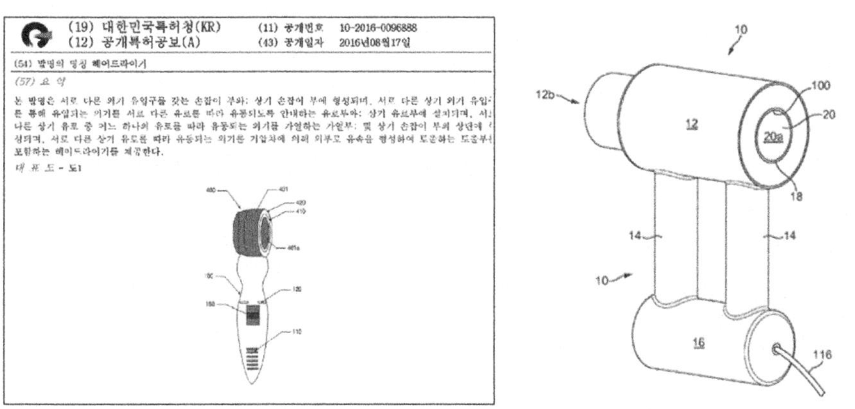

a b

Fig. 9.6 **a** Author's hairdryer patent (KR 10–2016-0,096,888). **b** Dyson's first hairdryer patent (US 10,016,040)

References

Fleming L (2004) Perfecting cross-pollination, Harv Bus Rev 82(9):22–24

Kim D, Kim J (2021) Is innovation design-or technology-driven? Citation as a measure of innovation pollination. World Pat Inf 64: 102010.https://doi.org/10.1016/j.wpi.2020.102010

Norman DA, Verganti R (2014) Incremental and radical innovation: Design research versus technology and meaning change. Des Issues 30(1):78–96.

Srinivasan S, Pauwels K, Silva-Risso J, Hanssens DM (2009) Product innovations, advertising, and stock returns. J Mark 73(1):24–43.https://doi.org/10.1509/jmkg.73.1.024

Talke K, Salomo S, Wieringa JE, Lutz A (2009) What about design newness? Investigating the relevance of a neglected dimension of product innovativeness. J Prod Innov Manage 26(6):601–615https://doi.org/10.1111/j.1540-5885.2009.00686.x

Verganti R (2006) Innovating through design. Harv Bus Rev 84(12):114.

Chapter 10
Predict Strategic Pivot Points: Bose

Abstract A premium audio tech giant, Bose Corporation, has certainly moved away from its crown of premium sound products and pivoted a new vision for future innovations beyond sound, such as suspension seats, high-tech cooktops, audio AR sunglasses, and sleepbuds. Starting from MIT's research laboratory, 50 years of intensive R&D endeavors and Bose's pioneering spirits are evidenced in wide and deep patenting activities. In this regard, this chapter uncovers Bose's strategic pivot points through patent network analyses.

10.1 Bose's New Neat! Innovation Pivots

Bose Corporation has finally unveiled its *Vortex* project. However, the project has no connection with sound at all; instead, it is a high-tech induction cooktop. The cooktop looks like a regular appliance but can transfer the energy required to cook food precisely while the rest of the cooktop remains completely insulated. This means that users have no risk of getting burned—even if they touch the cookware handle, bottom, or the upper plate of the cooktop (CNET 2016). Can this be regarded as a one-off invention by an eccentric researcher? Or is it a part of Bose's research and development (R&D) portfolio? To find the answers, we look at Bose's history and its philosophy.

Bose was founded in 1964 by Amar Bose, a professor in the department of electrical engineering and computer science at the Massachusetts Institute of Technology. His research lab on acoustics became the world's leading sound company.

From its foundation, Amar has maintained the company as private and independent. He has encouraged long-term investment in R&D rather than short-term performance. For instance, Bose's signature noise-canceling technology is one of the proven outcomes of his extensive research since 1979—one that continued for 12 years and incurred costs of $50 million.

Bose's innovation is well embodied in its intellectual property portfolio, including patents, designs, and trademarks. Bose's slogan *Better sound through research* is registered as a trademark, US-TM1767324, since 1993 and is being renewed to the

J. Kim et al., *Patent Analytics*,
https://doi.org/10.1007/978-981-16-2930-3_10

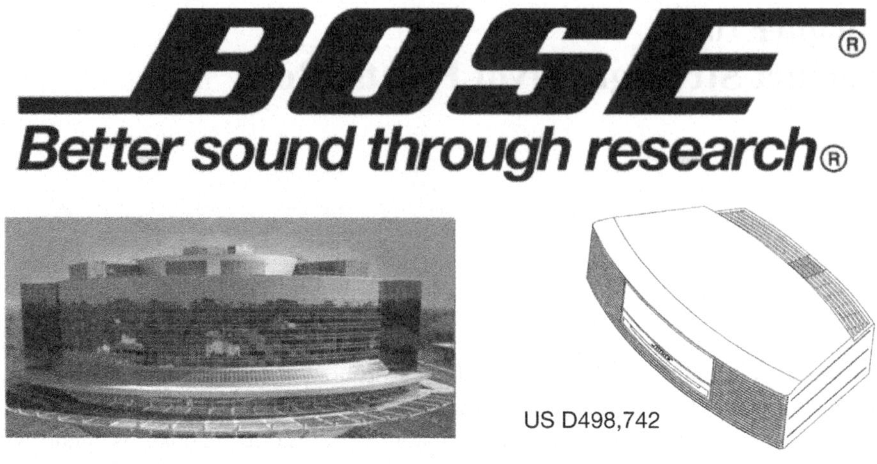

Fig. 10.1 Bose's intellectual property for designs and slogans

present. The headquarter building located in Framingham, Massachusetts, resembles Bose's signature product designs, like the example of US D498,742 (Fig. 10.1).

Bose's tireless R&D is not restricted to sound and can also pivot the business in diverse directions, such as automobiles, high-tech appliances, and sunglasses. A pivot in business is much like the act of rotating or moving around on one foot while remaining the other in place, which frequently occurs in sports or dance. Rice (2011) defined *pivot* in business as the manner in which a company changes business strategies while maintaining its current business as the central axis.

There are some famous business pivots that can be used as inspiration. Instagram began as a check-in app called Burbn. After a few trials and errors, the CEOs discovered that users preferred sharing photos rather than location-based services. The company decided to relinquish its core function of check-in services and relaunched Instagram as a photo-sharing app, which had hitherto only been a support function. Similarly, Groupon, the first social commerce platform, originated from a site called The Point, which was initially designed for collective actions for public services and social fundraising. YouTube started as a dating site. However, as increasingly more users started uploading funny videos, the company decided to pivot its business to a video-sharing platform. The pivoting concept seems simple enough, but companies require bold strategic decision-making and resolute determination to implement it.

Bose's innovation is deeply rooted in *Better sound* and pivoted *Beyond sound*. The company's pivoting strategies are well embodied in its intellectual properties. The next sections identify Bose's core technology and emerging pivoting areas based on a patent citation network in 1972–2016.

10.2 Core Innovation: Better Sound

Starting with its first patent application (US 4,456,872) in 1972, Bose filed 927 patent applications between 1972 and 2016. This includes 772 utility and 155 design patents to the United States Patent and Trademark Office (USPTO).

Bose's patent citation network was drawn based on the focal patent filed in 1972–2016 as nodes and the patent citations as the edges in forward and backward directions. Table 10.1 summarizes a stepwise data configuration of the patent network analyses. Network visualization was conducted by using Gephi™ v.0.9.2 and ForceAtlas 2 (Cherven 2015).

Figure 10.2 illustrates Bose's patent citation network in 1972–2016. The network consists of large and small groups of related patents in which the clusters are defined by patent classifications. *Clustering* refers to a group of entities (here, patents) linked by some common attribute (e.g., technology classifications) (Prell 2012). In addition, the value of the modularity is 0.9, indicating a strong group structure (Q value 0.30 ~ 0.50: a reasonably strong group; above 0.50: a very strong group; Valente et al. 2015).

Bose's patent citation network illustrates large and densely connected clusters in the middle, which forms the backbone of the network, and several sparse patent clusters, which are loosely connected with the central clusters. This central cluster represents its core sound technology that comprises three areas: (A) noise cancelation, (B) acoustic radiation, and (C) sound amplification. The product offerings in relation to sound technologies are positioned on the dotted clusters.

It is important to note that the size and position of clusters in a network indicate their power (or influence) and neighborhoods (see Chap. 5). For instance, the red-dotted cluster, where the core technologies of (B) acoustic radiation and (C)

Table 10.1 Overview of Bose's patent citation network analysis

Step 1: Data collection	Step 2: Data cleaning and mapping
Assignee: Bose Corporation Period: 1972–2016 Origin of Data: USPTO Number of patent data: 927 (772 utility patents, 155 design patents)	Backward citation: 1 depth Forward citation: 1 depth Number of nodes: 14,740 Number of edges: 30,688 Edge type: Direct
Step 3: Network analysis	**Step 4: Network visualization**
Average degree: 2.036 Network diameter: 10 Network density: 0.000 Modularity: 0.9	Software version: Gephi v.0.9.2 Layout: ForceAtlas 2 Node size: Betweenness centrality Edge type: Curved

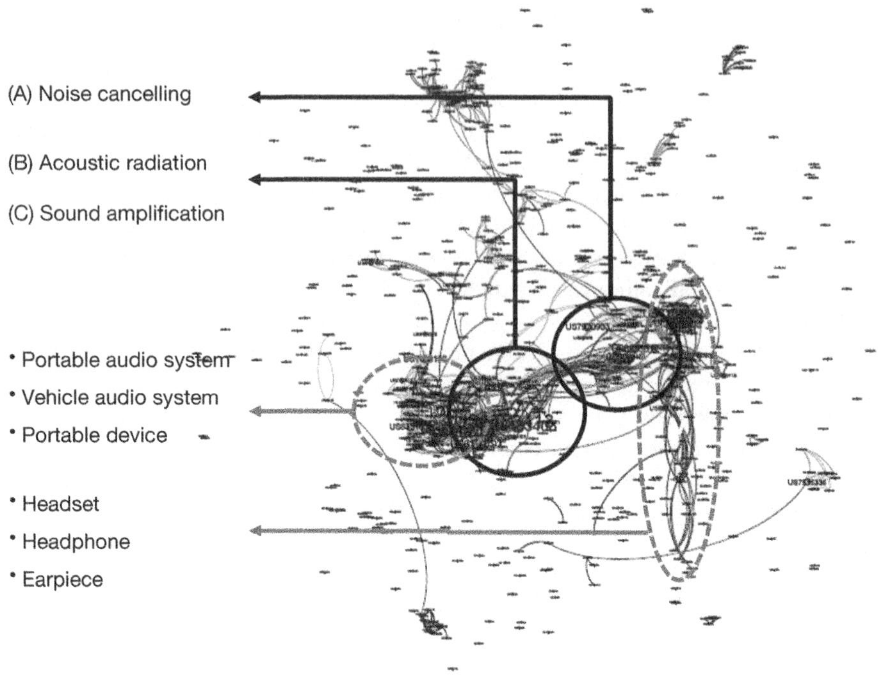

Fig. 10.2 Bose's patent citation network

sound amplification overlap, encompasses the home theater sound systems, small-size speakers (e.g., SoundLink), and car audio systems mounted on Nissan and Audi vehicles. Bose started supplying audio systems to automobile companies in 1982 and has now expanded its product line to premium car brands for which it produces custom-tailored audio systems.

The blue-dotted cluster at the right vertical edge represents Bose's staple products, such as headsets, headphones, and earpieces. These products are placed close to the cluster of (A) noise-canceling technology as both are closely related. Bose owns several important noise-canceling technologies that can offset noises electrically by generating inverse waves. This is considered a breakthrough innovation in the headphone industry.

Eighteen product categories and 155 design patents

Most of Bose's design patents are for a range of audio products: 71 for speakers, 21 for earpieces, and 18 for headsets. The remaining 45 design patents have no connection with sound. The Locarno classification of the design patents enables us to identify the product categories registered by Bose. They are: designs for TVs (08–07), car seats (06–01), kiosks (06–04), and virtual theatre (25–02). More examples are given in Table 10.2.

Table 10.2 Bose's design patents by the Locarno classification and corresponding product category

Speaker (14-01)	Earpiece (14-01)	Microphone (14-01)
US D514090 (2013)	US D659117 (2010)	US D563395 (2006)

Headphone (14-01)	Control module (14-01)	Audio signal process (14-01)
US D541255 (2006)	US D432523 (1995)	US D441374 (1996)
		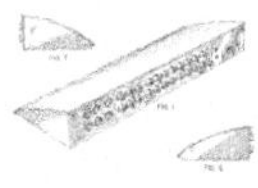
CD player (14-01)	GUI (14-04)	Portable audio device (14-31)
US D508905 (2003)	US D791781 (2014)	US D708228 (2013)

Remote control (14-03)	Radio (14-03)	Amplifier (14-03)
US D663288 (2010)	US D498742 (2003)	US D788066 (2016)
		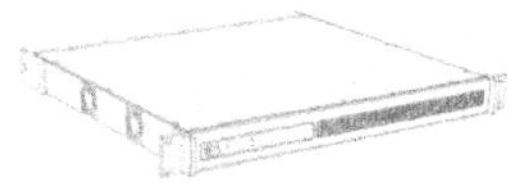
Accessory (03-01)	Seat (06-01)	Merchandise display (06-04)
US D740560 (2014)	US D605420 (2009)	US D727666 (2013)

TV (08-07)	Control console (21-01)	Virtual theatre (25-02)
US D646684 (2010)	US D801434 (2015)	US D674114 (2011)
	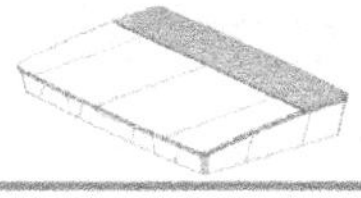	

How centrality measures might have predicted Bose–Beats patent infringement lawsuit

In 2014, Bose accused Beats Electronics of infringing on five noise-canceling technology-related patents (BBC 2014). The accused patents include dynamically configurable ANR filter block topology (US 8,073,151), method and apparatus for minimizing latency in digital signal processing systems (US 6,717,537), dynamically configurable ANR signal processing topology (US 8,073,150), digital high frequency phase compensation (US 8,345,888), and high frequency compensating (US 8,054,992), which relates to a technique called active noise reduction (ANR). It is often true that if Beats commits a patent infringement, and the patents in question are significant. Typically, the patent litigation prematurely discloses the core technology of the accuser company against their will.

Patent citation networks have further credence to the premise. Without going to court, centrality metrics are effective measures to identify core technology in the field of interest. As a zoom-in view in Fig. 10.3 shows, the five patents are all centered

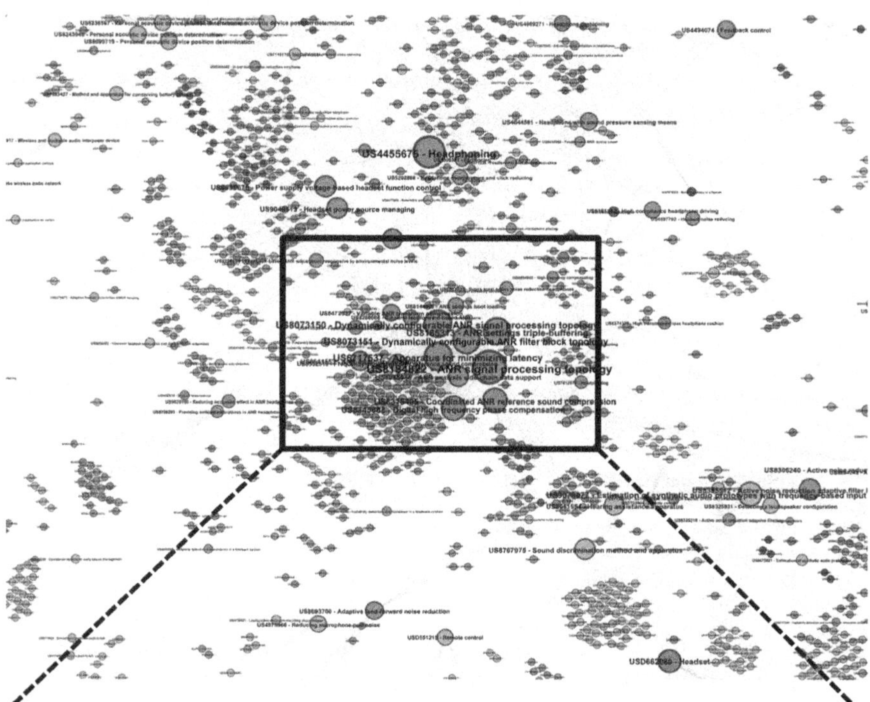

Number	US 6,717,537	US 8,054,992	US 8,073,150	US 8,073,151	US 8,345,888
Year	2001	2006	2009	2009	2009
Title	Apparatus for minimizing latency	Noise reduction	Active noise reduction	Active noise reduction	Active noise reduction
Drawing	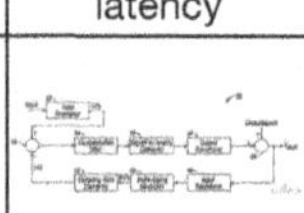	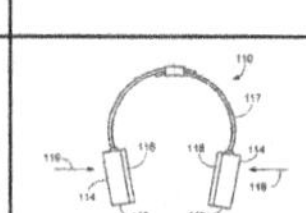	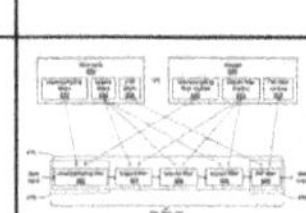	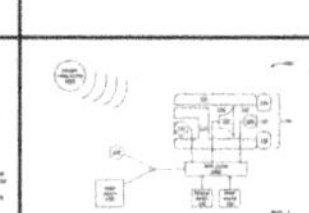	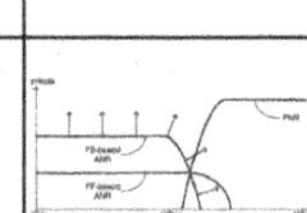

Fig. 10.3 Bose–Beats patent lawsuit on the five patents relating to active noise reduction (ANR) technologies

in Cluster A (noise-canceling technology) of Bose's patent network. In addition, given that the nodes are sized according to the value of betweenness centrality, the patents have relatively high betweenness centrality among related technologies, which indicates their pivotal roles in the diffusion of technology.

Eventually, both companies dropped the lawsuit, and the details of the settlement agreement are unknown. However, at the time, Apple had announced its plans to merge with Beats, so the lawsuit gained a lot of attention as it became a patent war between Apple and Bose. Simultaneously, Apple's new project was leaked fueling rumors that it is working on a high-end headphone with an ambient, noise-canceling technology and an over-the-ear design. Presumably, Bose attempted to protect themselves before the Apple-Beats coupling expanded into the sound market. The anticipation and wait for Apple's mysterious noise-canceling product has finally ended though, with the release of AirPods.

10.3 Four Innovation Pivots: Beyond Sound

This section looks at the *Beyond sound* patent clusters. These are the emerging and peripheral clusters with a loose connection with the core sound technologies, which can be potential pivoting points for the company. Figure 10.4 highlights the four

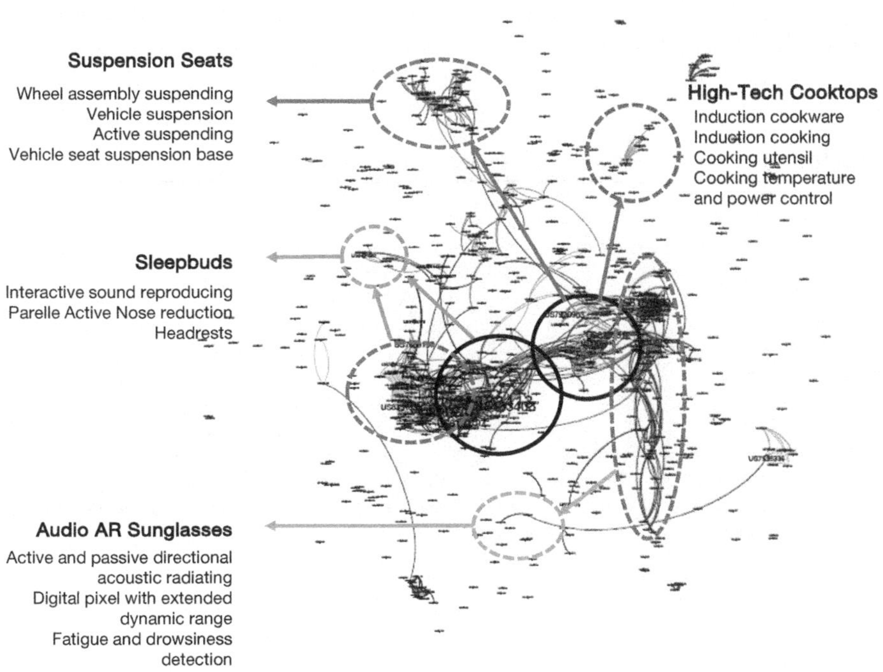

Fig. 10.4 Beyond sound: four pivoting points

innovation pivots: suspension seats, high-tech cooktops, audio AR sunglasses, and sleepbuds.

10.3.1 Technology Pivot: Suspension Seats for Vehicles

At the 2017 Consumer Electronics Show (CES) in Las Vegas, Bose surprised everyone by introducing an active suspension car seat called *Bose Ride*. A suspension is one of the structural devices of a vehicle that absorbs shock impulses and reduces the impact of driving on a rough surface. A well-designed suspension system significantly increases ride comfort, vehicle maneuverability, and stability for drivers and passengers. Adopting the science behind noise-canceling technology, Bose's active suspension offsets vehicle vibrations using an electromagnetic method that generates a wave in the inverse direction to the vehicle vibration by analyzing the amplitude and wavelength of vibrations delivered.

Bose's technology pivot to vehicle markets had been under development for 20 years—under the code-name *Project Sound*. Amar Bose had filed the first patent application for wheel assembly suspending in 1989 (US 4,960,290, 1989), followed by vehicle suspension (US 6,945,541, 2003), and active suspending (US 7,983,813, 2004). The latest suspension-related application was titled vehicle plant active suspension control based on vehicle position (US 2017–0,253,155, 2017). The evolution of product development becomes much clearer with a handful of design patents filed from 2009—from a vehicle seat to a vehicle suspension's seat base. (Table 10.3)

Table 10.3 Bose's design patents related to suspension seats for vehicles

US D605,420 Bose's first vehicle seat design patent	US D605,879 Vehicle seat base	US D695,558 Vehicle seat suspension base

10.3.2 Customer Segment Pivot: High-Tech Cooktops

Bose's core technology can generate and propagate sound from air, water, other fluids, or arbitrary solids. It deliberately controls the process to amplify or attenuate sound waves precisely. What if this sound technology is pivoted into kitchenware?

Speakers and induction cookware employ the principle of electromagnetic functions in a similar manner. Speakers move a vibration plate through electromagnetic induction and radiate sound by vibrating the air. Induction cookware generates resistance through the interactions between the magnetic field and coil underneath the pot, which is then converted into heat.

A zoom-in of the patent network map reveals Bose's pivoting toward high-tech induction as early as in 2008. The project had long been under the name Vortex before it became public in 2016. As Fig. 10.5 shows, Bose's cooktop is derived from three technology clusters: cooking temperature and power control (US 8,598,497; US 9,131,537), cool-touch materials and methods (US 8,754,351; US 9,006,622), and cooking utensils (US 8,602,248; US 8,796,598). It can be predicted that Bose would employ its accumulated sound-related technologies to roll out high-tech induction products that can increase heat transfer efficiency and control temperature precisely while maintaining thermal insulation.

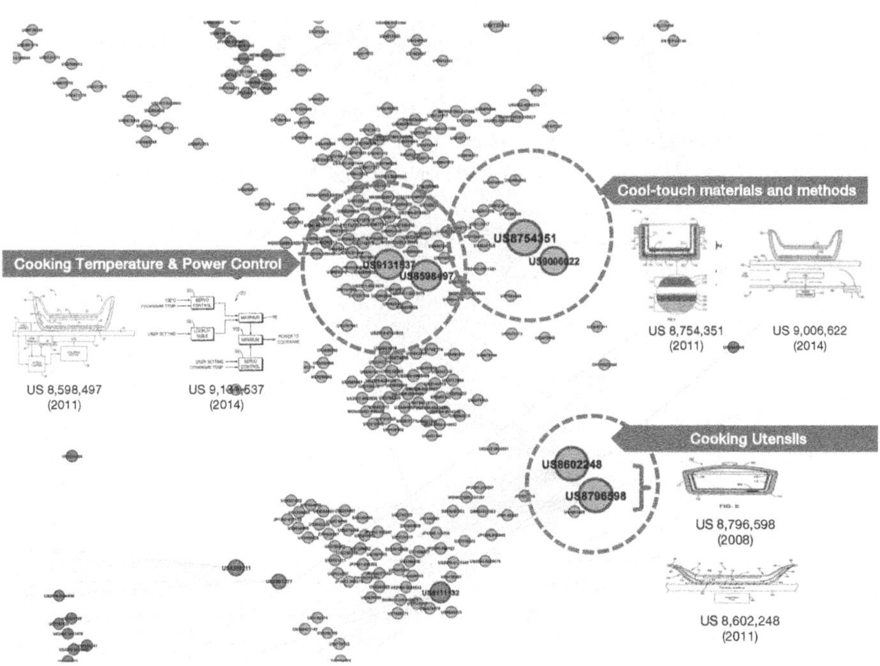

Fig. 10.5 Zoom-in of Bose's patent cluster of high-tech cooktops

10.3.3 Platform Pivot: Audio AR Sunglasses

In early 2016, Bose launched its audio AR sunglasses. While existing smart glass companies such as Google had focused on visual augmentation and gesture-based interactions, Bose differentiated its design by augmenting both audio and head motion through sound technology, which is Bose's strength.

At first glance, there are no significant differences from ordinary sunglasses other than the thick glass temples. However, the temples are equipped with directional speakers (active and passive directional acoustic radiating) to produce vivid sound and are correctly angled to the wearer's ears. The various built-in sensors, such as the gyroscope and motion sensors, detect the wearer's accurate location and viewing directions, thus providing contextual information on the viewed place via sound. Suppose a person wearing the audio AR glasses looks up at the sky. In that case, the glasses will provide weather information (e.g., "Today's weather in Kitsilano Beach, Vancouver is 27 °C, which is 2 °C higher than yesterday.").

This pivot is Bose's first attempt toward building a platform business. Its audio AR glasses create a business platform that can collect the wearer's location and activities and deliver app content to the wearer in real-time. Bose offers a software development kit to increase the variety of app content, such as music, trips, fitness, and restaurant recommendations and has also expanded its partnerships with popular app providers, such as TripAdvisor, ASICS Studio, and Yelp. In early 2019, Bose officially launched the early model called Frames, which combines both audio and sunglasses. However, this model does not provide interactive functions yet, other than receiving or canceling a phone call by nodding or shaking the head.

The latest patent applications in Fig. 10.6 hint at Bose's next service platform to implement the audio AR sunglasses. For instance, a digital pixel with extended dynamic range (US 2019–0,376,845) is for controlling the content of a near-eye display in wearable virtual-reality (VR), augmented-reality (AR), or mixed reality (MR) systems. Also, the patent US 2020–0,330,017 relates to a driver safety platform by detecting fatigue and drowsiness without using a camera.

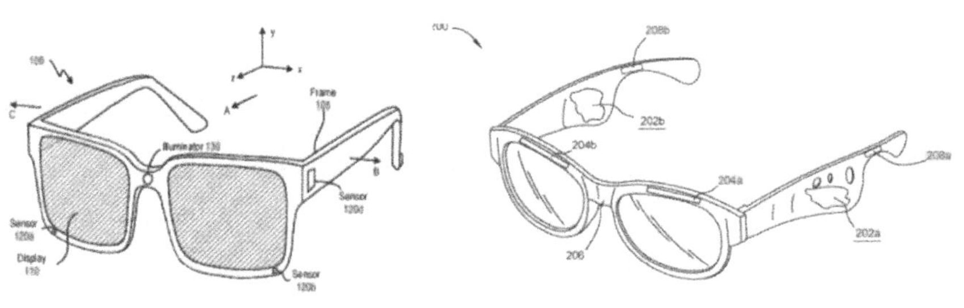

Digital pixel with extended dynamic range
US 2019-0376845

Fatigue and drowsiness detection
US 2020-0330017

Fig. 10.6 Bose's patents related to audio AR sunglasses

10.3.4 Zoom-In Pivot: Noise-Masking Sleepbuds

The latest pivot point of Bose makes use of the company's core technology—noise-masking—and develops it into a new product for sleep aid, Sleepbuds™. Noise-masking technology is completely different from noise-canceling technology. Noise-canceling offsets noise by generating inverse waves of the noise. In contrast, noise-masking covers noises with a low-frequency sound, which is especially effective in hiding the audio frequencies of snoring, dog barking, traffic, and so on (Bose 2018). Sleepbuds have preloaded soothing sounds like gentle rainfall, cracking fire, wind kicking up leaves, and airplane cabin ambient noise, which creates a low-frequency tone to mask noises (Carnoy 2018).

This idea came from a San Diego based start-up called Hush. Its early product employed technology to block sound by filtering noise via tiny, mounted speakers and then wrapping white noise. However, the early version was unable to filter sudden noises, and the ear tips were too large to be worn. Bose acquired Hush and put extensive work into miniaturizing and fine-tuning the noise-masking with sound reproducing technologies to handle environmental noises (Interactive Sound Reproducing, US 8,977,375, 2000). The patent US 10,354,640 (Parallel active noise reduction (ANR) and hear-through signal flow paths in acoustic devices) is the latest technology for Sleepbuds, enabling an input signal captured by one or more sensors associated with an ANR device (Fig. 10.7).

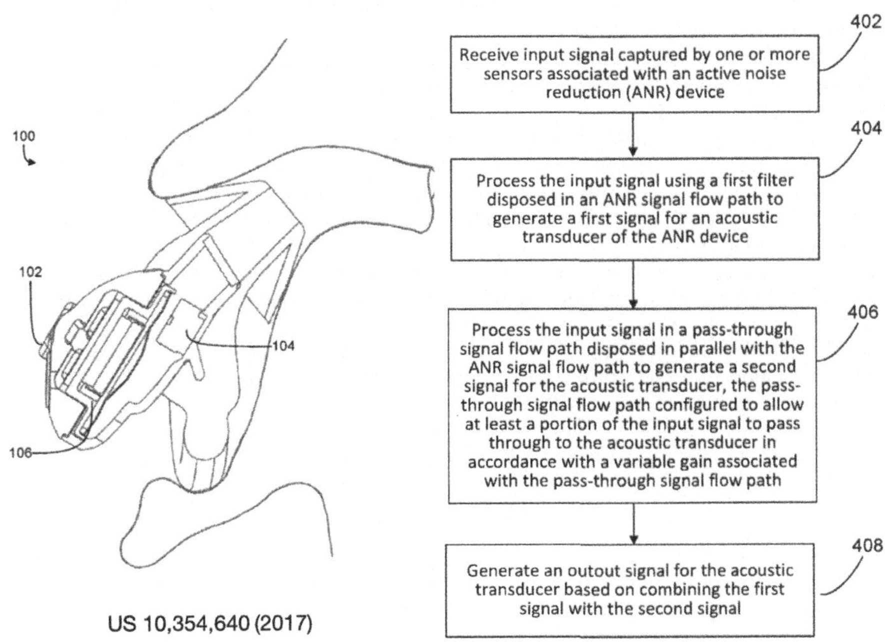

Fig. 10.7 Bose's latest patents related to Sleepbuds (US 10,354,640)

10.4 Summary

With the fast growth of smart speakers and wearable devices, premium audio companies are now facing a new challenge. Major speaker brands such as Harman Kardon, JBL, and Bose have launched wireless speakers mounted with Amazon Alexa or Google Assistant. In this hyper-competitive era, where competitive advantages change rapidly, Bose has attempted to differentiate its business strategy and has continuously sought potential pivoting points, such as its self-driving car suspension seat Bose Ride and the AR sunglasses Frames. In addition, Bose Ventures leads open innovation and investigates high-tech start-ups focused on wearables, wellness, audio, and the AR platform. Some of Bose's recent investments include the Detour audio walking tour app created by Andrew Mason and the Sync project, which helps patients with Alzheimer's or depression through personalized music play.

As evidenced by Bose's patent citation map, the company has certainly moved away from its past strategy of focusing on intense, internal R&D investment and depending largely on its own technologies. These active pivoting and technology acquisitions lead to significant changes in Bose's next innovation.

References

BBC (2014) Beats sued by Bose over noise-canceling patent. https://www.bbc.com/news/technology-28525440. Accessed 15 Jan 2021.

Bose (2018) Noise blocking, noise cancelling, and noise masking. https://www.bose.com/en_us/better_with_bose/noise-cancelling-vs-noise-masking.html. Accessed 05 June 2018.

Carnoy D (2018) Bose noise-masking Sleepbuds will be officially introduced June 20. https://www.cnet.com/news/bose-sleepbuds-will-be-officially-introduced-june-20. Accessed 04 June 2018.

Cherven K (2015) Mastering Gephi network visualization. Packt Publishing Ltd, Birmingham

CNET (2016) Hands-on with Bose's new super high-tech cooking systemhttps://www.cnet.com/videos/hands-on-with-boses-new-super-high-tech-cooking-system/?utm_source=reddit.com. Accessed 15 Jan 2021.

Prell C (2012) Social network analysis: History, theory and methodology. Sage, London

Ries E (2011) The Lean Startup: How Today's Entrepreneurs Use Continuous Innovation to Create Radically Successful Businesses. Currency, New York

Valente TW, Palinkas LA, Czaja S, Chu KH, Brown CH (2015) Social network analysis for program implementation. PloS one. 10(6):e0131712https://doi.org/10.1371/journal.pone.0131712.

Chapter 11
Who Drives Innovation? Apple

Abstract Apple has long credited a culture of innovation as a primary driver of its success. However, there is not much information on how Apple's internal innovation networks formed, how they have evolved over the years, who the core inventors have been, or the extent to which Steve Jobs influenced innovation. Throughout the many lawsuits surrounding the iPhone, court documents and patent filing history unravel Apple's innovation team's long, mysterious story. This chapter deploys a series of the inventor networks derived from Periscopic and Kenedict to demystify Apple's internal innovation network structure.

11.1 The Shapes of Internal Collaborations: Apple and Google

Organizational structure and interconnectedness vary on company philosophy, range of offerings, and pool of human resources. Only a few companies open up their core organizations or teamwork conditions, and it is very difficult to assess their internal innovation activities in detail.

Patents inform the world about inventors. The concept of inventor represents the individuals who contribute to the conception of an invention. Patents publicly recognize and reward inventors for their intellectual endeavors. Exploring patent information related to the inventors is helpful to look for potential experts and leaders or new employees with experience in a particular field of interest. Furthermore, inventor network analysis is frequently applied to identify collaborations between different inventors or groups of inventors and companies for which they work (Trippe 2015). Given that a team-based unit runs in most innovation activities within companies, we can speculate their internal collaboration patterns via a firm-level inventor network analysis.

Periscopic, a Portland-based data analysis and visualization company, is one of the pioneers in offering inventor network analysis through a visual lens. Its *Innovation Signature* depicts inventor network images of large companies like Google, Apple, Tesla, Facebook, and more (Periscopic 2020).

J. Kim et al., *Patent Analytics*,
https://doi.org/10.1007/978-981-16-2930-3_11

Periscopic: Periscopic is a company specialized in data analysis and visualization, located in Portland, Oregon. Its motto is "Do good with data." It provides data analysis, data visualization, and API development solutions to various institutions, including the USPTO and other companies. PatentsView was developed as a visualization platform of patent data for the USPTO as their representative portfolio. https://periscopic.com/

Figure 11.1 illustrates the recent ten-year patent inventor networks of Apple and Google. Each node reflects an inventor. The size of a node indicates the number of patents the inventor has created for the company (i.e., *degree centrality*, see Chap. 5). The links connecting the nodes represent their co-inventorships. In addition, Fluorescent green highlights the founders of Apple and Google: Steve Jobs, Sergey Brin, and Larry Page. Now, can you see any similarities or differences between Apple and Google?

A glimpse of the inventor network clearly shows that Apple and Google's collaboration structures are not identical. Apple's inventor network in Fig. 11.1a shows a tendency of concentration with a considerable number of instances of high connectivity and large nodes. Contrastingly, in Fig. 11.1b, Google displays an evenly distributed pattern where the inventor nodes are in a relatively uniform size. In addition, both companies have ringlike membranes that refer to independent activities at the periphery without any connecting relationships with core inventor groups.

Here are some numbers. Apple's teams, comprising 5,232 inventors, registered 10,975 patents in the last ten years, whereas 8,888 inventors at Google had registered 12,386 patents in the same period. A comparison shows that Apple has 4.2 inventors per patent, whereas Google has 2.8. In other words, Apple pursued a larger collaboration group rather than Google.

Steve Jobs registered 347 patents, and his node is placed close to Apple's industrial design team. We can recognize many names of the elite designers who have performed leading roles for designing the iPhone in Fig. 11.2, not to mention Jonathan Ive.

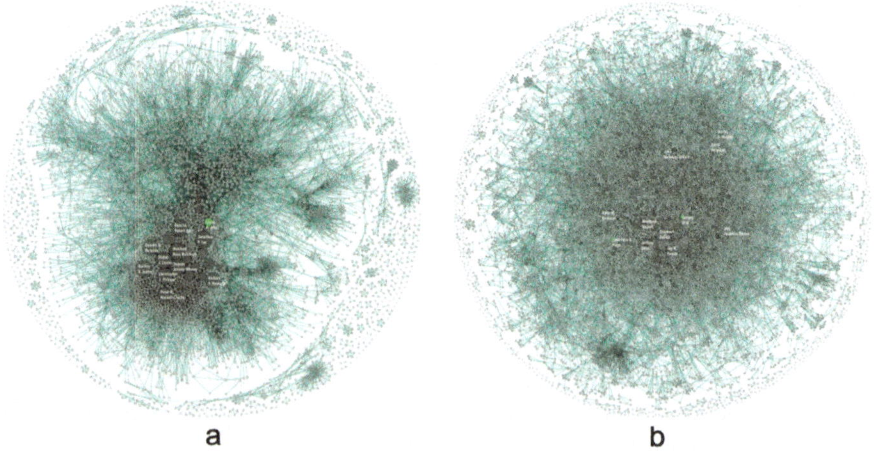

Fig. 11.1 Inventor networks of **a** Apple. **b** Google (Periscopic 2017)

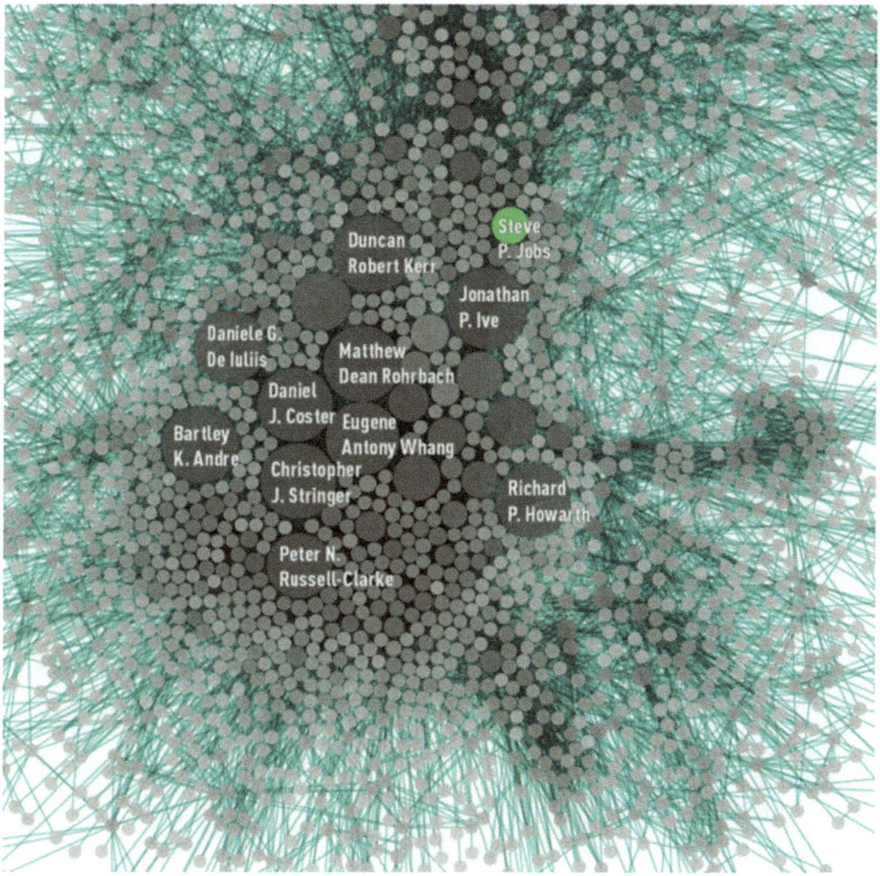

Fig. 11.2 A zoomed-in view of Apple's inventor network

At Google, many inventors seem to take part in the more evenly dispersed innovation structure (see Fig. 11.3). Sergey Brin and Larry Page registered only a total of 27 patents, and their nodes are not even apparent juxtaposed with Steve Jobs's. Indeed, Google has made substantial efforts to build an open innovation culture through broad cooperation among small teams and provide a horizontal environment that is advantageous for spreading and improving ideas.

Finally, it is worthy of note that both companies show a ringlike membrane in the outer periphery. It is partially due to that new inventors, after several M&As tend to form micro clusters in relative isolation (refer to innovation assimilation of M&As in Chap. 12), or a company deliberately operates an emerging team for secret missions (e.g., Google X team).

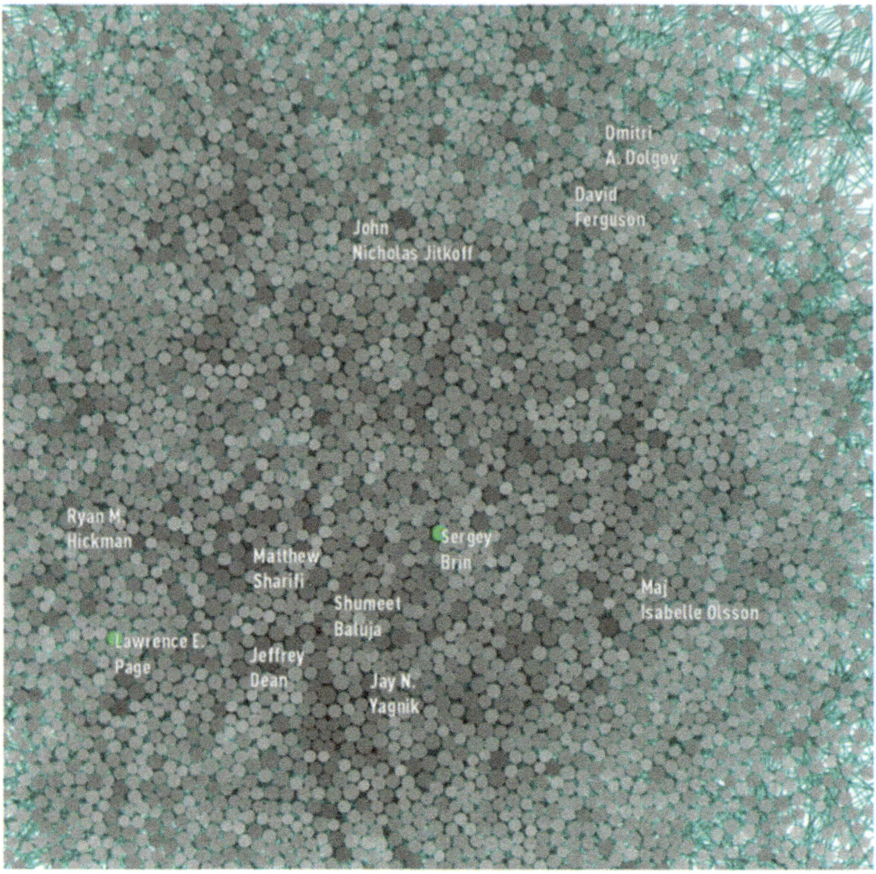

Fig. 11.3 A zoomed-in view of Google's inventor network

11.2 Apple's Inventor Network: One-Mode Network

Before Apple and Samsung's design patent war began, Apple's design team and key designers were barely known, though we can venture a guess. André Vermeij, the founder of Kenedict Innovation Analytics, released Apple's evolving internal innovation network, providing an insightful analysis of Apple's internal innovation network (Vermeij 2013a). He collected all the published patents granted to Apple from January 2007 to December 2012 in the United States and visualized the inventor network changes. Figure 11.4 shows Apple's inventor network, where each node represents an inventor, and a node's size changes according to the collaboration frequency (the node's so-called degree centrality, see Chap. 5.). The color reflects technology fields based on the International Patent Classification (IPC).

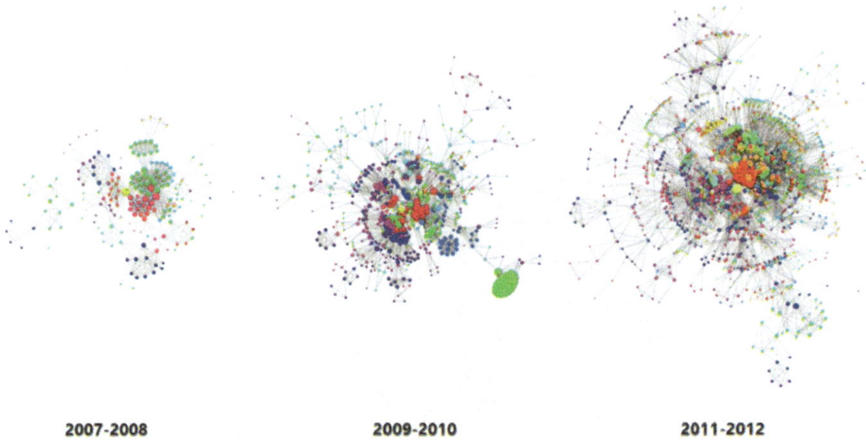

Fig. 11.4 Apple's evolving inventor network in 2007–2012 (Vermeij 2013a)

KENELYZE: an interactive network visbased on one type ofualization tool launched by Kenedict Innovation Analytics (founded in 2013 by André Vermeij). The tool was developed on the belief that inventors or patent networks consisting of simplified, static snapshots are limited to providing variable insights that reflect practical and dynamic innovation environments. The interactive visualization tool enables us to utilize network analytic metrics and browse hidden networks within patent datasets. https://www.kenelyze.com

Figure 11.4 clearly illustrates a significant increase in the number of inventors and connections over time. The number of inventors increased from 489 in 2007–2008 to 1,891 in 2011–2012 and the number of patents also increased from 409 to 2,096 in the same period.

Similar to Periscopic's innovation signature, Apple has a large cluster in the center of the inventor network, which accounts for over 82% of Apple's collaborations. This cluster exhibits substantive growth: 184 inventors with 930 connections in 2007–2008 and 1,167 inventors with 4,785 connections in 2011–2012. The average number of co-inventors per patent slightly dropped from 5.1 to 4.1 during the same period.

The large yellow node denotes the late Steve Jobs. He was positioned in the center of the largest cluster surrounded by the company's full design team (the pink/red colored nodes). A further deep dive into Apple's design inventor network is shown in Fig. 11.5.

Apple's industrial design team is based on the company's design patents and co-inventor information over a period of six years from 2007 to 2012. Apple has produced 615 design patents with 98 designers, which accounts for one-sixth of its total patents. We can identify Apple's core design team and some of the key members proxied by the size and position of the nodes in the network.

There is a tightly connected cluster (the pink and red nodes) in the center of the network, alluding to Apple's core design team led by Jonathan Ive, the former Chief Design Officer at Apple. The team of 15 designers has performed leading roles for designing Apple's signature i-devices, including the iMac, iPhone, and iPad. The

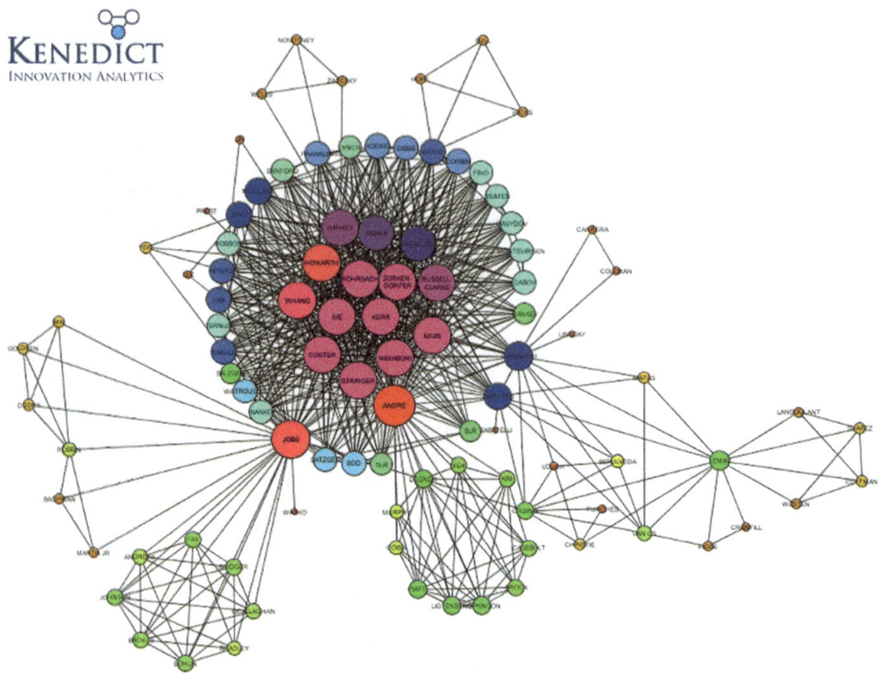

Fig. 11.5 A zoom-in view of Apple's industrial design team (Vermeij 2013b)

inventors in the outer circles in blue and green and in the smaller clusters worked on various product lines along with the core designers placed in the inner circle.

Here is the list of the top ten designers in the order of degree centrality (i.e., inventors in large-sized nodes): Bart Andre, Richard Howarth, Steve Jobs, Eugene Whang, Chris Stringer, Jonathan Ive, Daniele de Iuliis, Daniel Coster, Duncan Kerr, and Rico Zorkendorfer.

Some might be wondering why Steve Jobs or Jonathan Ive do not have the highest degree centrality. There are many different ways to define centralities in a network structure (Brandes 2001; Borgatti et al. 2018). *Degree centrality* counts the number of *direct* connections a node has, which refers to the level of activeness of the node. Other measures, such as betweenness centrality and closeness centrality, consider both direct and indirect connections of a node in the whole network. Some pertinent questions are "*who is critical for information flow*" or "*who has the shortest path to convey information*?"

In this regard, *a core inventor* varies in the way researchers define the centrality: one co-working as many as inventors (i.e., *degree centrality*) or one in charge of controlling the flow of information in the entire group (i.e., *betweenness centrality*). Refer to Chap. 5 for further information on network metrics and learn more about an inventor network with the measure of betweenness centrality and how other companies with a similar range of offerings—Samsung and LG—form their internal innovation networks in Chap. 13.

11.3 Apple's Inventor-Technology Network: Two-Mode Network

Let us extend Apple's inventor network to a *two-mode network,* consisting of a set of inventors and related technologies. While the earlier inventor networks in Figs. 11.1,11.2,11.3,11.4 and 11.5 are based on one type of data where all the nodes are tied to one another (i.e., *one-mode network*), a two-mode network consists of two types of nodes, and all the connections are made between the two nodes and not within.

Figure 11.6 shows Apple's inventor-technology network in various periods between 1978 and 2014. It consists of two types of nodes where a circular node represents an inventor, and a square node corresponds to a patent. Inventors are connected to one another via patents where they contributed. In the same way, patents are linked together via inventors (see Chap. 5 for more information on two-mode networks). In addition, colors were assigned to patents and inventors based on the network cluster. An interactive version is available on this website: https://www.kenedict.com/.

Fig. 11.6 Apple's inventor—technology network in 1997–2001 with a zoomed-in look at Jobs' connections

The two-mode network construction and interactive visualization function allow us to easily navigate clusters of inventors and corresponding technologies by zooming in or out, search for the inventor's name or patent title to highlight particular points of interest and explore the evolution of technology and knowledge clusters over time (Vermeij 2014).

Earlier, this chapter started with a question "what role did Steve Jobs play in the company?" With Apple's interactive network spanning multiple periods, further questions can be raised, such as when was the first time Steve Jobs formed his team, how did the team constitute and connect to other teams? From which moment onward did Steve Jobs play a pivotal role at Apple? After his decease, does his legacy still drive Apple's innovation or fade away? Figs. 11.6, 11.7 and 11.8 hint at the aforementioned questions.

Although Steve Jobs won few design patents during the 1980s relating to the Apple III and the Macintosh, his collaboration network made a first appearance in 1997–2001. Figure 11.6 shows a global view of Apple's inventor—technology network in 1997–2001 and a closer, zoomed-in look at Steve Jobs's connections (in full, Steve Paul Jobs). At that time, he just returned to Apple as a CEO and began to restructure the formation of the innovation team. Steve Jobs's initial cluster was small and placed at the periphery with disconnecting relations with other technology

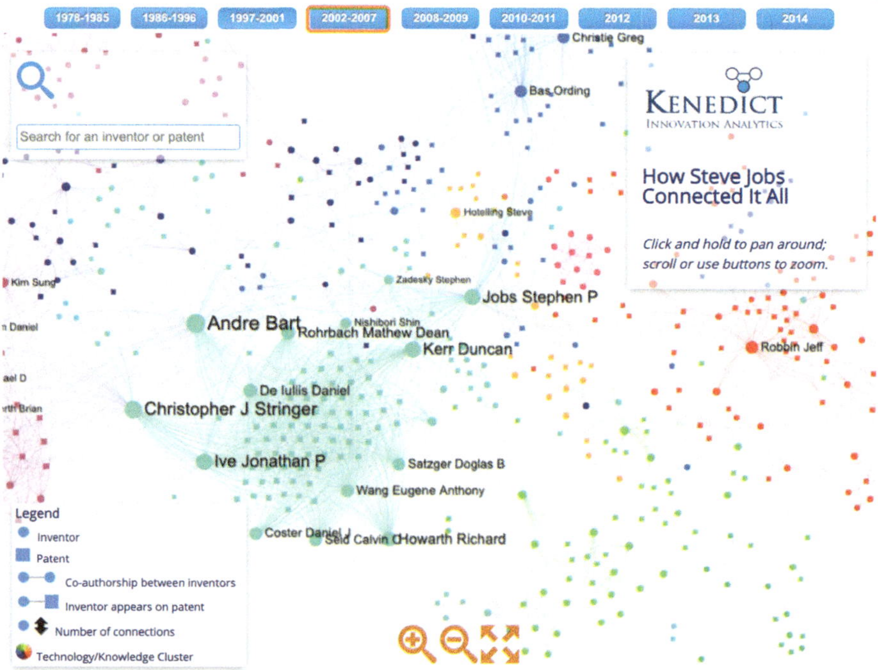

Fig. 11.7 Apple's inventor–technology network in 2002–2007

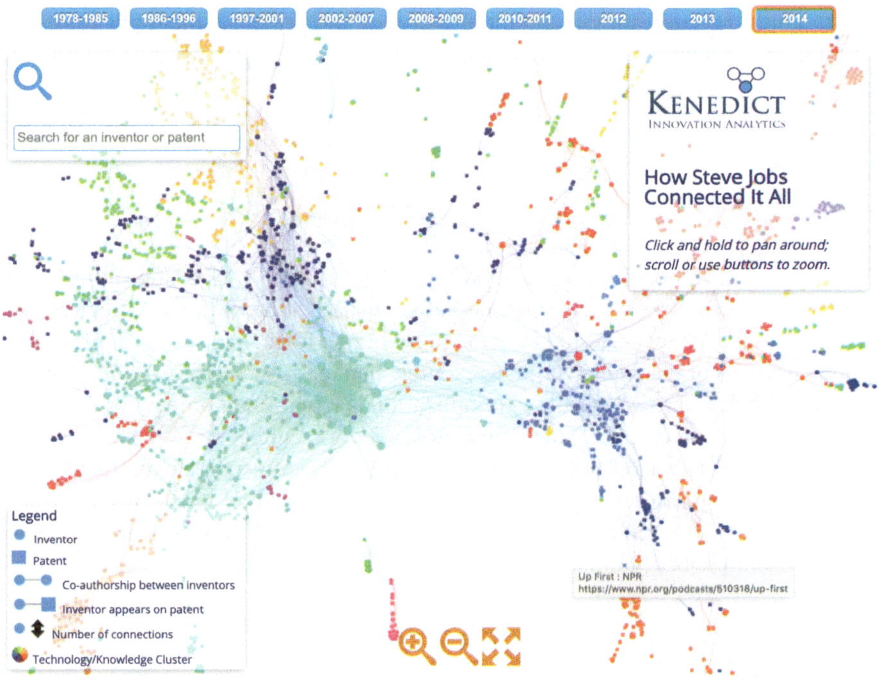

Fig. 11.8 Apple's inventor–technology network in 2014

clusters. Jobs endeavored to user interface (UI) together with Bas Ording and other innovators.

In 2002–2007, Apple's network remarkably shaped up. Figure 11.7 clearly shows the position of Steve Jobs between the design team (in cyan) and the Operation Systems (OS) and UI team (in blue) via Bas Ording, Jonathan Ive, Duncan Kerr, and Bart Andre. Bas Ording, a UI developer, was the sole inventor of patent US 7,469,381 (an inertial scroll, 2007), later known as the iconic rubber band effect that launched the iPhone. Steve Jobs collaborated closely with Jonathan Ive and Duncan Kerr from the industrial design team (in cyan) and Steve Hotelling (in yellow) from the touch technology team in the iPhone's early development. Notably, Jobs played a pivotal role in linking them, which made him a hub of Apple's network.

After he passed on in 2011, how did the formation of Apple's network change? Considering the pendency period of patent applications which is about two to three years (or more), let us jump to the network of 2014. Figure 11.8 demonstrates a somewhat loose collaboration between the design and OS/UI teams. The size of design team networks (in cyan) where Jonathan Ive and the famed designers surround significantly grew, but the interconnections with the OS team (in blue) were far less dense. Still, Steve Jobs's position is alive but placed much closer to the design team.

Many things have changed since the initial Kenedict report was published. There are no Steve Jobs, Jonathan Ive, Bas Ording, or Duncan Kerr who led Apple's golden age. It would be interesting to keep track of the latest changes in Apple's inventor network to see how Apple's new CEO, Tim Cook, has forged his own legacy and restructured its internal organization.

11.4 Summary

Conventional inventor network analysis can only acquire fragmented information on patenting activities. Instead, the interactive visualization of the inventor network identifies how core-inventors and their teams emerge, form, and split over time. This approach can be of great aid in human resource management and M&A due diligence by providing deeper insight into an organization's actual functioning.

Are all innovative companies' inventor networks alike, or is each company successful in its own way? In Chaps. 12 and 13, we further respond to this question by investigating the inventor networks of Adobe, Samsung, and LG Electronics which are all united by their culture of innovation but differ in their philosophies, range of offerings, and pools of human resources.

References

Borgatti SP, Everett MG, Johnson JC (2018) Analyzing social networks. Sage, London.

Brandes U (2001) A faster algorithm for betweenness centrality. J Math Sociol 25(2):163–177.

Vermeij A (2013a) Apple's Internal Innovation Network Unraveled–Part 1–Evolving Networks. https://www.kenedict.com/apples-internal-innovation-network-unraveled-part-1-evolving-networks. Accessed 18 Nov 2020.

Vermeij A (2013b) Apple's Internal Innovation Network Unraveled–Part 2–Apple's Industrial Design Team. https://www.kenedict.com/apples-internal-innovation-network-unraveled-part-2-apples-industrial-design-team. Accessed 18 Nov 2020.

Vermeij A (2014) How Steve Jobs Connected It All: An Interactive Look at Apple's Technology History. https://www.kenedict.com/how-steve-jobs-connected-it-all-an-interactive-look-at-apples-technology-history. Accessed 16 Jan 2021.

Periscopic (2017) Exploring the Innovation Signatures of Google and Apple. https://medium.com/@Periscopic/exploring-the-innovation-signatures-of-google-and-apple-e035240309a1. Accessed 18 Nov 2020.

Periscopic (2020) Exploring Innovation Signatures in Patent Data. https://periscopic.com/#!/articles/Exploring-Patent-Data. Accessed 18 Nov 2020.

Trippe A (2015) Guidelines for preparing patent landscape reports. Patent landscape reports. https://www.ompi.org/edocs/pubdocs/en/wipo_pub_946.pdf. Accessed 04 Jan 2021.

Chapter 12
Knowledge Acquisition and Assimilation After M&As: Adobe

Abstract Merger and acquisitions (M&A) have become an increasingly popular strategy for firms that seek to expedite business transformation and shape new organizational culture. Around the time of the Creative Cloud initiatives in 2011, Adobe paved the way for digital transformation by incorporating a substantial number of M&A activities. This chapter examines how Adobe assimilates the newly acquired technology and knowledge in pursuit of company initiatives. Specifically, this chapter deals with two questions: how did technology and knowledge clusters evolve between pre-and post-M&A periods, and how much has the collaboration between inventors increased over time? A deep dive into Adobe's co-inventor network analysis (1988–2018) sheds light on these questions.

12.1 Adobe M&A Activities

Merger and acquisitions (M&A) play an increasing role in contemporary business environments. Along with a sharp shift in technology—cloud computing, artificial intelligence, and blockchain—and digital consumer behavior, many IT giants seek disruptive innovation opportunities through an M&A strategy (Deloitte 2017). Indeed, acquiring creative design firms and start–ups has been a increasingly popular mode of innovation aiming to kindle creative thinking culture and design-led innovation (Kim et al. 2017; Kim and Kim 2019)

For instance, in 2014, Google acquired Gecko Design, a design firm for its Google X project, to enhance design competitiveness and creativity as it expanded beyond software (e.g., Google Glass, Project Loon). In the same year, McKinsey & Company acquired a Silicon Valley-based design firm, Lunar, to bring a design thinking approach to its corporate strategy. While there are a wide variety of reasons for their success, the two companies have been featured as a prime example of M&As, which manifest the role that design can play in shaping their innovation activities and creative organizational culture. Adobe was no exception to this type of move.

Figure 12.1 shows a list of Adobe's M&A activities over the past three decades. The first acquisition was made with Emerald City Software and BluePoint Technologies in 1990. Almost two decades later, Adobe's $1.8 billion acquisition of Omniture

J. Kim et al., *Patent Analytics*,
https://doi.org/10.1007/978-981-16-2930-3_12

1990-1999	2001-2005	2006-2010	2011-2015	2016-2020
Emerald City Software (1990)	Fotiva (2001)	Trade and Technologies France (2006)	Demdex (2011)	TubeMogul (2016)
BluePoint Technologies (1990)	Accelio (2002)	Pixmantec (2006)	EchoSign (2011)	Livefyre (2016)
LaserTools-Language Tech (1992)	Syntrillium Software (2003)	InterAKT (2006)	Iridas Technology (2011)	Sayspring (2018)
OCR Systems (1992)	Yellow Dragon Software-Tech (2003)	Serious Magic (2006)	Nitobi (2011)	Magento (2018)
Aldus (1994)	Q-Link Technologies (2004)	Scene7 (2007)	Typekit (2011)	Marketo (2018)
LaserTools (1994)	OKYZ (2004)	Virtual Ubiquity (2007)	Auditude (2011)	Allegorithmic (2019)
Photoshop (1995)	Macromedia (2005)	YaWah (2008)	Efficient Frontier Technology (2011)	workfront (2020)
Frame Technology (1995)	Navisware (2005)	Business Catalyst (2009)	Behance (2012)	
Ares Software (1996)		Omniture (2009)	Neolane (2013)	
Sandcastle (1997)		Day Software (2010)	Ideacodes (2013)	
HyWay Ferranti (1997)			Aviary (2014)	
DigiDox (1997)			Fotolia (2015)	
Sandcastle (1999)			Mixamo (2015)	
			Adobe's Creative Cloud Initiative	

Fig. 12.1 Adobe's M&A activities from 1990 to 2020

in 2009 was a creative flare for its business transition towards a cloud-based SasS company. In 2011, Adobe officially announced the Creative Cloud initiatives and foreshadowed fundamental changes from selling boxed software towards a subscription model. Since then, Adobe made a wide variety of types and sizes of acquisitions, including marketing automation software companies, such as Neolane ($600 million, 2013), TubeMogul ($540 million, 2016), and Marketo ($4.8 billion, 2018) as well as a social portfolio service platform, Behance ($150 million, 2012).

For a broader push into cloud-based offerings, Adobe aggressively acquired several design agencies to set its sights on creative professionals and designers. Adobe acquired Typekit in 2011, which offers web-based typography and holds 250,000 web font subscribers (Takahashi 2011). In 2013, Ideacodes, a San Francisco-based design consultancy, which is specialized in the user experience design of smart applications and digital products, was acquihired.[1] An $800 million acquisition of Fotolia in 2015 further amassed Adobe Stock's library with an extensive stock photo, vector illustrations, and videos.

Adobe has successfully shifted and reconfigured its Creative Cloud business, as evinced by its high market share with a growing number of subscriptions and creative cloud contents. However, an objective, data-driven overview of how Adobe assimilates the newly acquired technology and knowledge in pursuit of the company initiatives is still missing.

This chapter[2] specifically focuses on how did technology and knowledge clusters of Adobe evolve between pre-and post-M&A periods and how much has the

[1] Acqui–hiring refers to the process of acquiring a company primarily to recruit its employees, rather than to gain control of its products or services.

[2] Chapter 12 originally published in journal form in 2019. See Kim and Kim (2019).

collaboration among inventors increased over time? The next section introduces a few measures of inventor network analysis to answer these questions.

12.2 Inventor Network Analysis as a Proxy of Innovation Assimilation

The term *assimilate* from its definitional roots suggests that something is taken in and absorbed by a system. In the field of IT innovation, Fichman and Kemerer (1997) defined *assiliation* as "the process spanning from an organization's first awareness of an innovation to, potentially, acquisition and widespread deployment (p1346)." Agarwal et al. (1997) emphasized the interpretation of assimilation as *purposeful organizational action*, focusing on *transfer* or *facilitating adoption and diffusion of new or emerging technology and knowledge among sub-units within the company.*

Through the multiple M&As, the acquiring companies are exposed to diverse external knowledge bases and obtain opportunities for the increase in organizational learning (Barney 1986; Cloodt et al. 2006). M&A activities often lead to a redistribution of tacit knowledge (e.g., design or technology) among individuals and within an organization accompanied by an inventor's mobility (He and Fallah 2009).

In this respect, the question of how M&As come to be assimilated is related to the company's organizational change to acquire, transfer, and integrate the acquired knowledge base. In addition, measuring organizational changes related to technology or knowledge clusters between pre-and post-M&A periods can be key indicators to comprehend innovation assimilation of M&As. This chapter examines the evolution of co-inventor networks by connecting co-inventors and corresponding technology and design fields.

Several measures have been developed to characterize the evolution of the inventor network (Kim and Kim 2019). Table 12.1 lists the key measures for inventor network analysis used in the study. First, counting the number of inventors indicates an organizational growth in size. The more a company participates in M&As, the acquiring company increases the number of inventors in relatively short order. Second, *network density* measures structural aspects of the inventor network. Network density indicates whether inventors are closely or broadly connected. Third, *modularity* can

Table 12.1 A list of measures for measuring the evolution of inventor network

Measures	Description
Number of inventors	Organizational growths
Density of network	Close or broad internal collaboration
Modularity	Clusters of inventors with technology or design relatedness
Degree centrality	Core inventors within an organization
Betweenness centrality	Influential inventors who control the flow of knowledge within an organization (e.g., a team leader)

Fig. 12.2 Adobe's first typeface design patent (US D317,621, 1988)

be used to *cluster* inventors according to technology or design relatedness. We can compare the changes in technology and knowledge clusters between pre-and post-M&A periods.

Finally, *degree centrality* and *betweenness centrality* are widely used measures that capture core or influential inventors. Degree centrality indicates the number of direct connections incident to an inventor. Betweenness centrality measures the extent that an inventor falls on the shortest path between other pairs of inventors in a network. Based on these concepts, inventors with a high degree centrality in a network can be regarded as active and core members of the organization. In comparison, inventors with a high betweenness centrality are likely to be team leaders of the organization and play a crucial role in controlling knowledge flow (Choi and Park 2016) (see Chap. 5 for more details).

12.3 Evolution of Adobe's Inventor Network

This case study investigated Adobe's inventor network's evolution between 1988–2010 and 1988–2018. The aim of the study is to understand Adobe's innovation affiliation after the multiple acquisitions in pursuit of the Cloud Creative initiatives since 2011.

We have collected all Adobe patents published in the United States between 1988 and 2018.[3] Adobe won the first patent in 1988, a typeface design (US D317,621) (Fig. 12.2). Since then, a total of 2,411 patents, of which 94 were design patents,

[3]Data collected March 2, 2018.

Table 12.2 Overview of Adobe's inventor network analysis

Step 1: Data mining	Step 2: Data cleaning and mapping
Assignee: Adobe Period: 1988–2018 Origin of Data: USPTO Number of patent data: 4,526 (4,391 utility patents, 135 design patents)	Node: Inventor Edge: Co-inventorship Number of nodes: 3,175 Number of edges: 6,621 Type: Undirect
Step 3: Network analysis	**Step 4: Network visualization**
Average degree: 4.171 Network diameter: 18 Network density: 0.001 Modularity: 0.787	Software version: Ggephi v.0.9.2 Layout: Circle pack layout (Hierarchy 1: modularity class, Hierarchy 2: Degree centrality) Node size: Degree centrality Node color: Modularity class

were registered between 1988 and 2010. The number of cumulative patents from 1988 to 2018 was 4,526 patents, of which 135 were design patents.

Table 12.2 summarizes the stepwise data configurations, followed by a four-step patent network analysis (see Chap. 8). Network visualization was further conducted using Gephi™ v.0.9.2 and Circle pack layout (Hierarchy 1: Modularity class, Hierarchy 2: Degree centrality).

Question 1: How did technology and knowledge clusters of Adobe evolve between pre-and post-M&As?

The comparative analysis of Adobe's co-inventor network for the two periods: 1988–2010 and 1988–2018 is summarized in Table 12.3.

First, in 1988–2010, Adobe produced 2411 patents with a team of 1780 inventors having 2730 connections. Drawing the analysis to the entire period from 1988–2018, the total number of patents was 4526, with a team of 3175 inventors having 6621 connections. Over the two decades, the volume of inventors and patent applications in force grew by 78.4% and 87.7%, respectively.

Second, the average degree centrality of an inventor was 3.07 (sd = 3.05) and 4.17 (sd = 4.97) in 1988–2010 and 1988–2018, respectively. This means that three inventors co-worked on one patent on average from 1988 to 2010. In comparison, a

Table 12.3 Comparative analysis of the inventor networks in 1988–2010 and 1988–2018

Categories	1988–2010	1988–2018
Number of patents	2,411	4,526
Number of inventers (node)	1,780	3,175
Number of co-inventors (edges)	2,730	6,621
Average degree centrality (sd)	3.07 (3.05)	4.17 (4.97)
Density	0.002	0.001
Modularity	0.898	0.787

slightly larger inventor group of four on average co-worked in the post-acquisition period.

Third, Adobe's network density was 0.002 and 0.001 in 1988–2010 and 1988–2018, respectively. The result showed that as the inventor group's size grows, its connectedness appears to be loosened.

These causes may be twofold. First, after the massive M&As since 2011, 445 inventors (16.3%) were newly introduced and took part in the diverse patenting activity in 1988–2018. Many of the patent applications were acquired rather than developed in-house. For instance, Typekit's patent (US 8,683,006: Method and systems for serving fonts during web browsing sessions) was added after the Adobe's acquisition deal in 2011. Second, in pursuit of new Creative Cloud initiatives, Adobe attempted to diversify several business units, such as beyond mobility, cloud native, intelligence everywhere, and open ecosystem. It is common that a large organization having a wide range of business units shows a small value of network density. For instance, Choi and Park (2016) empirically revealed that the network density of Samsung (2010–2014) was 0.0002, which shows much sparser connections among inventors than Adobe.

Question 2: How are the innovation teams transformed in line with a company's business initiatives?

Figure 12.3 shows Adobe's inventor network in two periods of 1988–2010 and 1988–2018. Each node indicates an inventor. Whenever there were joint inventors involved with a single patent, we connect them with edges. The node's size indicates the number of connections an inventor co-worked with other inventors (i.e., degree centrality). Node colors denote different clusters containing more than 100 nodes. The rest of the smaller clusters are marked in gray.

The modularity value implies how strong a team structure is. In both periods, the values were more than 0.70, which pointed to a very strong group structure in the network (Q value 0.30~0.50: a reasonably strong group; above 0.50: a very strong group; Valente et al. 2015). The inventor network comprises four clusters (Clusters 1–4) in 1988–2010 and six clusters (Clusters A–H) in 1988–2018.

In 1988–2010 (refer to Fig. 12.3a), cluster 1 (209 inventors, 11.74%) centers on the document generation, security, and encryption technologies of PDF readers, mainly empowering a well-known Acrobat product line. The core inventors with a high degree centrality include Sunil C. Agrawal (degree centrality = 18), John P. Brinkman (degree centrality= 17), and Roberto Perelman (degree centrality = 15). Cluster 2 (202 inventors, 11.35%) has a similar-sized team structure, covering the subjects of computer vision and image synthesis techniques. The inventors in this cluster mainly attach to Adobe's Photoshop and other digital media products (e.g., Illustrator, InDesign). Inventors in cluster 3 (137 inventors, 7.7%) relate to mobile applications and interactions across various platforms. Cluster 4 (108 inventors, 6.7%) consists of inventors from the field of human-computer interaction.

Figure 12.3b illustrates Adobe's inventor network in the period from 1988–2018. The most marked difference between the two periods is the presence of one giant cluster (cluster A) and many smaller-sized clusters (clusters B–E). Cluster A (739

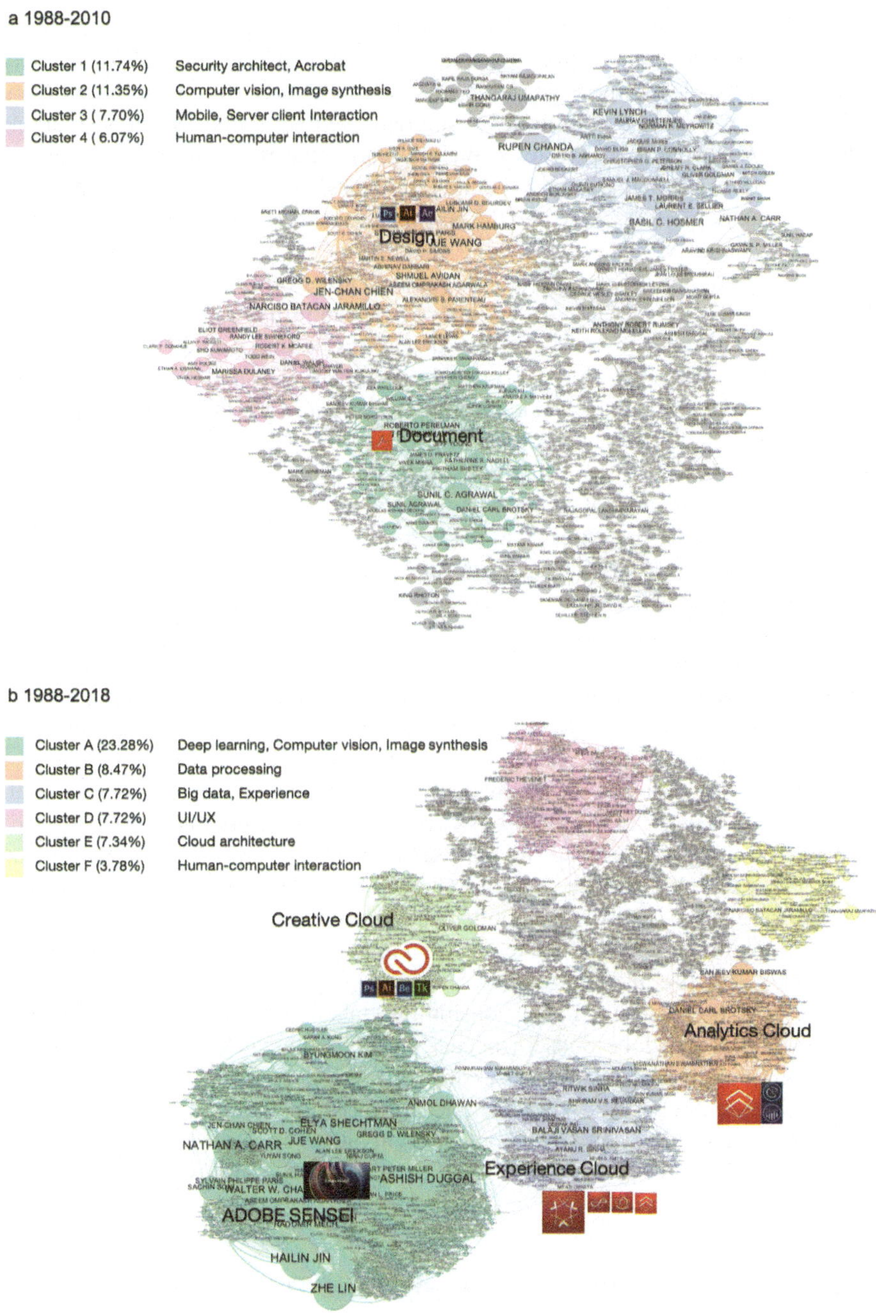

Fig. 12.3 **a** Adobe's inventor network in 1988–2010. **b** Adobe's inventor network in 1988–2018

inventors, 23.28%) is on the bottom left of the network and represents the inventors in the fields of deep learning, computer vision, and image synthesis. This cluster closely associates with Adobe's new business unit, Sensei. *Adobe Sensei* is the artificial intelligence-driven framework that is being deployed across all Adobe's solutions (Adobe 2017). Inventors in cluster A mainly rearranged from cluster 1 (document generation, security) and cluster 2 (computer vision, image synthesis) in the earlier inventor network of 1988–2010 and the new inventors from the acquired companies, such as Aviary and Mixamo.

The top two inventors with the highest degree centrality were Hailin Jin (degree centrality = 58) and Zhen Lin (degree centrality = 57). Both inventors belong to cluster A and co-worked (25 co-inventions) within Adobe's Creative Intelligence Lab. Hailin Jin, a senior principal researcher who has been at Adobe for more than 14 years. Before 2011, he mainly worked on Adobe's flagship products, including Photoshop and After Effect (refer to cluster 2 in Fig. 12.3a). After the release of Adobe Creative Cloud initiatives, his works focus on computer vision, deep learning, alignment, 3D reconstruction, and motion estimation. He is constantly playing a pivotal role in Adobe Sensei Platform (refer to cluster A in Fig. 12.3b). Zhen Lin has worked for only six years at Adobe since 2012. Surprisingly, he filed the most significant number of patents (113 utility patents). His area of interest includes image recognition techniques derived from machine learning and deep learning.

Cluster B includes 269 inventors (8.47%) who specialized in data processing technologies linked to Adobe Analytics Cloud. Cluster C (245 inventors, 7.72%) consists of the inventors who interfaced between big data technology and user experience design. This cluster is closely in line with Adobe Experience Cloud business unit, which focuses on data-driven marketing to cultivate customers with personalized offers. Cluster D (245 inventors, 7.72%) relates to the graphical user interface for Adobe's software. Cluster E includes 233 inventors (7.34%) concerning cloud architecture technologies (e.g., Creative Cloud). Between 1988 and 2010, only 137 inventors in relation to cluster 3 (mobile and server-client interaction) were present. Since 2011, a larger cluster E emerged with a drastic increase in the number of new inventors by 70% (96 inventors).

There is a big shift in the responsibilities taken to focus more on the new direction—notably Adobe Sensei. Indeed, the triangulated connection with small clusters among cluster B (Data processing), cluster C (Big data, Experience), and cluster E (Cloud Architecture) is also noticeable. The evolution of Adobe's inventor network revealed a visible move of how the company assimilates the newly acquired knowledge and influx of inventors to pursue the company initiatives.

12.4 Knowledge Diffusion in Design and Technology

We further questioned how core inventors diffuse their knowledge to others and whether such diffusion comes across design and technology fields. A total of 3,175 inventors was further divided into three groups as follows: *designer group* (the inventors who filed design patents only), *engineer group (*who filed utility patents only), and *designer-engineer group* (who filed both design and utility patents). The engineer group consists of 3,098 inventors, which accounts for around 98% of Adobe's inventors. The designer group comprised 41 inventors, followed by the designer-engineer group of 36 inventors.

Table 12.4 presents the average degree centrality of the three inventor groups. The inventors in the designer group have the least degree centrality 1.02, compared to the engineer group 4.18 and the designer-engineer group 6.42. A similar tendency was found in the value of betweenness centrality.

What is remarkable is that the designer-engineer group, which was merely present in the share of Adobe's inventors, has the highest value in both degree centrality and betweenness centrality. That being said, the inventors in the designer-engineer group co-work within a large group of six or seven on average and are likely to play a crucial role in knowledge diffusion across design and technology.

Another interesting point is that the inventors in the designer group are mainly associated with Adobe's typeface team. For instance, a principal typeface designer, Robert J. Slimbach, excels at design patenting activity with 23 design patents that are the second-largest share of design patents in Adobe. However, he has formed a very closed design team with around three people for one design patent (degree centrality = 3), implying a relatively weak influence on other designers. Similarly, Ryoko Nishizuka, who is also ranked top ten inventors in the design group, produces five typeface design patents with no collaborators; therefore, her degree centrality was zero. It might be because that the nature of font design requires artistic endeavor rather than collective intelligence.

In juxtaposition, for those who work in the field of user experience design, a multidisciplinary approach is an essential part of their work. Daniel Walsh, a former manager for the experience design team at Adobe and moved on to YouTube, has

Table 12.4 Comparison of degree centrality and betweenness centrality by inventor groups

Groups	Designer group (n = 41)	Engineer Group (n = 3,098)	Designer-engineer Group (n = 36)
Illustrations		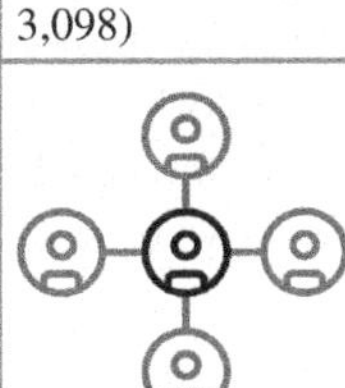	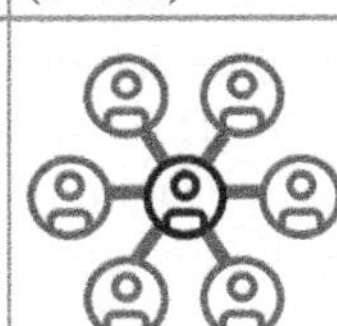
Average degree centrality	1.02	4.18	6.42
Average betweenness centrality	0.00000	0.00075	0.00194

the highest degree centrality of 16 with seven utility patents and 24 design patents (designer-engineer group). He substantially contributed to the journey of Adobe's digital transformation by delivering a new breed of digital experience from Adobe document products to cloud marketing platforms.

To summarize, the inventors in the designer-engineer group tend to form a large team with high betweenness centrality, implying a greater tendency to share knowledge with others. However, a smaller team, working in a silo way, was observed for those who belong to either the designer or engineer group. Of course, many large companies tend to operate independent design teams to encourage their creative spirit and communication culture. This decision varies with organizations, and it holds the potential for success or failure in the long-term view, which is presently still under debate.

12.5 Summary

Since Adobe announced the Creative Cloud initiatives in 2011, the company has pursued M&As at the forefront of the digital transformation strategy. However, it poses a challenge of how the company assimilates this newly acquired R&D personnel and technology and knowledge in line with its strategic directions. Specifically, this chapter responds: how did technology and knowledge clusters evolve between pre-and post-M&A periods, and how much has the collaboration between inventors increased over time?

Through Adobe's inventor network analysis, we confirmed that the inventor network's size in the post-M&A period grew by around 80% with 445 new inventors, and the directly connected collaboration group has been enlarged from a group of three to four. However, the network density becomes lower due to a significant increase in the number of business units to strengthen the emerging technology areas, such as big data, cloud computing, data security, and artificial intelligence.

In a similar line, the number of technology clusters has increased from four to six in the periods of 1988–2010 and 1988–2018. There is a visible shift in the responsibilities taken to focus more on the new digital platform – Adobe Sensei, which is the artificial intelligence-driven framework being deployed across all Adobe's solutions (Adobe 2017). This cluster predominates in the network and closely connects to other clusters in application levels, notably Adobe Creative Cloud, Experience Cloud, and Analytics Cloud.

References

Adobe (2017). Adobe Investor Presentation. https://www.adobe.com/content/dam/acom/en/investor-relations/pdfs/ADBE-Investor-Presentation-October2017.pdf. Accessed 25 May 2018.

Agarwal R, Tanniru M, Wilemon D (1997) Assimilating Information Technology Innovations: Strategies and Moderating Influences. IEEE Trans Eng Manag 44(4):347–358.

Barney JB (1986) Strategic factor markets: Expectations, luck, and business strategy. Manage. Sci 32(10):1231–1241.

Cloodt M, Hagedoorn J, Van Kranenburg H (2006) Mergers and acquisitions: Their effect on the innovative performance of companies in high–tech industries. Res policy 35(5):642–654.

Choi S, Park H (2016) Investigation of strategic changes using patent co-inventor network analysis: The case of Samsung electronics. Sustainability 8(12): 1315.

Deloitte (2017) Fuelling growth through Innovation: Deloitte M&A Index. Outlook for 2017. p 30.

Fichman RG, Kemerer CF (1997) The Assimilation of Software Process Innovations: An Organizational Learning Perspective. Manage Sci 43(10):1345–1363.

He J, Fallah M H (2009) Is inventor network structure a predictor of cluster evolution? Technol. Forecast. Soc. Change 76(1): 91–106.

Kim D, Ryu H, Kim J (2017) Design-utility patent citation analysis from the case study of apple©. J Intellect Prop Rights 12(1):155–182.

Kim D, Kim J (2019) Measure of design M&As:Exploratory investigations of ip analysis in design. Strateg Des Res J, 12(1): 43–61.

Takahashi D (2011) Adobe acquires cloud font site Typekit as part of larger creative cloud service offering. https://venturebeat.com/2011/10/03/adobe-acquires-cloud-font-site-typekit-as-part-of-larger-creative-cloud-service-offering. Accessed 25 May 2018.

Valente TW, Palinkas LA, Czaja S, Chu KH, Brown CH (2015). Social network analysis for program implementation. PloS one. 10(6):e0131712. https://doi.org/10.1371/journal.pone.0131712.

Chapter 13
Learn to Build Design Innovation Team: Samsung Versus LG

Abstract For nearly 50 years, Samsung and LG Electronics have been in fierce competition to take the lead in the consumer electronics market. This chapter explores their competitive landscape using in-depth network analysis of co-inventors and the Locarno classifications in their design patents filed between 2014 and 2017 in Korea. This case study juxtaposes the clusters of design teams, product line-ups, and core inventors of both companies and examines their different product diversification strategies and collaboration patterns.

13.1 A Look at Samsung and LG's Patenting Activities

Global tech giants Samsung and LG Electronics have long been in fierce competition, operating in a huge range of consumer and enterprise products. Both companies have continued to hold on to their positions among the top ten US patents granted (Lunden 2020). The rivalry is far more than just technology. According to the number of international applications for the registered designs, Samsung and LG were the world's top two applicants, heading the list for many consecutive years (WIPO 2019).

Both companies have their territories in terms of markets. Samsung continues to dominate smartphone and tablet sales, whereas LG has significant shares in the household appliance segment, such as televisions and air conditioners. Sometimes, the two companies simultaneously bring out similar products and beat the competition to grab the title of the world's first, notably OLED displays.

As innovations are still mostly conceptualized as being technological, previous studies on the patent portfolio of competing companies have mainly relied on the counts of utility patents and their co-occurrence of technology classifications. Consequently, design patents and their classifications—the Locarno Classifications, have seldom attracted practical attention as innovation indicators (Jeong et al. 2018).

This chapter examines Samsung and LG's competitive landscape based on its bibliographic information derived from their design patents, including the details of inventors, co-inventor groups, and corresponding design classifications. The purpose of the study is twofold. First, it aims to discover how two companies build design teams and where collaborations happen among designers across product areas.

J. Kim et al., *Patent Analytics*,
https://doi.org/10.1007/978-981-16-2930-3_13

Table 13.1 Overview of Samsung-LG's patent network analysis

Step 1: Data collection	Step 2: Data cleaning and mapping
Assignee: Samsung, LG Electronics Period: 2014–2017 Origin of data: Korea Intellectual Patent Office (KIPO) Number of design patents: Samsung (2,938), LG (2,578)	Node: Inventor Edges: Co-inventorship Number of nodes: Samsung (554), LG (310) Number of edges: Samsung (3,715), LG (1,957) Edge type: Undirected
Step 3: Network analysis	**Step 4: Network visualization**
Average degree: Samsung (6.249), LG (5.436) Network diameter: Samsung (15), LG (10) Network density: Samsung (0.005), LG (0.008) Modularity: Samsung (0.887), LG (0.804)	Software version: Gephi v.0.9.2 Layout: Fruchterman-reingold Edge weight: Number of degree centrality Edge color: Product category

Second, it charts product innovation areas of the two companies in which the designs are intended to be applied. This mapping may help forecast future product innovation areas in which the two companies' investigations are in conflict or focus more on or are ignorant of a particular area over the other.

Table 13.1 summarizes a stepwise data configuration for the case study. First, we collected Samsung and LG's design patents issued at Korea Intellectual Patent office (KIPO). Data were collected from July 2014 to June 2017, as of January 2018. Given that the KIPO joined the Geneva Act of the Hague Agreement[1] in March 2014, the Locarno classifications in design bibliographic data are only available from July 2014 onward.

Over the three years, Samsung published 2,938 design patents with 554 inventors, and LG published 2578 design patents with 310 inventors. There is no noticeable difference in the volume of design patents. However, Samsung has 244 more inventors than LG. Interestingly, 10.5% of Samsung's inventor group constitutes foreign inventors while LG has 3.2% foreign inventors.

13.2 Diversification of Product Innovation

In Fig. 13.1, we structured co-inventor networks at Samsung and LG Electronics. Each dot represents one inventor, and the lines connecting inventor nodes when there exists at least one co-invented design patent. The large-sized dots highlight the top ten inventors who have a higher betweenness centrality, and the red dot

[1] The Geneva Act of the Hague Agreement offers the owner or the applicant of an industrial design a means to obtain protection in several countries through a single application in one language with one set of fees in one currency, which can be submitted to WIPO or one of the contracting parties. The Hague Agreement came into force in the Republic of Korea on July 1, 2014. Since then, KIPO has adopted the Locarno classification system and the Korea Design code in parallel in design patents.

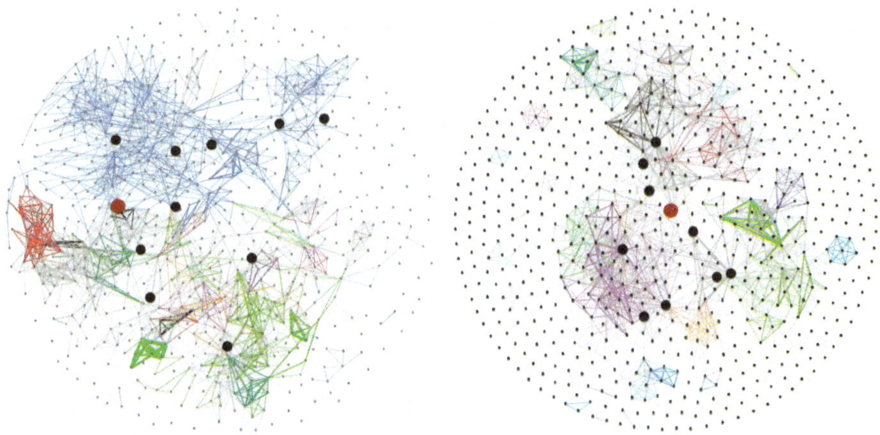

Fig. 13.1 **a** Inventor networks of Samsung. **b** LG Electronics (the large-sized dots denote the top 10 inventors with high betweenness centrality)

denotes the core inventor having the highest betweenness centrality. Additionally, each colored collection of links represents a cluster of inventors who work closely together. Thicker lines indicate the relative strength of links among the inventors, and color codes are applied to substantial clusters marked with the corresponding Locarno classes. Table 13.2 lists the inventor's percentage, which accounts for each cluster with color codes for the Locarno classes and relevant design areas.

Table 13.2 Substantial inventor clusters corresponding to the Locarno classes and product design areas in Samsung and LG

Code	Locarno classes	Product design areas	Samsung (%)	LG (%)
	14-04	Graphical User Interface (GUI)	36.61	4.65
	14-03	Smartphone	10.12	5.42
	14-03	Television apparatus	3.01	11.39
	14-02	Wearable band, smartwatch	2.18	2.10
	15-07	Refrigerator	2.18	3.32
	15-05	Washing machine	1.56	2.61
	23-04	Air conditioner	0.84	4.34
		Total	56.5	29.49

As the Locarno classification system institutes two levels of industrial design classes, it is fairly broad to identify a wide range of electronic products. Thus, this study manually subdivided some of the Locarno classes with respect to the Korean design codes and scrutinized specific design categories. For instance, Locarno subclass 14-03, referring to *telecommunications equipment, wireless remote controls, and radio amplifiers,* is divided into two categories with different color codes: 14-03 in yellow-green indicates smartphone (another handheld device), and 14-03 in puple relates to televisions apparatus. In addition, some class headings were relabeled to render Samsung and LG's products better (e.g., 14-02 *wrist tablet computer* is relabeled as a wearable band and a smartwatch).

Both companies have a substantial number of design patents in Class 14 (Digital communication devices) and Class 15 (Home appliances). Marked differences emerge regarding the extent to which the size and relative placement of inventor clusters in each company. In Fig. 13.1a, Samsung shows one large cluster of inventors (color-coded in sky-blue) that spans multiple small clusters in the network. Contrastingly, Fig. 13.1b shows that LG forms middle or small-sized clusters tightly knitted within the clusters, while much of the network is fragmented.

Samsung has a noticeable number of design patents on the graphical user interface (GUI) in the Locarno subclass 14-04 (36.61%, in sky-blue) followed by smart equipment, such as smartphones, tablets, which are associated with the subclass 14-03 (10.12%, in yellow-green). One-third of Samsung's inventors involved display panel designs with GUI for *a product name.* The latest Apple and Samsung patent litigation affects the active patenting activities relating to GUI-related designs.

In juxtaposition, only 4.65% of LG's inventors is associated with the GUI design patents (14-04, in sky-blue), splintered into smaller clusters according to the target product: one small GUI cluster a bit under the television cluster (11.39%, 14-03 in puple); another on the left to the smartphone cluster (5.42%, 14-03 in yellow-green); and the third on the right to the air conditioner cluster (4.34%, 23-04, in black).

To sum up, while Samsung focuses more on GUIs (14-04) and smartphones (14-03) and, a considerable number of inventors at LG involved in television apparatus (14-03) and household appliances, including air conditioners (23-04), refrigerators (15-07), and washing machines (15-05).

Figure 13.2 shows a Venn diagram of the product designs of Samsung and LG. The overlapping portion represents the common Locarno classes that both companies work. The non-overlapping portions show the unique classes that each company pursues. Several product design areas relating to smart devices and home appliances, on which both companies have long competed, are found at the intersection, along with emerging products that are set to grow independently.

First, we examine the unique product design areas of each company. Samsung focuses on two areas: cameras (e.g., 16-05, 16-06) and medical devices (e.g., 12-12, 24-02). The rest are related to parts or accessories of the main product lines, such as textile fabric for the speaker (05-05) and decorative film for a refrigerator (05-06). Healthcare and medical sectors are Samsung's long-discussed business area to diversify from consumer electronics. In December 2010, Samsung bought MEDISON Co., a South Korean medical equipment company, which is now called Samsung Medison.

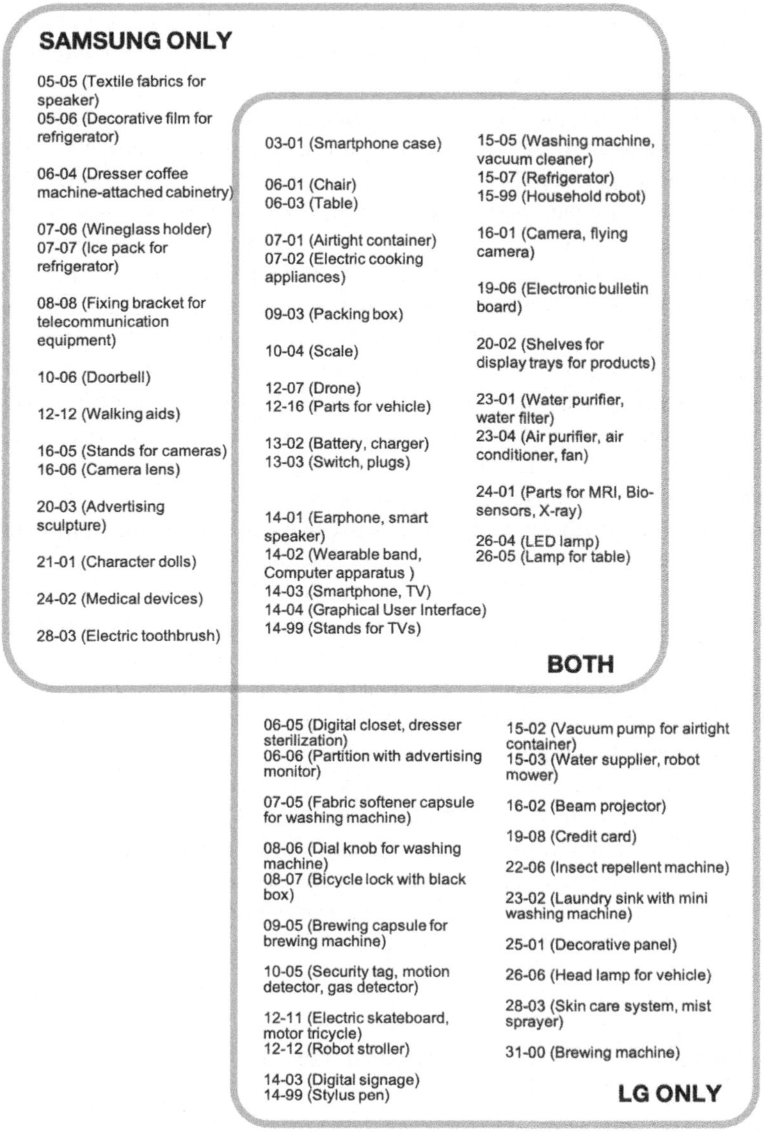

Fig. 13.2 Venn diagram of product designs of Samsung and LG

Moreover, Samsung Medical Centre is the second-largest hospital in Korea and well known for its fully digitalized-paperless health care workstation. As part of its digital healthcare ecosystem, many design activities relate to smart personal activity monitoring devices (e.g., Galaxy Fit fitness bands, Smartwatches, Samsung Health apps) and medical equipment, such as a wearable hip-assist robot (12-02) in collaboration with Samsung Medical Center, and Ultrasound system (24-01) and diagnostic devices (24-02) with Samsung Medison.

In contrast, LG's unique classes are pivoted toward high-tech and convergence appliances for niche markets. LG focuses on high-end home appliances such as a clothing care system (15-05, Styler™), a dual load washer (23-02, TWIN Wash™), a premium built-in kitchen appliance (Signature Kitchen Suite), as well as home beauty-tech lines (28-03, Prael™). LG has also ventured into new home beverage markets, where major electronic companies may not have thought. In 2016, LG first filed design patents for a beer brewing machine (Class 31-00) and beer capsules (Class 09-05). After three years, LG HomeBrew™, a capsule-based craft beer system, was unveiled at CES 2019. This state-of-the-art product reflects the culmination of years of refrigerators and water purification technologies. LG's kimchi refrigerator technology enables the maintenance of a low and stable temperature for an optimized fermentation process. A sterilization technology that has been drawn from a water purifier ensures convenient self-cleaning features.

Some design classes that have overlaps between the two companies aim at different products and market segments. For example, in Class 13-02 (battery and charger), while Samsung focuses on a wireless charger for a mobile phone, LG pursues a charger or energy storage system (ESS) for an electric car. Another example is Class 12-16 (parts for a vehicle), where LG has a wide range of parts and accessories for cars, such as dashboards, smart keys, steering wheels, and room mirrors, whereas Samsung's design patents are limited to dashboards.

The future vehicle designs conceived by LG are partially unveiled in its design patents. Figure 13.3 highlights the sub-clusters that have vehicle-related Locarno classes, which include class 12-16 (parts for a vehicle), 13-02 (battery), 26-06 (headlamp for a vehicle), and 14-04 (GUIs). Their relative positions indicate potential proximity to television appliances (Class 14-03) and other household appliances (air conditioner in Class 24-05 and refrigerator in Class 15-07) rather than mobile communication design (smartphone in Class 14-03).

13.3 Different Structure of Design Team

The subsequent analysis focuses on the structure and size of design teams and core inventors of Samsung and LG. Figure 13.4a shows the distribution of the number of co-inventors in design patents. The graph shows a somewhat puzzling result given that it did not follow the normal distribution. In most cases, three or four inventors contributed to one design patent in both companies (median number of co-inventors per design patent: 3.36 at Samsung vs. 3.52 at LG). However, Samsung shows more cases of a design patent with one or two inventors. Solo inventors made as many as 30% of Samsung's design patents. In comparison, LG tends to build larger teams of inventors per design patent.

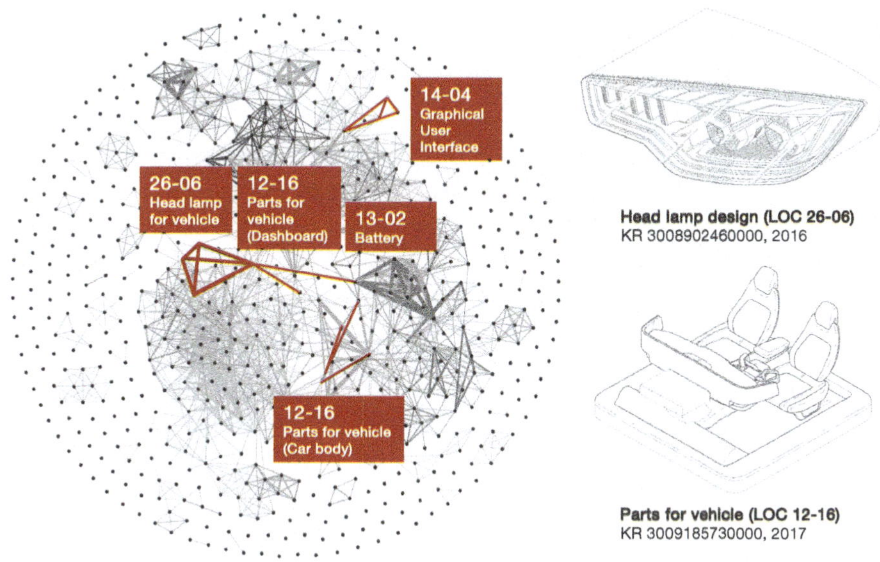

Fig. 13.3 LG's innovation pivots: vehicle-related design patents

We further compared the number of inventors per design patent (Fig. 13.4b). Most inventors in both companies have recorded fewer than five design patents. However, 12.6% and 34.9% of inventors published ten or more designs over the three years from 2014 to 2017 in Samsung and LG, respectively.

Each company has one super inventor who publishes more than a hundred design patents. For instance, Heo Byeongmu, the former principal designer at LG, co-worked with 34 inventors for 158 design patents which incorporate earphones & speakers (14-01), television (14-03), beam projectors (16-02), and smartphone case (03-01) designs. Kim Seunggwon, a director at Samsung, took part in 160 design patents with 13 inventors, focusing mainly on smartphone design (14-03) and smartwatches (14-02).

Figure 13.5 shows a zoom-in of Kim's co-inventor relationship. There is a robust and closed-loop inventor network for smartphone design (14-02, in yellow-green)—it constitutes a group of seven inventors. The super inventor Kim Seunggwon has actively co-worked with Hong Gwanui for 143 design patents, followed by Kim Cheongha (95 counts), Woo Giha (81 counts), Lee Seung Chan (42 counts), Cho Yonghui (42 counts), and Lee Seo (42 counts).

Before proceeding further, it is important to note that our analysis is based on the three-year design patenting activities of Samsung and LG. It is not intended to consider the professional background, position, and employment years of inventors. However, we attempted to identify the current positions and activities of some of the inventors with a high centrality in a network to comprehend the meaning of the network in real-world business contexts. This information is based on corporate magazines, blogs, and a web search, given that the high executive positions and

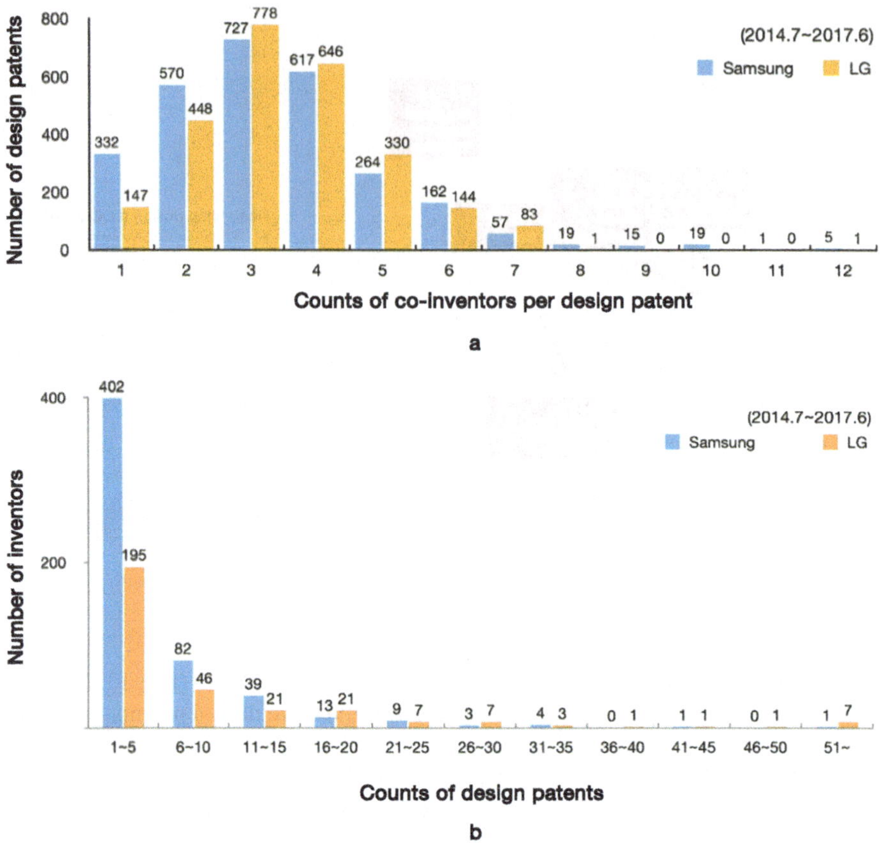

Fig. 13.4 **a** Distribution of the design patents per co-inventor. **b** distribution of the inventors per design patent between Samsung and LG

the recent promotion of Samsung and LG are open to the public. Additionally, as all bibliographic information was written in Korean, the inventor's name was Romanized using a Korean Romanization Converter. Thus, this study could be different from the names on their official document.

Different definitions of *a core inventor* accentuate different centrality measures: one having the most number of patents, like the aforementioned super inventors, co-working with many inventors, or controlling the flow of information in the entire group. In the network graph theory (Brandes 2001; Borgatti et al. 2018), the first two refer to *degree centrality,* which counts the number of direct connections to a node and ignores all other nodes in a network. This resembles real-world scenarios where a super inventor publishes as many patents and is likely to run a big team with many co-inventors.

However, the third way of defining a core inventor conveys the different meaning of centrality, called *betweenness centrality.* It measures the number of shortest paths

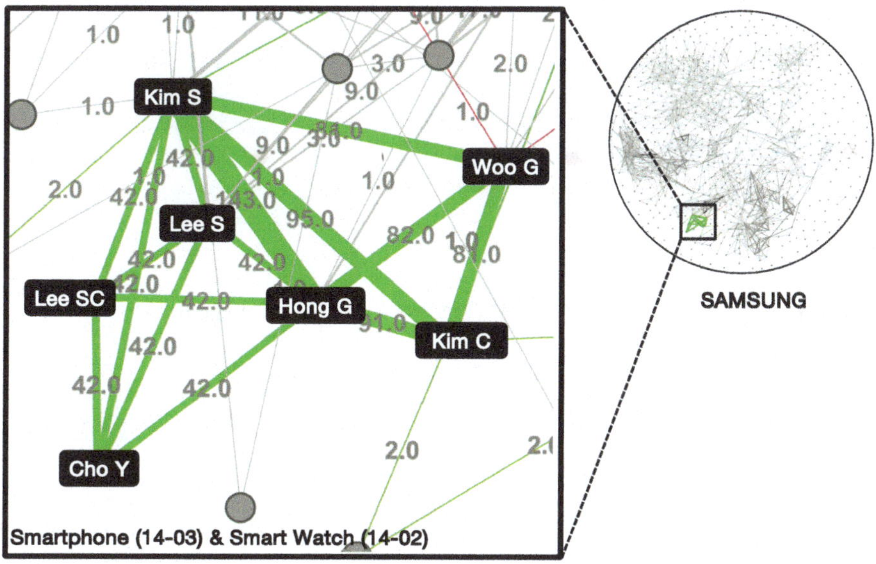

Fig. 13.5 Zoom-in of Samsung's super inventor relationship

that pass through a node. A node having high betweenness centrality is considered a broker or gatekeeper of information in the network. In inventor networks, an inventor having a higher betweenness centrality is often a team leader, who becomes an intermediate channel of information distribution (Choi and Park 2016).

Earlier in Fig. 13.1, we marked the top ten inventors with high betweenness centrality in each company. They are as follows: At Samsung, Lee Joonho (in red dot) has the highest betweenness centrality (betweenness centrality = 0.075), followed by Seung Jeonga (0.069), Jieun Kim (0.065), Bang Yongseok (0.064), Lee Minhui (0.053), Kim Myeonggyu (0.052), Hwang Juncheol (0.051), Lee Sangyeong (0.051), and Lee Sukgyeong (0.042). At LG, the inventor who has the highest betweenness centrality was Kim Jinju (in red dot, 0.047), followed by Bae Sehwan (0.045), Heo Byeongmu (0.041), Jeong Dana (0.036), Lee Hopil (0.035), Cho Seonggu (0.035), Jung Hyein (0.033), Lee Jeonghun (0.032), Lee Myeonghun (0.030), and Kim Gyeongjung (0.027) in that order.

We further draw ego networks with depths of 1, 2, and 3 for the two inventors with the highest betweenness centrality in each company: Lee Joonho (Samsung) and Kim Jinju (LG). An ego network consists of the focal actor as the *ego,* and the nodes to which the ego is directly connected are called *alters* (see Chap. 5). The ego-networks can be expanded with 2, 3, or more depths. An ego network is formed by the ego (a core inventor), alters (who have co-worked with the core inventor), and alters of the alters (direct and indirectly connected inventor group) according to the number of depths of networks.

Figure 13.6a shows the ego network of Lee Joonho (Samsung). Between 2014 and 2017, Lee Joonho has published seven design patents with 19 inventors in the

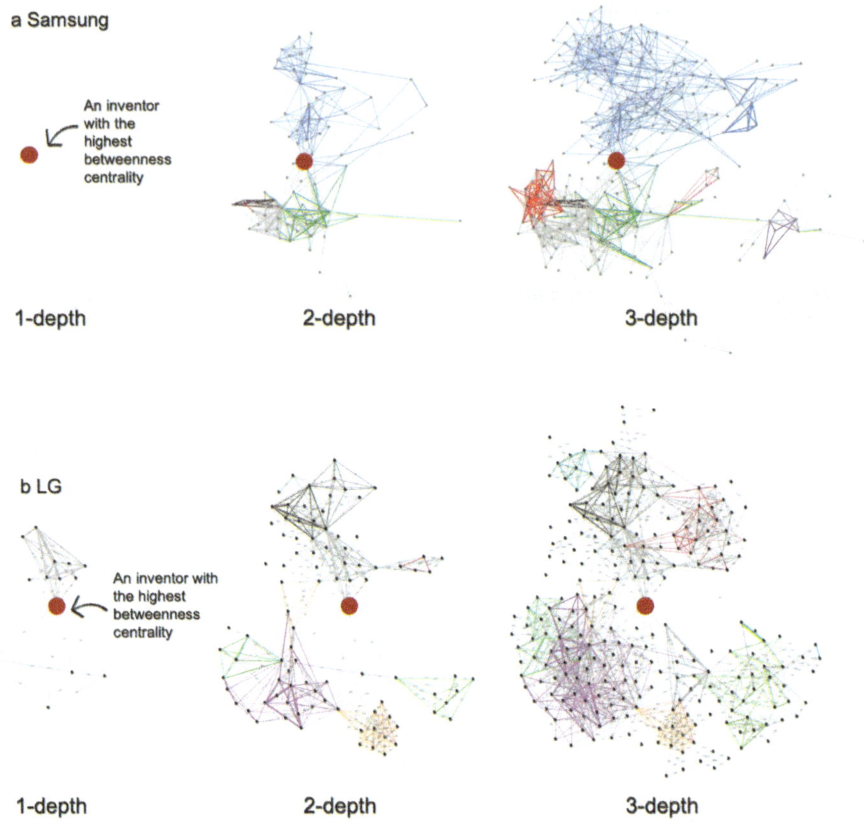

Fig. 13.6 Evolution of ego networks for an inventor having the highest betweenness centrality: **a** Samsung. **b** LG

fields of GUIs (14-04) and washing machines (15-05). The ego network with depth 1 has 19 nodes and 56 edges. At depth 2, the network grows and connects his co-inventors' inventors, resulting in 81 nodes and 295 edges. In two steps, he can reach 81 inventors who are involved in the areas of the smartphone (14-03), wearable band (14-02), smartphone case (03-01), air conditioners (23-04), and refrigerators (15-07) in addition to his initial design fields. Finally, the depth three network includes 263 nodes and 940 edges, expanding to air purifiers (23-04), vacuum cleaners (15-05), and cooking appliances (07-02). With three steps, he can reach out to 47.4% of Samsung's inventors who work on different design projects, such as GUIs, smartphones, and home appliances. For instance, Lee Joonho takes part in several GUI design projects in Samsung's smart living appliance division. His notable design portfolio includes the first touch keypad design for washing machine (FlexWash™) and the advanced interface with color aurora lighting for the wind-free air conditioner.

The ego network of Kim Jinju (LG) is shown in Fig. 13.6b. In the same period, Kim Jinju has published 28 design patents that fall into two design areas: wearable bands (14-02) and vacuum cleaners (15-02). In the ego network with depth 1, the inventor has 14 nodes and 46 edges. That said, there are 14 co-inventors with whom she directly co-worked. At depth 2, she has 93 direct and indirect connections in the network (i.e., 93 nodes and 379 edges) where six more Locarno classes incorporate, such as televisions (14-03), smartphone (14-03), beam projector (16-02), air conditioner (23-04), speaker (14-01), and refrigerators (15-07). Finally, the depth three network includes 239 nodes and 1146 edges, covering robots for guiding people (15-99), air purifiers (23-04), washing machines (15-05), and even drones (12-07). With three steps, she can reach out to 77.1% of LG's inventors in the areas of vacuum cleaners, air conditioners, televisions, smartphones, and counting. At LG, she is a senior researcher in the home appliance & air solution business division and leads LG's signature cordless vacuum cleaner product design (e.g., CodeZero series™).

13.4 Summary

This chapter reports Samsung and LG's competitive landscape using inventor network analysis derived from their design patent activities between 2014 and 2017 in Korea. The co-inventor network and subsequent measures help us understand the two companies' product innovation portfolio and structure of design teams. The main findings can be summarized as follows:

First. while Samsung and LG have a fierce competition in both digital communication devices and home appliances, their choice of product lines and target markets is dissimilar. In particular, Samsung focuses on GUIs, followed by smart equipment, such as smartphones and tablets. Contrastingly, LG's main focus is TV sets and the rest of the products, such as smartphones, air conditioners, and refrigerators, have a similar share.

Second, both companies follow different strategies for product diversifications: Samsung intensifies health and medical product designs in pursuit of a digital healthcare ecosystem, enabling the connections between its wearable activity monitoring devices and medical equipment for use in various healthcare settings. This innovation area will continue to grow in the age of COVID-19. LG pursues a growth strategy through diversification more vigorously. A handful of convergence home appliances emerge, ranging from a clothing care system, home brewing to high-tech cosmetics. Surprisingly, LG seizes the rise of autonomous car markets as a new opportunity to expand its electronic business. In 2018, LG acquired ZKW, an automotive lighting and headlight system company, and created a vehicle component solution division to strengthen this emerging innovation area. Our network analysis infers that this new division is closely connected to the home appliance and entertainment divisions and reinforced by bringing their considerable workforce.

Finally, Samsung and LG design teams vary in magnitude and collaboration pattern. Notable differences emerge regarding the extent of the size and position of the GUI cluster. One-third of Samsung's inventors are involved in the area of GUIs and are densely connected within the cluster whereas LG operates one-eighth of that of Samsung for the GUI team and is dispersed within other product design teams. Samsung's GUI-centric design team offers a harmony of various product lines through consistent user interface design. Also it ensures any design patent litigation lawsuit in the future, as a lesson learned from the latest Apple and Samsung patent litigation. In addition, similar patterns were observed in the ego-networks of the core inventors. Samsung's core inventor is grounded in the GUI cluster and pivots around other digital device designs, whereas LG's core inventor has more chances to reach out to collaborate with diverse design teams in pursuit of LG's convergence appliance initiatives.

References

Borgatti SP, Everett MG, Johnson JC (2018) Analyzing social networks. Sage, London.

Brandes U (2001) A faster algorithm for betweenness centrality. J Math Sociol 25(2):163–177.

Choi S, Park H (2016) Investigation of strategic changes using patent co-inventor network analysis: The case of Samsung electronics. Sustainability 8(12): 1315.

Ingrid Lunden (2020) US patents hit record 333,530 granted in 2019; IBM, Samsung (not the FAANGs) lead the pack. https://techcrunch.com/2020/01/14/us-patents-hit-record-333530-granted-in-2019-ibm-samsung-not-the-faangs-lead-the-pack/. Accessed 19 Nov 2020.

Jeong B, Kim D, Kim J (2018) Comparative Analysis of Design IP portfolio based on Locarno International Classification. KSDS Conference Proceeding, 6:50–51.

WIPO (2019) Hague Yearly Review 2019. https://www.wipo.int/edocs/pubdocs/en/wipo_pub_930_2019.pdf. Accessed 15 Jan 2021.

Part IV
Future Developments with AI

Chapter 14
Is Trademark the First Sparring Partner of AI?

Abstract The rapid growth of global trademark filing activities poses a great challenge to monitor, protect, and manage trademarks effectively. Recent developments in computer vision and natural language processing have significantly improved the performance of trademark similarity search resolving the complexity of trademarks with respect to their visual, aural, and conceptual features. This chapter reviews the state-of-the-art AI advancements and their implementation in the trademark domain. Finally, a use case guides how AI-powered trademark search tools incorporate brand protection and mitigate risks of infringements for global businesses.

14.1 The Great Wall: A Trademark Powerhouse

A trademark is a type of intellectual property for a sign used to represent goods, service, or organizations. Types of trademarks are broad, including words, names, letters, numerals, slogans, symbols, colors, 3D shapes, or a combination of these. Any sign capable of distinguishing the source of the goods or services of one party from those of others can be registered as a trademark. Trademarks do not protect the goods or services themselves but play an important role in preventing competitors from marketing similar goods or services, which could lead to customer confusion. Hence, trademark management is an integral part of brand strategy for any business, large or small, to leverage its brand equity and global competitiveness.

Start-ups entering a highly concentrated business-to-customer market are better off focusing on the acquisition of trademarks as early as possible. De Vries et al. (2017) have empirically confirmed that start-ups filing initial IP in the form of trademarks rather than patents have positive correlations in firm valuations, survival rates, and venture capital funding. Indeed, obtaining a trademark is a faster and cheaper option than a patent, and the duration of trademark rights is infinite—available for renewal every ten years—so long as the trademark is used in actual commerce.

The latest WIPO statistics report that the number of global trademark applications has reached a record high of 11.5 million in 2019, which is almost 630,000 more than filed in 2018 and represents a growth rate of 5.9% (WIPO 2019). Trademark applications each year have almost quadrupled since 2005. This is primarily driven

J. Kim et al., *Patent Analytics*,
https://doi.org/10.1007/978-981-16-2930-3_14

by a massive rise in filings in China, which accounts for over half of all the world's trademark filings.

Along with the rapid growth of global trademarks, there is an increase in conflicts of ownership claims with high-cost infringement lawsuits (Trappey et al. 2020). For example, note that China adopts a first-to-file system in which whoever first files a trademark will own the trademark, even if it was previously used by third parties. Between 2000 and 2004, long before Apple launched its popular tablet computer in China, a Shenzhen-based Proview Technology registered the iPad trademark in the European Union, China, Mexico, Republic of Korea, Singapore, Indonesia, Thailand, and Vietnam. Finally, Apple was caught in a $60 million lawsuit over the iPad trademark in the Chinese market in 2012.

Between the increase in global trademark filings and the disconnected nature of national patent offices, searching for existing trademarks and monitoring potentially misleading or conflicting new registrations by hand and human eyes are no longer viable. The next section reviews the state-of-the-art AI technologies to address these growing concerns in the trademark domain.

14.2 How AI Changes Trademarks Searches

Since the first introduction of the term Artificial Intelligence (AI) in the 1950s, AI has experienced several hype cycles, including the so-called *AI winters*. The first AI winter started in the early 1970s, mainly due to overly ambitious and unrealistic promises by leading scientists in the field, like telling machine translation and intelligent chess players. Since the late 1980s, the AI industry has boomed again with more satisfying results of expert systems, vision systems, pattern recognition, machine translation, and robots. However, soon after that came a period called the second AI winter where many companies fell by the wayside as they failed to deliver on extravagant promises (Russell and Norvig 2002).

Notwithstanding these two AI winters, AI has continued to develop without cease. Figure 14.1 shows the trends in AI applications based on patent filing activities

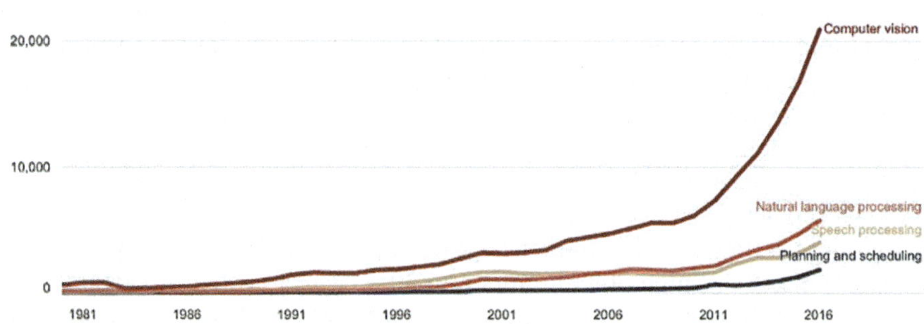

Fig. 14.1 Trends in AI applications (WIPO 2019)

since the 1980s (WIPO 2019). Around half of the AI-related patents associate with computer vision, with an annual growth rate of 24% from 2013 to 2016, followed by natural language processing. Indisputably, computer vision is one of the emerging research fields with the development of deep learning algorithms.

Currently, there are a few similar image search solutions armed with deep neural networks (e.g., Google Image Search). However, trademark similarity search is far more complex due to the concept of *deceptive similarity*. Deceptively similar trademarks can be understood as a trademark created similar or a look-alike of an already existing trademark in order to deceive and confuse the consumers.

The similarity of the figurative trademark containing a figure or a figure combined with one or more words needs to be evaluated with respect to its visual, aural, and conceptual aspects. Understanding how the human eye uses to quantify trademark similarity aids in tackling this complex nature of trademarks. In this regard, Mosseri et al. (2019) propose three aspects of trademark similarity to consider as follows:

- Visual similarity: Do the two trademarks look visually similar?
- Semantic/Content similarity: Do the two trademarks contain the same semantic content?
- Text similarity: Do the two trademarks contain similar text in one way or another?

From the algorithm perspectives, there are a variety of challenges associated with different levels of image complexity (Fig. 14.2). A multi-stage approach with different algorithms is necessary to recognize fine-grained figurative trademark similarities. Optical character recognition is simple and effective to identify words in figurative marks. In addition, color or texture pattern recognition algorithms capture visual and structural similarities of the marks. Image recognition at a higher level

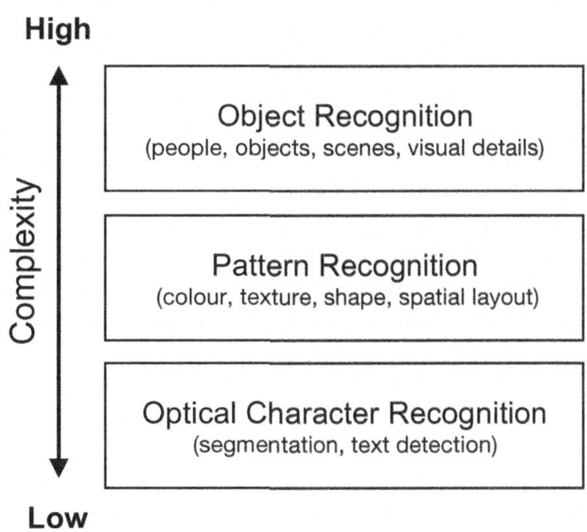

Fig. 14.2 Computational complexity for image recognition

further uses computer vision techniques for detecting and classifying objects in images.

Furthermore, recognizing content similarity benefits from a trademark classification system. For instance, the Vienna Classification is an international classification of the figurative elements of marks. The aim is to facilitate trademark search and to obviate substantial reclassification work when documents are exchanged at the international level. The classification constitutes a three-level hierarchical structure comprising categories, divisions, and sections. For instance, the Nike swoosh logo is assigned multiple Vienna classifications: 26.11.01, 26.11.06, and 26.11.12. Category 26 refers to geometrical figures and solids, and lines and bands are placed within its divisions under 26.11. If a trademark comprises several figurative elements, each of them should be placed in different categories, divisions, and sections based on their shape.

Finally, the third aspect, text similarity, measures spelling and phonetic characters of trademarks. Both measures capitalize on a lexical knowledge source (e.g., thesauruses) and machine learning for natural language processing (e.g., Word2Vec) (Trappey et al. 2020). Pronunciation-based similarity algorithms are particularly useful in the trademark domain, allowing us: to search similar pronunciations of trademarks with dissimilar spellings, and to assess trademark phonetic similarity in multi-languages. For instance, Ko et al. (2018) proposed an N-gram-based phonetic feature generation technique with Convolutional Neural Networks (CNNs) using Romanization and the international phonetic alphabets.

Too often, multinational corporations with English/Latin trademarks struggle with the protection of their trademarks in the Chinese market (see Apple's trademark lawsuit case in Sect. 14.1). This is partially due to the lack of knowledge about Chinese expressions and numerous dialects. A simple text-based search for trademarks cannot safeguard their legal rights and businesses in China. For instance, Apple is called "Pingguo" in a direct translation of the Chinese word for the fruit, apple (i.e., translation). Google renamed itself "Gu Ge" while entering the Chinese mainland market as it phonetically resembles the English trademark "Google" when spoken out loud in Chinese (i.e., transliteration).

Multi-layered algorithms of natural language processing improve machine translation and transliteration of foreign words in trademarks, facilitating greater certainty in strategic planning for brand expansion into foreign markets.

Figure 14.3 describes a workflow of AI-based trademark similarity search, which summarizes the works of Mosseri et al. (2019) and Trappey et al. (2020). Mosseri et al. (2019) further developed a commercial trademark similarity search engine, TradeMarker, as shown in Fig. 14.4.

There are also several big players in this field with a partnership with large trademark offices. WIPO's Global Brand Database offers an AI-powered trademark search by text or image. It covers the national collections of 45 trademark offices, representing a total number of almost 38 million trademarks to date (Fig. 14.5). Many trademark offices are implementing a range of state-of-the-art AI technologies

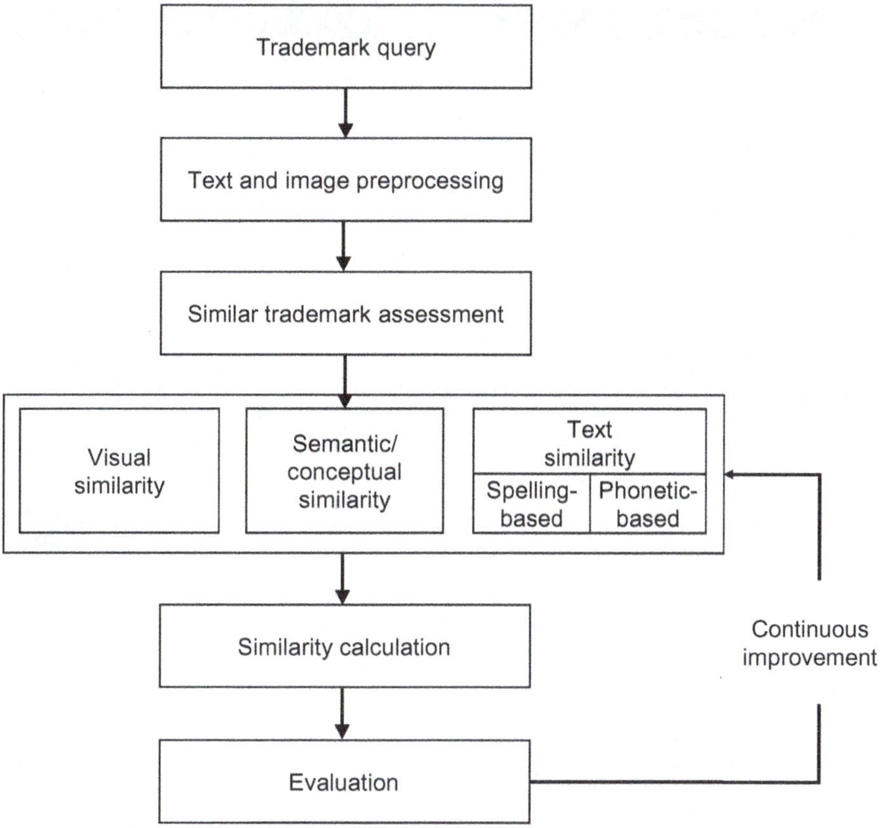

Fig. 14.3 AI-based trademark similarity search

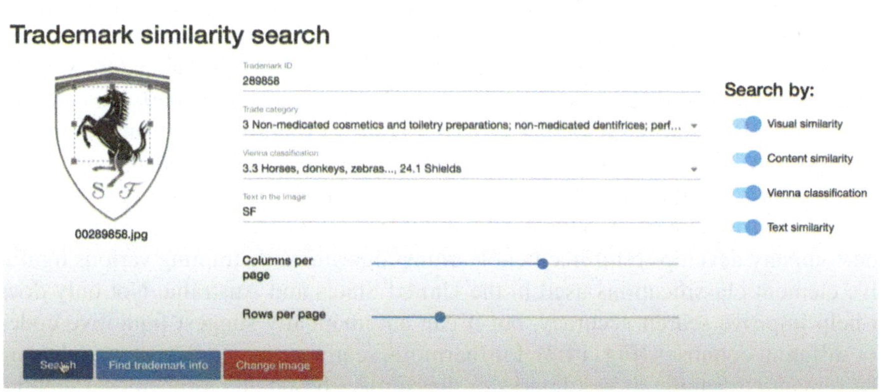

Fig. 14.4 TradeMarker: AI-based trademark similarity search engine

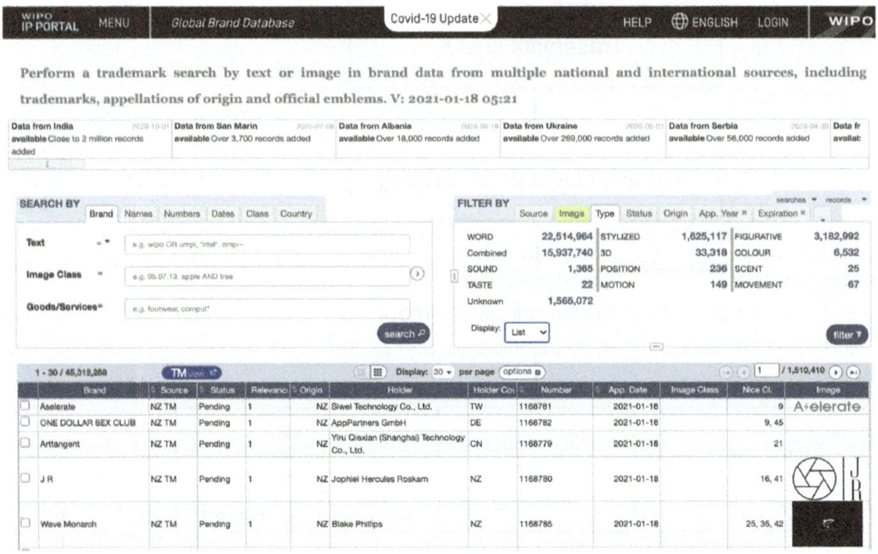

Fig. 14.5 WIPO's Global Brand Database

for trademark search, examination and prosecution with the aim of improving the efficiency and consistency of handling them.

TM go365 (formerly named Trademark Vision) is one of the notable pioneers in the field of AI-powered trademark searches. Particularly, this tool is designed for brand and trademark professionals to effectively launch, expand, and protect their brands with deep trademark expertise. A strategic partnership with the European Union Intellectual Property Office (EUIPO) and IP Australia seamlessly helps the company source thousands of trademarks and design drawings. The training data are not limited to data from patent offices. They are also gathered from the real world, such as logos posted in App Stores and websites. TM go365 signifiable improves the trademark search and recommendation by applying for this trademark big data and domain-specific learning (Clarivate 2020). Figure 14.6 presents an example for the visual search of a given trademark. The AI algorithm suggests potential infringements of brands according to the relevance of visual similarity.

Given that trademark classification is still clumsy and not uniform in patent offices, the company develops reinforcement learning algorithms by training various figurative element classifications used in the United States and Australia. Not only does it help improve search accuracy, but it can automatically suggest figurative codes for different countries (Fig. 14.7). Furthermore, search accuracy has improved using the semantic meaning of wordmarks or thesauruses based on morphemes. Potential infringement risks of a given word can be identified by calculating their semantic distances, the closeness of figurative classes, and their legal status.

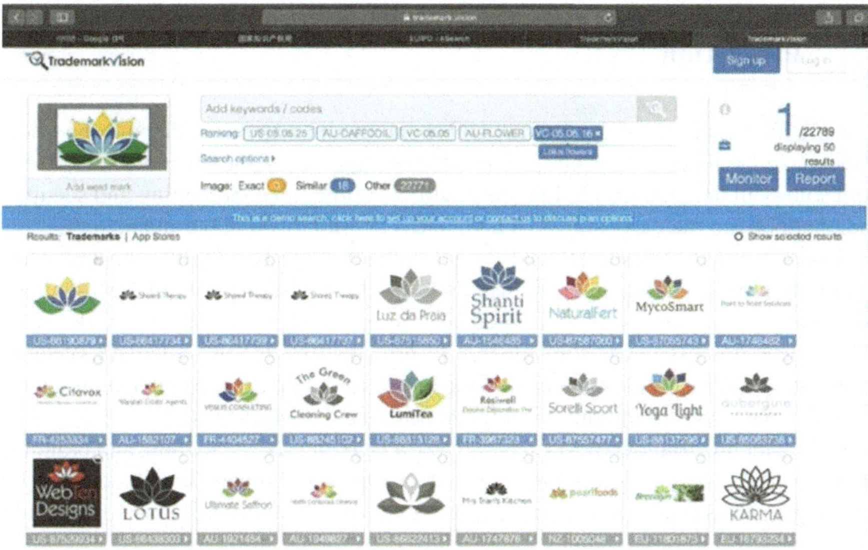

Fig. 14.6 TM go365: a similarity search for figurative marks

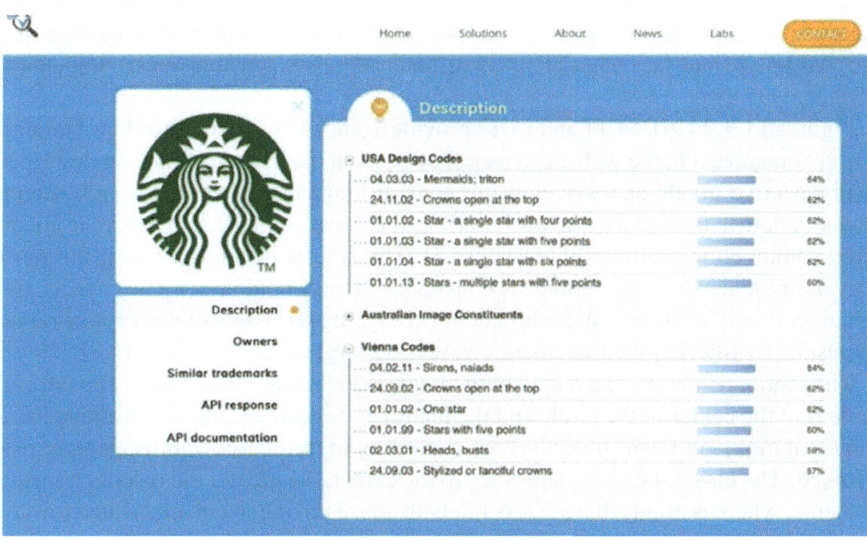

Fig. 14.7 TM go365: suggestions of country-specific trademark codes

14.3 Use Case: AI-Based Trademark Search for Brand Protection

Today, with the advent of the internet and social media, expensive disputes on trademarks have been seen regardless of the size or capacity of the businesses involved, from solo-founder start-ups to big multinational companies. Screening and securing trademarks from the early stages of a business are not elective but mandatory.

However, trademark search tends to get inundated easily with its ever-increasing volume and irrelevant hits to the fields of interest due to the disparity of the trademark system across countries and its limited search option. This entire trademark search and analysis process needs some degree of prior knowledge of trademark systems. Important considerations include allowing either sufficient time to conduct the search on one's own or a fair amount of budget to hire legal experts.

SB Master, the founder of Master-McNeil, a Berkeley-based naming and branding agency, rightly seized the opportunity to derive new trademark search services for branding professionals, marketing departments, or anyone who wishes to protect their company and brand names.

Naming Matters offers a web-based trademark search for meeting broad search purposes. It applies natural language processing and machine learning to determine the degree of risk associated with the desired name by mapping the trademark classifications, phonetic similarity, and legal status. The results are visualized in a dartboard-style interface whose relative distance indicates possible risks of trademark infringements (Fig. 14.8).

Figures 14.9, 14.10, 14.11 and 14.12 provide a quick walk-through of how Naming Matters operates. On the website, a user first types in the desired name and describes its prospective goods or services using general language. Then, the search screen shows the close trademark classes based on the description. For instance, if a user enters "homebrew" for capsule beer goods. The results instantly suggest the most relevant trademark classifications as Classes 21 (Household or kitchen utensils and containers) and 32 (Beers and non-alcoholic beverages). Users can accept or refine the results by filtering the trademark classes and target countries (Fig. 14.9).

The search results are presented onto an interactive concentric circle. The desired name is in the center of the circle and the identical or similar items are displayed as a point that moves outward from the core according to the degree of infringement risk involved. The closer the prior names are to the center, the greater the risk of choosing the name, whereas points that are less likely to cause infringement are located toward the periphery.

Users can freely zoom in and scroll over points of conflict to see the full trademark record (e.g., TLR Homebrew in class 32, Fig. 14.10). In the list mode (Fig. 14.11), users can assess the bibliographic information and the legal status of trademarks and cross-check whether there are already pre-occupied URLs or social media handles (Fig. 14.12).

(12) **United States Design Patent** (10) **Patent No.: US D768,646 S**
Master (45) **Date of Patent: ** Oct. 11, 2016**

(54) **DISPLAY SCREEN WITH A GRAPHICAL USER INTERFACE TO DISPLAY NAMING DATA**

(71) Applicant: **Master-McNeil, Inc.**, Berkeley, CA (US)

(72) Inventor: **Syndi Beth Master**, Berkeley, CA (US)

(73) Assignee: **Master-McNeil, Inc.**, Berkeley, CA (US)

(**) Term: **14 Years**

(21) Appl. No.: **29/506,554**

(22) Filed: **Oct. 16, 2014**

(51) **LOC (10) Cl.** **14-04**

(52) **U.S. Cl.**
USPC **D14/485**

(58) **Field of Classification Search**
USPC D14/485–495
CPC G06F 3/04842; G06F 3/04817; G06F 3/0482; G06T 11/00; G06T 11/20; G06T 13/00; G06T 13/80
See application file for complete search history.

(56) **References Cited**

U.S. PATENT DOCUMENTS

D435,257 S *	12/2000	Woods	D14/485	
D700,197 S *	2/2014	Akcasu	D14/486	
D725,133 S *	3/2015	Smirin	D14/486	
D732,557 S *	6/2015	Shunock	D14/486	
D735,213 S *	7/2015	Kim	D14/485	
D737,316 S *	8/2015	Li	D14/488	
2002/0054117 A1*	5/2002	van Dantzich	G06F 3/0482	715/766
2003/0197724 A1*	10/2003	Reed	G06F 3/0481	715/738
2009/0244072 A1*	10/2009	Pugach	G06T 15/10	345/475
2011/0116769 A1*	5/2011	Sugiyama	G06F 3/0481	386/282
2011/0173567 A1*	7/2011	Sasaki	G06F 3/0482	715/810
2011/0238690 A1*	9/2011	Arrasvuori	G06F 3/04812	707/769
2013/0038599 A1*	2/2013	Krakowski	G06T 11/00	345/419
2014/0062897 A1*	3/2014	Muller	G06F 17/246	345/173
2014/0282132 A1*	9/2014	Daly, IV	G06F 3/04817	715/763
2015/0058769 A1*	2/2015	Kim	G06F 3/048	715/765
2015/0301592 A1*	10/2015	Miller	G06F 3/011	345/156
2015/0301698 A1*	10/2015	Roques	G06F 3/0482	715/736

OTHER PUBLICATIONS

Author Unknown, LegalSherpa, LegalSherpa Trademark Search & Report, Jul. 4, 2014, retrieved from: https://web.archive.org/web/20140704093658/http://www.legal-sherpa.com/trademark-search.

(Continued)

Primary Examiner — Sheryl Lane
Assistant Examiner — Nicole Shiflet
(74) *Attorney, Agent, or Firm* — Van Pelt, Yi & James LLP

(57) **CLAIM**

I claim the ornamental design for a display screen with a graphical user interface to display naming data, as shown and described.

DESCRIPTION

FIG. **1** is a front view of a first embodiment of a display screen with a graphical user interface to display naming data.
FIG. **2** is a front view of a second embodiment thereof; and,
FIG. **3** is a front view of a third embodiment thereof.
The broken line on the outer boundary of the figures illustrates a display screen and forms no part of the claimed design. The broken line drawings of text in all views are included for the purpose of illustrating environmental structure form no part of the claimed design. The difference in shading and types of shading indicate a contrast of appearance.

1 Claim, 3 Drawing Sheets

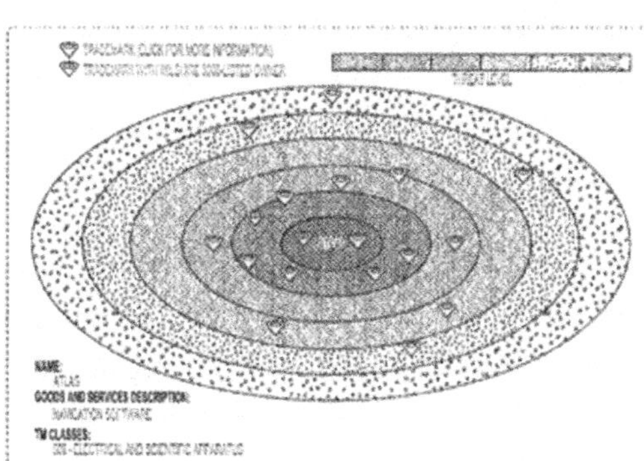

Fig. 14.8 Naming Matters' design patent (US D768,646): an interactive dartboard-style graphic interface for displaying naming data

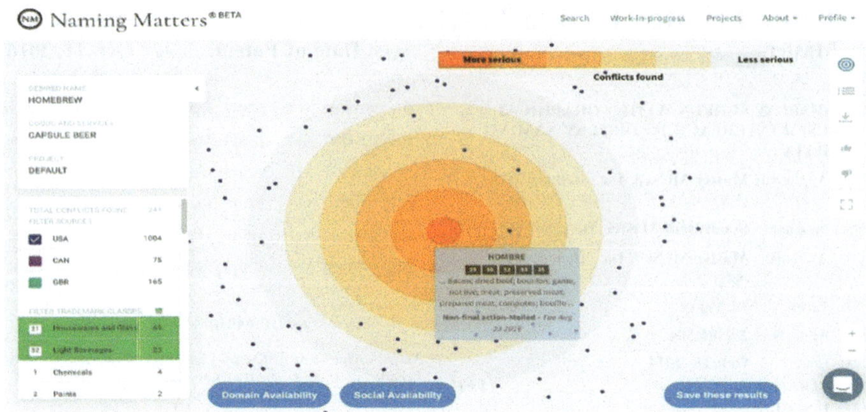

Fig. 14.9 Overview of Naming Matters

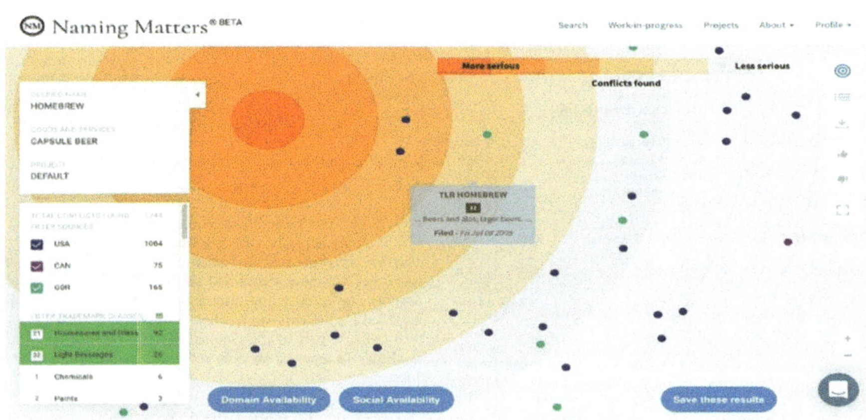

Fig. 14.10 Zoomed-in view of Naming Matters

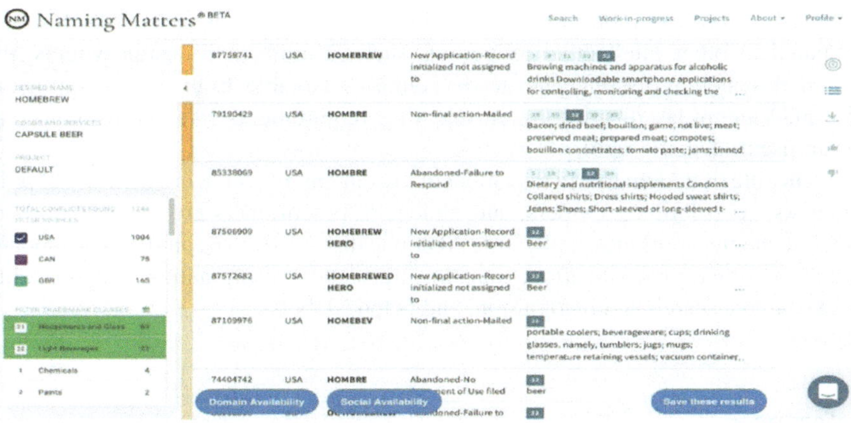

Fig. 14.11 List mode of Naming Matters

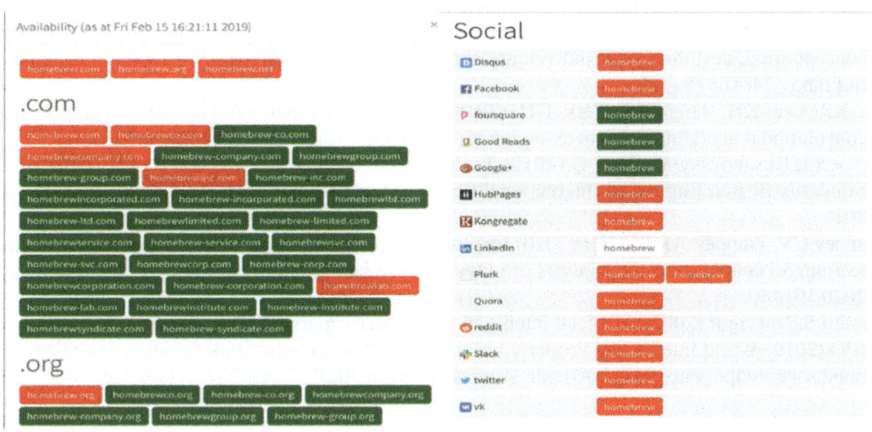

Fig. 14.12 Cross-search of social media handles and available URLs

14.4 Summary

Recent developments in computer vision and natural language processing have greatly advanced the performance of trademark similarity search. AI-powered trademark search tools support a wide number of stakeholders in the trademark domain, including companies, brand professionals, trademark attorneys, and examiners. The tools serve to identify similar trademarks before filing new trademarks ensuring uniqueness to avoid infringement disputes and screen potential infringement of trademark images and wording for adequate global brand protection.

Nevertheless, there are several challenges of implementing AI tools in trademark practice. First, with the growing popularity of global e-commerce, AI tools require increased vigilance of monitoring and tracking the illegal use of trademarks. Second, compared to other intellectual properties, such as utility and design patents, the trademark system is disconnected across countries. Notable differences adopting the Nice and Vienna classification system and filing requirements, like first-to-file versus first-to-use trademark regime.

As the role of trademarks in the global market intensifies, concerted efforts of policymakers, AI solution providers, and trademark practitioners are urgently needed. The next chapter continues explicating AI applications on the rise in IP environments, namely automatic classification, machine translation, examination and formality checks, image search and recognition, and helpdesk bots.

References

Clarivate (2020) TM go365. https://clarivate.com/compumark/ko/solutions/trademark-searching/diy-trademark-searching/tm-go365/. Accessed 18 Nov 2020.

de Vries G, Pennings E, Block JH, Fisch C (2017) Trademark or patent? The effects of market concentration, customer type and venture capital financing on start-ups' initial IP applications. Ind Innov 24(4):325–345.

Ko KP, Lee KH, Jang MS, Park GH (2018) 2-gram-based phonetic feature generation for convolutional neural network in assessment of trademark similarity. arXiv:1802.03581.

Mosseri I, Rusanovsky M, Oren G (2019) TradeMarker-Artificial Intelligence Based Trademarks Similarity Search Engine. In International Conference on Human-Computer Interaction, 26 Jul 2019.

Trappey CV, Trappey AJ, Liu BH (2020) Identify trademark legal case precedents-Using machine learning to enable semantic analysis of judgments. World Pat Inf. https://doi.org/10.1016/j.wpi.2020.101980.

Russell S, Norvig P (2002) Artificial intelligence: a modern approach. Pearson, London.

WIPO (2019) World Intellectual Property Indicators 2019. Available: https://www.wipo.int/edocs/pubdocs/en/wipo_pub_941_2020.pdf. Accessed 15 Jan 2021.

Chapter 15
Legal Technologies in Action

Abstract The incorporation of big data and artificial intelligence (AI) has sparked interest in building a new era for legal technologies. Particularly, this chapter focuses on five areas of AI implications where the concerted efforts of the World Intellectual Property Organization and several national patent offices have been made: Automatic classification, machine translation, examination and formality checks, image search and recognition, and helpdesk bots. In addition, how legal technologies are making new waves to change the delivery of legal services are discussed.

15.1 Background: AI and IP

Artificial intelligence (AI) is increasingly driving important developments in technology and business. It is being employed across a wide range of industries with an impact on almost every aspect of the creation. The availability of large amounts of training data and advances in high computing power are fueling AI's growth.

AI intersects with intellectual property (IP) in a number of ways. In May 2018, the World Intellectual Property Organization (WIPO) held the first meeting involving directors of regional and national patent offices to spark a conversation in pursuit of coherent ICT strategy, management of IP big data, and the cooperative development of AI applications (WIPO 2019). Since then, the WIPO has hosted a series of conversations on AI and IP with a broader range of stakeholders, including representatives of member states, academic, scientific, and private organizations.

Many international and national patent offices have been active in developing in-house AI capabilities bespoke to each IP environment as technology becomes more accessible. Section 15.2 focuses on major AI applications on the rise in IP environments, namely automatic classification, machine translation, examination and formality checks, image search and recognition, and helpdesk bots.

J. Kim et al., *Patent Analytics*,
https://doi.org/10.1007/978-981-16-2930-3_15

15.2 Five AI Applications in IP

15.2.1 Automatic Classification

The primary goal of an automatic classification system is twofold. The first is to allow inventors, companies, and R&D organizations to conduct reliable IP search. The second is to aid patent offices to streamline the IP sorting process and achieve comparable accuracy to the current manual process.

In the pre-classification stage, the incoming patent applications are preliminarily assigned the International Patent Classification (IPC) to route them to the appropriate patent examiners. Additional codes may be appended to satisfy a given regional or national patent system. For instance, the United States Patent Classification (USPC) is employed in the United States Patent and Trademark Office (USPTO), Cooperative Patent Classification (CPC) in the European Patent Office (EPO) and the USPTO, and F-Term in the Japan Patent Office (JPO).

A patent classification is a hierarchical system in which all technical knowledge for the field of inventions is divided into several classes and sub-classes, for instance, containing 250,000 classes in the CPC and 350,000 entries in F-Terms (Gomez and Moens 2014). The assignment of classification requires domain-specific knowledge and enough time to accomplish this complex task. Indeed, thousands of patent applications arrive daily to patent offices; automatic IP classification algorithms would be an effective, labor-saving IP administrative tool.

Today, AI begins to mimic legacy IP classification practices. The WIPO and several patent offices have introduced their in-house systems and automatic classification tools using AI technologies. For instance, WIPO released the AI-based IPC classification tool (a.k.a. IPCCAT-Neural). As Fig. 15.1 demonstrates, IPCCAT-Neural provides a prediction of the IPC codes that correspond to an inputted short description or keyword. The tool is based on neural network technology with a large

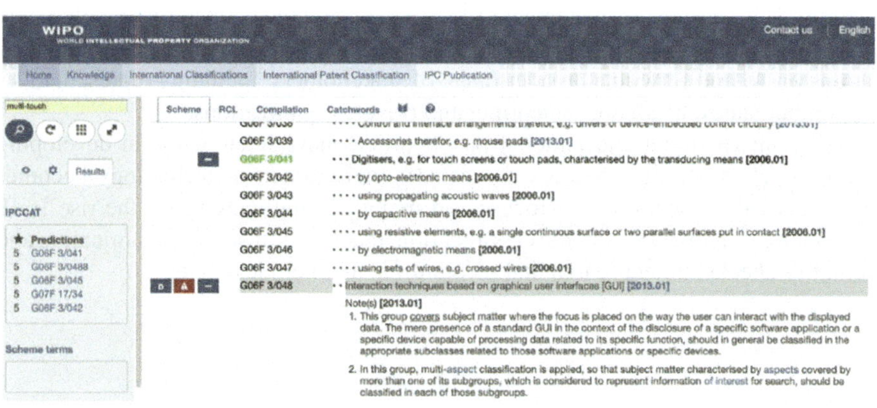

Fig. 15.1 WIPO's IPCCAT-Neural: AI-based IPC classification tool

training set of available patent documents that were classified by human experts and continues retraining the algorithm with the revised IPC. Furthermore, IPCCAT-Neural incorporates WIPO Translate services to offer cross-lingual text categorization through automatic translation in 10 languages including English, French, Korean, Japanese, and Chinese (see Sect. 15.2.2 for more information on WIPO Translate services).

In the case of trademarks, there are two classification systems: The Nice Classification and the Vienna Classification. The Nice Classification is used to classify goods and services for the purposes of the registration of marks. It consists of 34 goods and 11 services with explanatory notes about the type of goods and services covered. The Intellectual Property Office of Singapore (IPOS) has developed a trademarks class recommendation tool, which employs natural language processing and other machine learning technologies to aid automatic Nice Classification for trademarks. This tool automatically extracts the text description field included in the incoming trademark applications. It matches them with the Nice Classification explanatory notes to provide a prediction of the relevant classes. Up until now, IPOS reports that the automatic trademark classification tool saves approximately 5000 examiner man-hours annually and expects to increase drastically as the number of trademark applications is on the rise (IPOS 2017).

In addition to the Nice Classification, the Vienna Classification applies to figurative elements of marks, like logos, to facilitate similarity searches based on the images. The Vienna Classification constitutes a highly hierarchical system that classifies the marks with 31 categories, 147 divisions, 818 main sections, and 715 auxiliary sections.

Recently, WIPO released an AI-powered Vienna Classification assistant. As Fig. 15.2 demonstrates, by dropping an image in the web-based assistant tool, a walk-through of different selection steps from the main categories to auxiliary sections

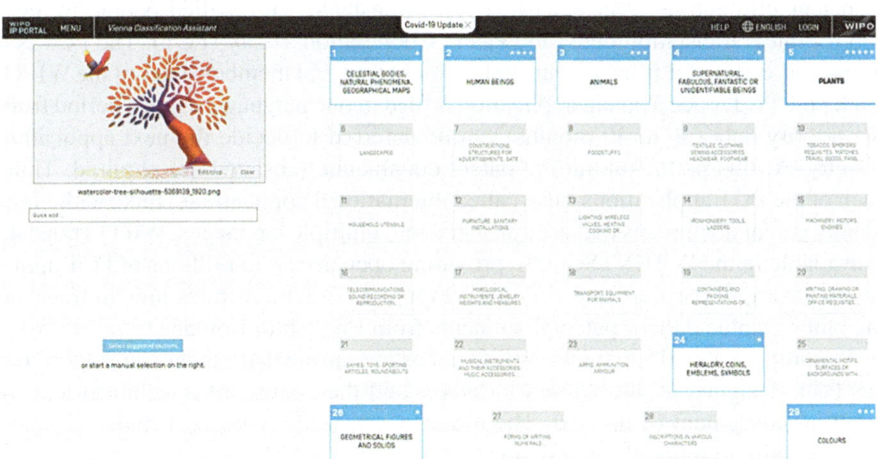

Fig. 15.2 WIPO's AI-based vienna classification assistant

aids to identify appropriate Vienna Classification codes to the given image. This tool provides the recommended categories and sections by highlighting them with color and star rating.

The automatic classification system helps applicants choose correct classes for patents and trademarks and reduce the rejection rate or turnaround time for amendment. Simultaneously, patent offices can save significant time and effort for handling an ever-increasing number of patent and trademark applications.

15.2.2 Machine Translation

Machine translation is an automatic translation from one language to another. Comparing to general-purpose machine translation services, such as Google Translate or Microsoft Translator, patent translations pose many challenges. First, many experts consider the choice of terminology that requires domain-specific knowledge to reduce lexical ambiguity during the translation process. Another challenge is the number of visual elements–drawings–that need to be reproduced and translated within the document. It makes sure that nothing gets lost in translation because small mistakes or missing elements cause a series of legal complications and even reduce the scope of protection (see Chap. 4).

Since 2008, international and national patent offices have made a concerted effort to improve machine translation capacities for patent documents. With the latest developments in deep learning, the first WIPO Translate (Pouliquen 2017) successfully experimented for English–Chinese translations in 2016, followed by an extension to 10 languages (Arabic, Chinese, English, French, German, Japanese, Korean, Portuguese, Russian, and Spanish) in 2017.

WIPO Translate has been exclusively trained multilingual texts using a corpus of patent title and abstract pairs that were translated with skilled people in legal and technical translation under the Patent Cooperation Treaty (PCT). The PCT is a unified procedure for filing patent applications to several member states of the WIPO. Under the PCT, once a patent application is filed in one language, a grace period from the priority date (up to 30 months) can be deferred to decide the next application country. At this point, submitting patent documents translated are required. Thus, each of the PCT applications (also called international applications) links with high-quality patent documents that are translated into multiple languages. WIPO Translate is available in the PATENTSCOPE, providing open access to millions of PCT applications from all participating countries. Figure 15.3 demonstrates how to translate the bibliographic data of patent documents from English to Korean.

In addition, Fig. 15.4 shows WIPO Translate: an instant patent translation that has been designed to allow users to understand the context of a technical text by inputting a segment of the text. The tool can detect the relevant technical domain automatically to refine the translation results.

The highly structured and cumulative volume of patent documents available in multiple languages improves machine translations in patent texts at an unprecedented

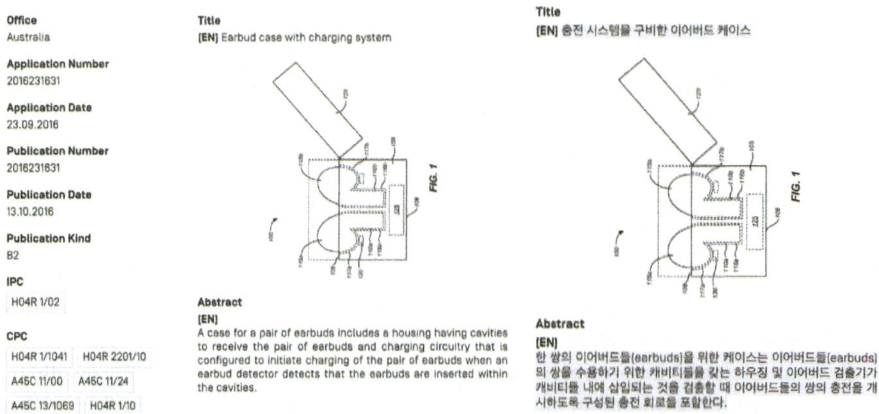

Fig. 15.3 WIPO translate on PATENTSCOPE (https://www.wipo.int/patentscope)

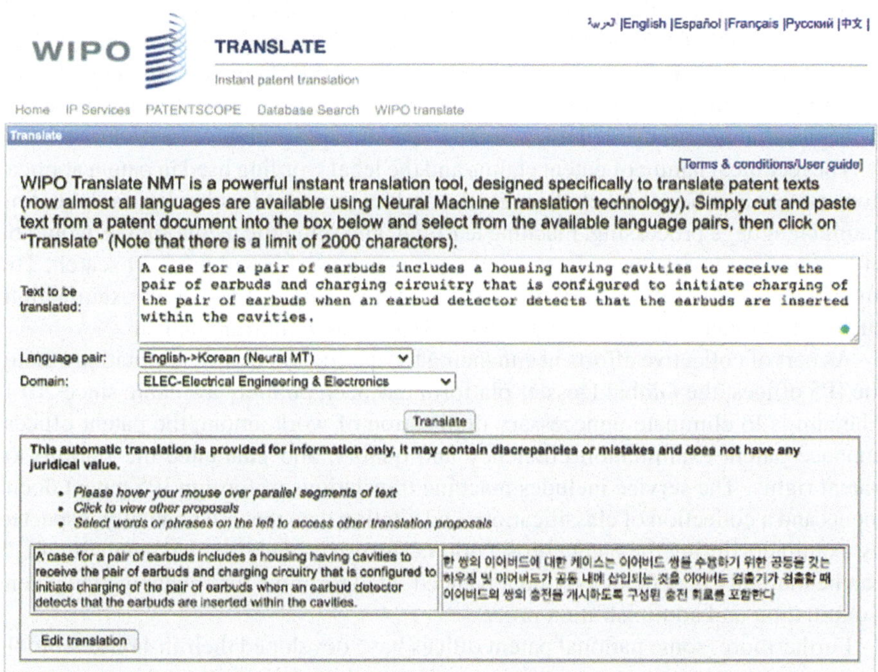

Fig. 15.4 WIPO translate: instant patent translation (https://patentscope.wipo.int/translate)

pace. Yet, neural machine translation needs to overcome some persistent problems, such as low translation quality in the case of infrequent technical terms and long sentences as well as on low-resource language pairs (Ngo et al. 2019).

15.2.3 Examination and Formality Checks

The burden of examiners in patent offices has increased with the growing technical complexity and the rise in the number of applications. In 2019, a total of 2.7 million patent applications were filed at the IP5 offices.[1]

Several AI applications aim at improving the examination quality while easing up the time-consuming and labor-intensive tasks, such as prior art search and formality checks.

First, we consider how AI algorithms can automatically generate search statements. This is particularly important considering that the construction of a search statement is one of the most time-consuming and knowledge-intensive parts of the prior art search process. In the pilot project at the USPTO, a system named *Sigma* not only performs basic keyword searches but also allows experts to create search strategies that are best suited to examine a specific application.

The technical nature of patent claims and the legal wording used in patent applications raise a number of AI challenges. A combination of AI technologies, including natural language processing, machine learning, and semantic technologies, would be of best use in moving away from cumbersome keyword-based prior art search. The algorithms can be refined further by learning a vast record of patent examination, such as examiners' query records, citation search, and multilingualism.

As part of collective efforts in enhancing the quality of patent examination among the IP5 offices, the Global Dossier platform has been publicly available since 2014. The aim is to eliminate unnecessary duplication of work among the patent offices, enhance patent examination efficiency and quality, and guarantee the stability of patent rights. The service includes machine translations of foreign IP5 patent documents and a collection of classifications and citation data that are manually inspected by examiners during the patent prosecution. The use of the extended database of IP5 can be mutually beneficial to build advanced AI algorithms for enhancing the patent examination and administration processes.

Furthermore, some national patent offices have developed their in-house AI tools programs to enhance general administrative tasks of IP filing, prosecution and formality checks. For example, WIPO's AI-assisted OCR technology and IPOS's patent auto checker have the ability to streamline automatic proofreading for patent applications. In addition, the Swiss Federal Institute of Intellectual Property (IPI)

[1] IP5 is a forum of the five largest intellectual property offices in the world. The five patent offices are the US Patent and Trademark Office (USPTO), the European Patent Office (EPO), the Korean Intellectual Property Office (KIPO), the Japan Patent Office (JPO), and the China National Intellectual Property Administration (CNIPA).

has employed a rule-based AI for process automation in order to reduce repetitive administrative work (e.g., applications for rulings/decisions with fees or deadlines).

15.2.4 Image Search and Recognition

Several patent offices investigate AI-based image search and recognition systems at various degrees of implementation, mainly focusing on the following areas: *search for design patents, figurative elements of trademarks,* and *chemical structures.*

Search for Design Patents
The Korean Intellectual Property Office (KIPO) introduced an image similarity search system for design patents in a world premiere in 2016. It is now integrated into its design patent database portal, called Design Map (designmap.or.kr). Using reference materials, such as forward and backward citations and examiners' prior search database, KIPO deploys a function to retrieve relevant design patents that may be similar to the inputted design patent (Fig. 15.5). The next system for intelligent design patent search is under development with neural networks being trained on design patent documents with the examiner records, semantic form factors, and multi-label classifications.

Today, many patent offices have adopted a classification system for design patents, such as the Locarno Classifications or regional classifications (e.g., the USPC, Korean Design Code, or Japan Design Classification, see Chap. 3). Each design patent is labeled with two or more classes that best represent its subject matter. For instance, Apple's AirPods design patent (US D801,314) is associated with three classifications: the Locarno 14-01 and USPC D14/223 and D14/205. These multi-classifications assigned to design patents will be of best benefit from the use of deep neural networks, such as Convolutional Neural Networks (CNNs) and recurrent neural networks (RNNs) to enhance design patents-specific retrieval tasks.

Search for Figurative Elements of Trademarks
In the case of trademark searches, WIPO newly released the AI-powered *Global Brand Database* by leveraging deep neural networks for image search and figurative element classification data from the Madrid System (Fig. 15.6). Whereas the earlier version primarily determined visually similar trademarks based on shapes and colors identified in figurative elements, the current system can understand the conceptual level of trademarks (e.g., an apple, a tree, or a car) and thus present a narrower and more precise group of potentially similar marks.

Search for Chemical Structures
Finally, the latest challenge of image recognition is a search for chemical structures in patent documents. Chemical structure search had been only made with a name or the entirety of a drawn structure. Recently, as Fig. 15.7 demonstrates, WIPO's chemical compounds search allows researchers to upload a drawing of either a complete or

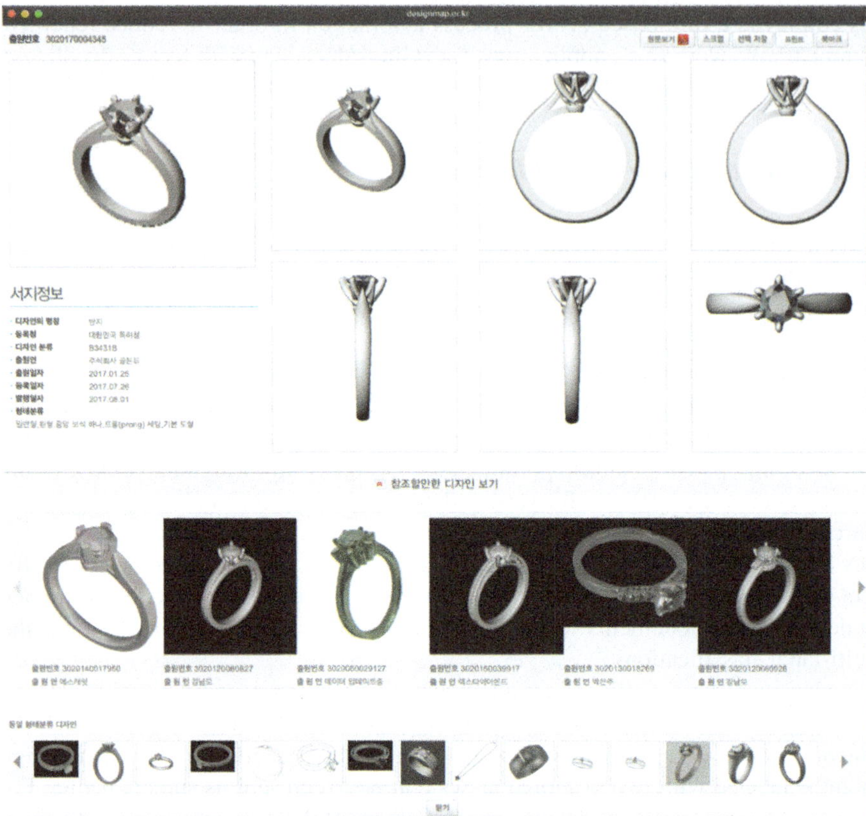

Fig. 15.5 KIPO's Design Map: a web-based design patent portal applying image similarity search

sub-structure of a chemical compound as a search query, and they can be matched with a complete structure in the patent database. This service is available in the PATENTSCOPE (WIPO 2019).

Chapter 14 further reviews the state-of-the-art AI technologies, particularly computer vision and natural language processing, to enhance trademark similarity searches.

15.2.5 Helpdesk Bots

A *chatbot* is an AI application used to conduct an online chat conversation via text or text-to-speech, in lieu of providing direct contact with a human agent. Many patent offices envisage utilizing helpdesk chatbots and automated request routing for

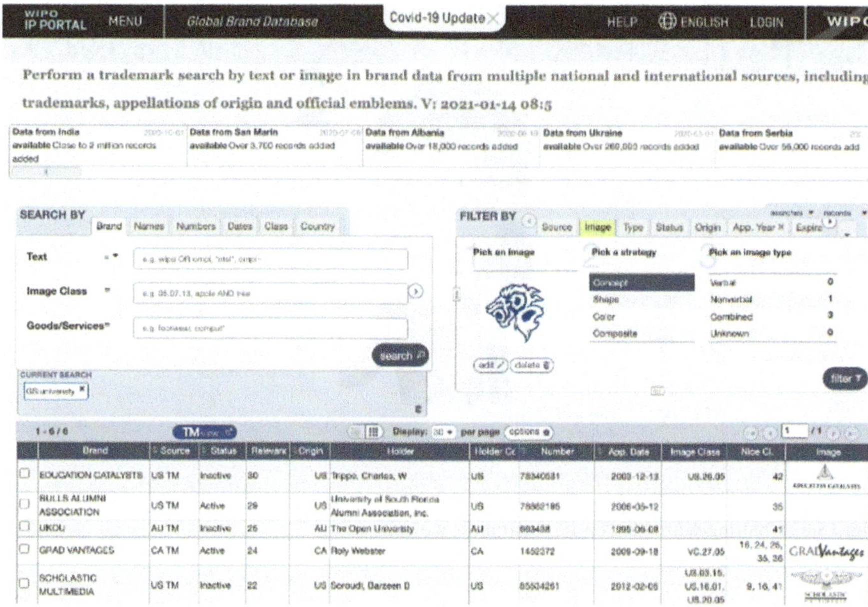

Fig. 15.6 WIPO's Global Brand Database

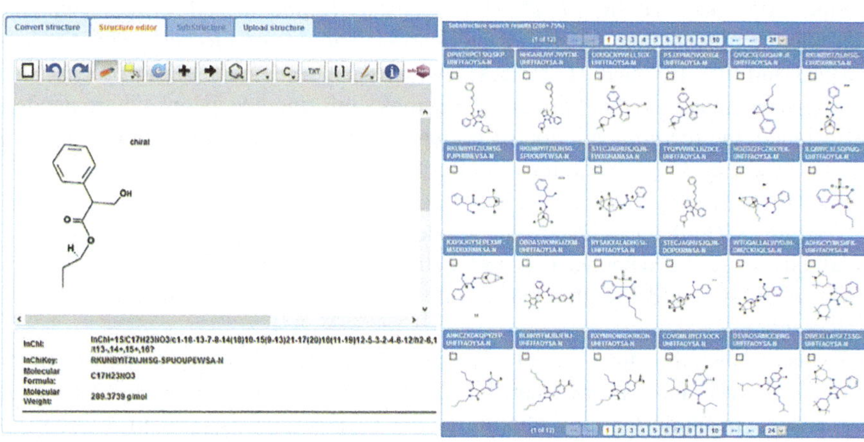

Fig. 15.7 WIPO's chemical compounds search

handling numerous routine questions, such as a filing process, application fee, and tracking applications.

IP Australia first brought an intelligent assistant named Alex into their practice in May 2016 (Kelly 2018). Alex works 24/7 on the IP Australia websites and manages basic customer inquiries. It uses a combination of advanced natural language processing and machine learning based on digitalized data from prior consultation,

Fig. 15.8 Chatting with Alex on IP Australia's website

conversations, and the core IP content. With every conversation, Alex evolves and enhances their capacity to respond to future conversations with greater accuracy (IP Australia 2020).

Since 2017, the Australian Trade Mark Assist tool embedded Alex to cope with the high volume of self-filed trademark applications and respond to customer inquiries in a fast and effective way (Fig. 15.8). Alex assists trademark filling process in a step-by-step manner so that applicants can make informed decisions where needed, for instance, the recommendation of trademark classifications of designated goods and services (Fig. 15.9a), search for similar trademarks, and notification of estimated application fee (Fig. 15.9b).

The biggest challenge with current helpdesk bots is training and support. However, not all businesses have been set up with automation in mind. It is time to rethink the way in which we build a chatbot knowledge base and curate contextualized functions in IP practice.

To accomplish this, first, patent offices should utilize records of responses in the current helpdesk and various manuals for AI training. An example of this would be the deep machine learning chatbot at the USPTO that is used in training for the US Manual Patent of Examination of Procedures. Second, note that international and national patent rules are regularly amended to meet the changing industrial demands and new environments. AI chatbots necessitate substantial adaptation and maintenance in order to keep their knowledge up to date and provide accurate information.

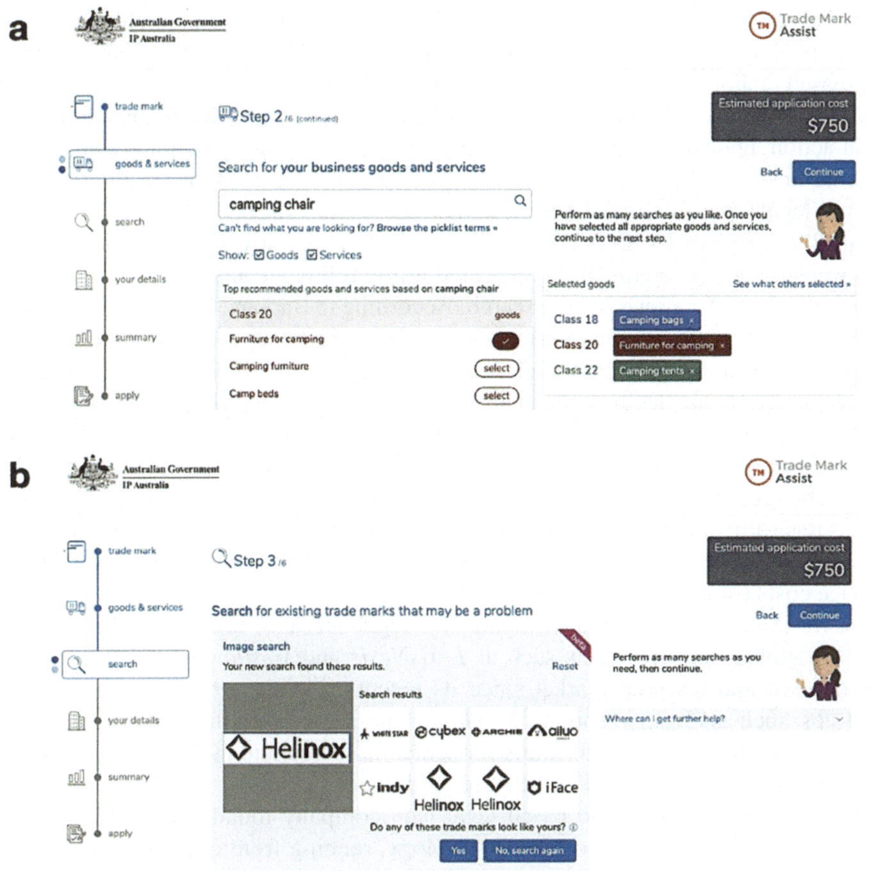

Fig. 15.9 IP Australia's trade mark filing assistant with alex: **a** recommendation of trademark classifications. **b** search for similar trademarks

15.3 The Rise of Legal Technology

Heaps of legal technologies (in short, legal tech) companies have emerged with AI and automation tools for better engagement with the legal profession. Legal Tech refers to the use of technology to provide legal services and support for the legal industry (Bahatti et al. 2020). Since the early 2010s, legal informatics communities have continued developing data and technical standards in the legal field. A few examples of already available legal tech include intellectual property management, legal document review and search, e-Discovery, e-Billing, and legal service chatbots. The biggest and most widely known database for the legal tech landscape is the Stanford CodeX Index (2020) in which a list of legal tech companies, including IP specialized service providers, is curated according to their main service categories and target stakeholders. The list comprises over 1300 companies.

Legal service chatbots have vigorously branched out, and several intelligent assistant applications have emerged. For example, DoNotPay (donotpay.com), a free, app-based chatbot, has gained popularity by offering intelligent legal counsel since 2015. The app provides numerous legal aid services and drafts documents to pursue legal action against an individual or company. It started out by helping with unfair parking tickets and delayed flights and was then extended to offer consultations on various legal issues such as real estate and refugee rights. In 2020, DoNotPay covered legal filing services for COVID-19 relief, such as unemployment insurance, delay and waivers on rent, credit card issues, and utility bill payments.

Another popular area is legal research. According to Barkan et al. (2018, p1), legal research is "the process of identifying and retrieving information necessary to support legal decision-making. In its broadest sense, legal research includes each step of a course of action that begins with an analysis of the facts of a problem and concludes with the application and communication of the results of the investigation." In the process of legal research, legal firms and professionals face issues that are exactly the challenges that legal tech companies claim their solutions address: confronting issues regarding the ever-increasing volume and complexity of legal documents and the pressure from clients to improve the efficiency of their work and lower legal service costs (Massey 2020; Hodges and Morgan 2020).

North America is the largest market for legal services, accounting for around half the global market. Giants such as *LexisNexis* and *Westlaw* have led the legal information and research market since its inception in the 1970s. To date, some start-ups, such as *Casetext* and *Lex Machina*, have highlighted their incorporation of AI and machine learning algorithms for semantic search and intelligent analysis of IP-related documents, including litigation judgments.

Casetext, a San Francisco-based legal tech company founded in 2013, is well known for its litigation automation technology, ranging from case law research to drafting a legal brief. Casetext's early version, Case Analysis Research Assistant—CARA—offers a keyword-based case search like Westlaw and Lexis, but in ways that enhance presentation through intuitive interface and visualization.

For each case returned by a search, CARA displays the case title and citation, along with preview paragraphs. As Fig. 15.10 shows, the color gradient heatmap adds value for users in identifying frequently cited pages and portions of opinion texts in multiple cases.

In 2016, Casetext launched its AI-backed version called CARA A.I. Its natural language search had enhanced flexibility for the choices of search queries, other than crafting complex keyword queries that often miss important cases. It has further noteworthy analytical features that are specialized in handling legal documents. For instance, based on what users upload as their own draft briefs, motions, and legal memoranda, CARA A.I. scans, analyses, and reports facts, legal issues, missing citations, and relevant languages (Fig. 15.11).

Casetext's latest product, *Compose*, automates writing the first draft of a legal brief, which often takes 10–80 hours of billable work, and reduces it to 20 minutes (Bloomberg 2020). Compose provides a list of arguments and relevant legal standards and citations customized based on the jurisdiction and the position in which

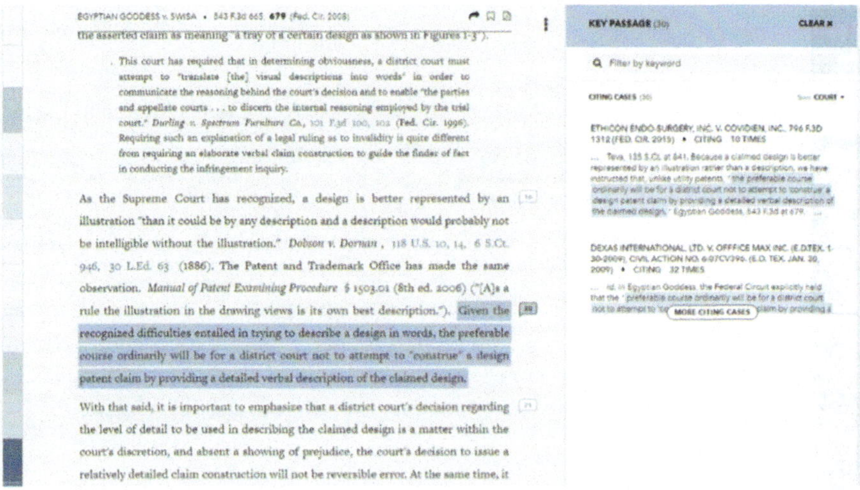

Fig. 15.10 Early version of Casetext's CARA: a heatmap-like visualization feature to indicate highly cited cases

Fig. 15.11 Casetext's CARA A.I.: automatically searches relevant cases omitted from a document

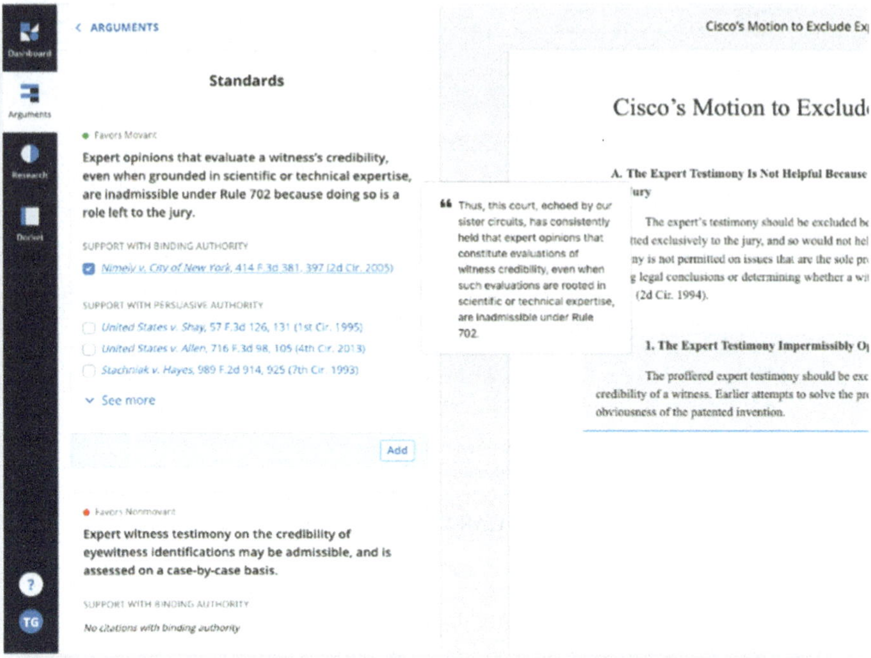

Fig. 15.12 Casetext's Compose: a litigation automation product for writing the first draft of a legal brief

the attorney is going to file. Simple drag-and-drop interfaces help build blocks of arguments with supporting citations (Fig. 15.12).

Lex Machina (Latin for *law machine*)[2] is a legal analytic company that is specialized in IP litigation. With powerful big data analytics that can mine multiple sources of litigation data, including the Patent Trial and Appeal Board (PTAB-USPTO), PACER (an electronic public access service of the US federal court documents), and USITC-EDIS (the repository for all documents filed in relation to an investigation conducted by the United States International Trade Commission), Lex Machina provides practice-specific information on the judges, law firms, lawyers, parties, timing, and more.

The advanced use of natural language processing and machine learning serves to predict litigation processes and outcomes such as time to trial, the likelihood of success or damage in given IP litigation, and the pattern of outcomes by judges or law firms that can be referred to while selecting a company or looking for legal representatives who have the most relevant experience given the type of claims and the opposing counsel involved.

---

[2]Lex Machina initially began in 2006 as part of a project by both the Law School and Computer Science Department at Stanford and was incorporated in 2008. In 2015, the company was acquired by LexisNexis.

It also supports multilateral decision-making while crafting litigation strategies according to the propensity of the judges or court, inter partes review (IPR) rates by technology categories, and infringement damage awards (Fig. 15.13).

In addition, Lex Machina's legal analytics safeguards unnecessary litigation through a preemptive assessment on how long a given case is likely to take or how large compensation for damage is going to be decided. Data on the likely process and outcomes thus allow companies to opt for alternative dispute resolution through negotiation or mediation. Recently, the unprecedented increase in non-practicing entities (NPEs) initiated court cases resulting in a surge of interest in harvesting litigation intelligence services to monitor NPE's activities and prepare for potential threats.

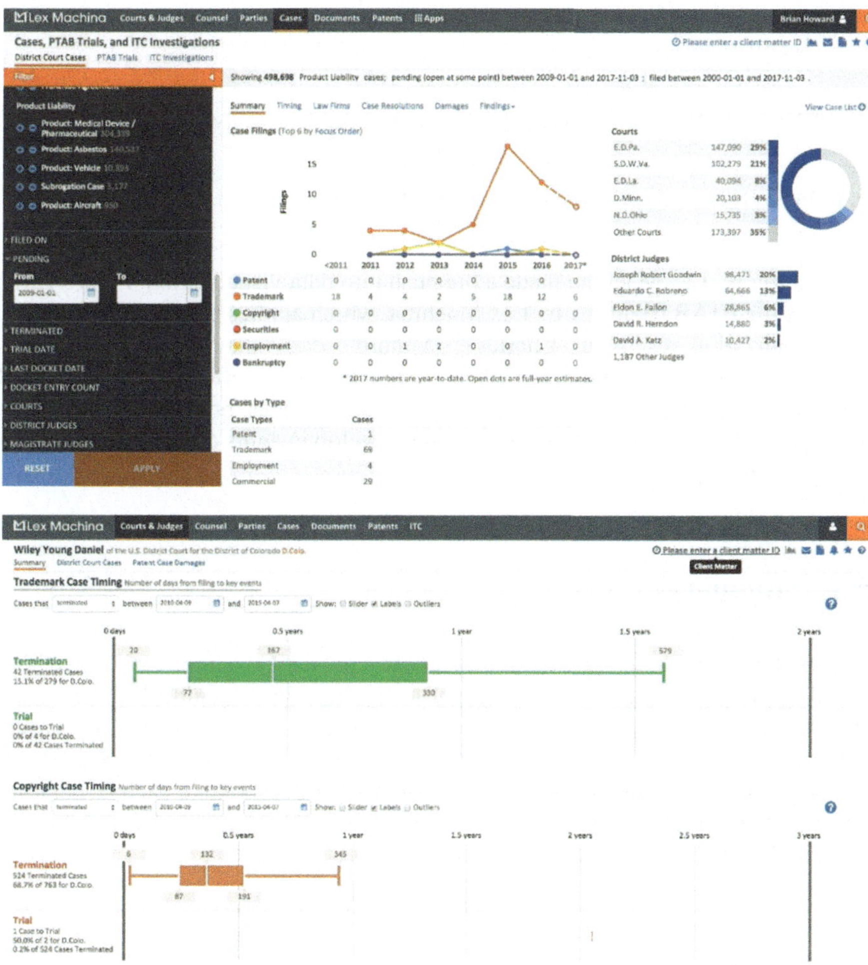

Fig. 15.13 Overview of Lex Machina's legal analytics platform

Fig. 15.14 A Sankey diagram representing apple's PTAB trials flow via Lex Machina

Furthermore, Lex Machina made a big push into data visualization. Figure 15.14 illustrates the PTAB trial flow by Lex Machina, which applies to a Sankey diagram. This visualization resembles Charles J. Minard's early diagram on Napoleon's Russian campaign, as explained in Chap. 7. To summarize, effective uses of visual elements, such as graphs, text highlighting, and color codes, provide users with the ability to quickly engage key information and develop insights on the cohesive story underlying the complex legal data.

15.4 Summary

Along with high-volume, -velocity, and -variety legal data, it is imperative to rethink AI and big data in legal industries. Legal technology in the field of IP has made headway compared to other legal deliveries. However, rather than implementing a variety of disparate solutions, legal technology needs to streamline IP prosecution and management and polish technology capacities bespoke to each IP environment. Future research of legal technologies should take an interdisciplinary approach to bridge the gap of legal, technology, and business needs.

References

Barkan SM, Bintliff B, Whisner M (2018) Fundamentals of legal research. Foundation Press, Saint Paul, MN.

Bahatti SA, Chishti S, Datoo A, Indjic D (ed) (2020) The legaltech book: the legal technology handbook for investors. entrepreneurs and fintech visionaries. John Wiley & Sons, Hoboken, NJ.

Bloomberg (2020) Casetext is automating litigation. https://www.bloomberg.com/press-releases/2020-02-25/casetext-is-automating-litigation. Accessed 18 Nov 2020.

Gomez JC, Moens MF (2014) A survey of automated hierarchical classification of patents. In: Paltoglou G, Loizides F, Hansen P (eds) Professional Search in the Modern World, Springer, Cham.

Hodges P, Morgan C (2020) Dispute resolution 2.0: The era of big data, AI, and analytics. In: Bahatti SA, Chishti S, Datoo A, Indjic D (ed) The legaltech book: the legal technology handbook for investors. entrepreneurs and fintech visionaries, 1st edn. John Wiley & Sons, Hoboken, NJ.

IPOS (2017) classification of goods and services. Available via IPOS. https://www.ipos.gov.sg/docs/default-source/resources-library/trade-marks/resources/classification-of-goods-and-services.pdf. Accessed 15 Jan 2021.

IP Australia (2020) Trade mark assist. http://assist.ipaustralia.gov.au/trademarks/welcome. Accessed 18 Nov 2020.

Kelly (2018) IP Australia puts digital intelligence to work. https://www.wipo.int/wipo_magazine/en/2018/03/article_0004.html. Accessed 18 Nov 2020.

Ngo TV, Ha TL, Nguyen PT, Nguyen LM (2019) Overcoming the rare word problem for low-resource language pairs in neural machine translation. arXiv preprint arXiv:1910.03467.

Massey (2020) In-house counsel can drive industry change through legal technology. In: Bahatti SA, Chishti S, Datoo A, Indjic D (ed.) The legalTech book: the legal technology handbook for investors. entrepreneurs and fintech visionaries, 1st edn. John Wiley & Sons, Hoboken, NJ.

Pouliquen B (2017) WIPO Translate: Patent Neural Machine Translation publicly available in 10 languages. In Proceedings of the Seventh Workshop on Patent and Scientific Literature Translation, Nagoya, 22 Sept 2017.

Stanford CodeX Index (2020) Stanford law tech index. http://techindex.law.stanford.edu/. Accessed 18 Nov 2020.

WIPO (2019) WIPO technology trends 2019: Artificial Intelligence. https://www.wipo.int/tech_trends/en/artificial_intelligence/. Accessed 18 Nov 2020.

Afterword

A patent professional in disguise but a designer at heart

I am a designer. I graduated from Korea Advanced Institute of Science and Technology (KAIST) in industrial design when global consumer electronic companies such as Samsung and LG built their own design competence in the race. When Apple's iPhone began to ignite attention to design again, I started a master's and Ph.D. program in the subject at Arts et Métiers ParisTech in Paris. When design thinking was in vogue, I was a Leverhulme postdoctoral researcher at the Royal College of Art in London. My journey as a designer was on a flowery path.

Before long, I realized I was being blinded. When I joined my university's technology management department as a faculty member, all content around innovation was strictly technology-centric, with no emphasis on design. It was 2013, but use of the word *design* was strongly biased toward the aesthetic aspect of products for non-designers. This was an extremely frustrating experience. I have long struggled to pull design off the sidelines and into the mainstream of innovation.

From my vantage point, one day I realized that it will never happen if I work on the design in isolation and then bring my designs down from the mountain and say, 'Here there are! Let me convince you why designs are great.' If I want to convince others, an easy way is to talk to them using their language and back it up with evidence.

Many companies have thrust intellectual properties into an increasingly critical position in innovation activities. In particular, patents account for a high percentage of the company's value. However, thousands of books about patents in innovation management do not teach how to manage design patents for innovation, nor show the linkages and interconnectivity between design and technology.

After ten years of teaching design using their respective *languages*, I can firmly announce that design and technology are very closely intertwined, and that design patents often play an even more significant role than utility patents in influencing the innovation pipeline. Companies would benefit from embracing both design and utility patents in their innovation management studies.

J. Kim et al., *Patent Analytics*,
https://doi.org/10.1007/978-981-16-2930-3

Nevertheless, from the front cover to the back of the book, I deliberately minimize the use of the word *design* but rather make readers think about the value of design without biasing them. In the case studies, a series of design and technology patent citation maps allows the readers to understand how design has played the leading role in Dyson's innovation from the bagless vacuum cleaner to the bladeless hairdryer. Another example is with Samsung and LG's innovative team, based on inventor information from design patents, highlighting the central role of UX designers to build out their innovation capabilities.

To the extent that I managed at all is because a number of people have helped and encouraged me. I am particularly grateful to Brigitte Borja de Mozota, who incited me to write initial book proposal and get the deals, and kindly accepted to write a foreword of this book.

For their invaluable assistance, I would like to acknowledge the foundational efforts of my co-authors, Buyong Jeong and Daejung Kim, and past and present graduate students at Hanyang University, who contributed exemplary work from research and in case contributions. Those who have helped in various ways to improve the book have been: Emirhan Aksu, Eunok Kim, Myungjin Hyun, Wooyoung Kim, Namhoon Park, Sunghoon Chung, and Taek-kyun Shin.

An excellent publishing team produced this book and worked impeccably throughout the publication process. Special thanks go to my ever-patient editor, Juno Kawakami.

I would also like to extend my thanks to Hokyoung Ryu, who has editorial X-ray vision and teaches me the pangs of authorship while showing an uncanny ability to ferret out areas for improvement. My best friend, Tatiana Hernandez, was always on the other end of the Zoom or e-mail to listen to my ramblings and stood by me during every struggle and all my success.

None of this would have been possible without my academic parents: Kunpyo Lee and Carole Bouchard, who gave me full confidence in every step of my academic career.

Finally, and most importantly, this book comes with the pleasure of thanking my family and their willingness to tolerate my frequent absences from home. It constitutes a small part of the debt of gratitude I owe them.

Seoul, Korea (Republic of) Jieun Kim
June 2021

The manufacturer's authorised representative in the EU is Springer Nature Customer Service Centre GmbH, Europaplatz 3, 69115 Heidelberg, Germany. If you have any concerns regarding our products, please contact ProductSafety@springernature.com

Printed and bound by CPI Group (UK) Ltd, Croydon, CR0 4YY
30/09/2026
02225294-0004